SIGNPOSTS TO THE MESSIANIC AGE

Signposts to the Messianic Age
Sermons and Lectures

RABBI JOHN D. RAYNER

VALLENTINE MITCHELL
LONDON• PORTLAND, OR

First published in 2006 in Great Britain by
VALLENTINE MITCHELL
Suite 314, Premier House, 112–114 Station Road,
Edgware, Middlesex HA8 7BJ

and in the United States of America by
VALLENTINE MITCHELL
c/o ISBS, 920 NE 58th Avenue, Suite 300
Portland, OR 97213-3786

Website: http://www.vm.books.com

British Library Cataloguing in Publication Data
A catalogue record has been applied for

ISBN 0-85303-703-5 (cloth)

Library of Congress Cataloging-in-Publication Data
A catalog record has been applied for

Typeset in 11/13pt Palatino by FiSH Books, Enfield, Middx.
Printed in Great Britain by MPG Books Ltd, Bodmin, Cornwall

Contents

Notes

The sermons were all given at the Liberal Jewish Synagogue, St John's Wood, London. The lectures were given at various places:

Hebraism: Our Common Heritage and Hope
The annual Lily Montagu Memorial Lecture of the London Society of Jews and Christians, at the Liberal Jewish Synagogue.

A Jewish View of Jesus
The Cardiff branch of the Council of Christians and Jews.

The Truth About the Pharisees
The Kingston branch of the Council of Christians and Jews.

The Suffering Servant
London Society for the Study of Religion, Athenaeum.

Good and Evil in the Classical Sources of Judaism
Colin Gold Memorial Lecture, North Western Reform Synagogue.

Principles of Jewish Ethics
The Learning Circle, Radlett and Bushey Heath Reform Synagogue.

Judaism and Animal Welfare
Freehof Institute for Progressive Halachah, Zurich.

Some Glimpses of the History of the Jewish Liturgy
Limmud Conference, Oxford Brookes University, Wheatley, Oxford.

The Four Children of the Passover Haggadah
Aryeh S. Dorfler Memorial Lecture, Leo Baeck College, Finchley, London.

Universalising Tendencies in Anglo-Jewish Liturgy
British Association of Jewish Studies, Hatfield College, Durham University.

The Ethical Issues Surrounding the Middle East
Maimonides Foundation, School of Oriental and African Studies, London.

Open Letter to David A. Harris
Self-explanatory.

To Jane, in deepest love and gratitude

Also to Lev and Max, in pride and affection

Foreword

This volume of sermons and essays needs no foreword: but I feel privileged to have been invited to contribute one, since it gives me an opportunity to pay tribute not only to the spiritual leadership that Rabbi John Rayner has given to his own, liberal Jewish congregation, but also to the stimulus which he has afforded to those in the wider Anglo-Jewish community to seek, within the terms of reference of their own particular religious tradition, ways of addressing issues that should not be evaded by any who take seriously the ethical values, and challenges, which are integral to Judaism.

John Rayner's years of service have witnessed a significant development in the character of progressive Judaism. It is understandable, in retrospect, that its founders, feeling themselves inspired with a mission to proclaim those ethical values and universalist implications of the Hebrew bible which, in their view, received too little emphasis in conventional Jewish attitudes and assumptions, devoted their efforts exclusively to redressing the balance. That they had, for some decades, but a limited impact on contemporary Anglo-Jewry, was probably due in no small part to their apparent lack of feeling – amounting to neglect – of Jewish historical consciousness. In the nineteenth century Oxford to which Claude Montefiore owed so much, the leading lights amongst those trained in the Greek and Latin classics who taught the discipline of *litterae humaniores* commonly called 'greats' had little interest in history. His own tutor and mentor, Benjamin

Jowett, published English translations of Plato, Aristotle and Thucydides, but it was the impact of philosophy rather than the effect of history on religious thought that preoccupied him. Montefiore certainly did, after Oxford, make it his business to acquire an impressive familiarity with rabbinic writing, but he was, it seems, sufficiently aware of his own missing dimension to involve as collaborators, in his address to making rabbinic religious values more widely accessible, scholars who were themselves imbued with both an intellectual and an emotional appreciation of the implication of the liturgical formula 'our God and the God of our fathers'.

The last 60-odd years have witnessed a growing realisation in the liberal camp that this so-to-say tone-deafness constituted a defect requiring remedy. Whilst it is right to take note of the circumstance that this reawakening was no doubt stimulated by the European Jewish *sho'ah* and by the establishment of a Jewish sovereign state in the Land of Israel, it would surely have atrophied but for two things: the views, initiative and the authority as a survivor of Leo Baeck, and, more importantly, the conviction of its indispensability on the part of the emergent younger religious leadership and, I suspect, above all of John Rayner, who put himself to school to strengthen the professional training that he had received from his seniors by acquiring a first-hand knowledge of rabbinic Hebrew and Aramaic, and so a familiarity with the classical sources of the Jewish religion and with the thought-categories passed down by its exponents.

This collection of essays constitutes an appropriate apex to John Rayner's earlier volumes. Where significant differences between progressive and traditional, so-called orthodox views exist, this is made clear: not merely with the avoidance of all captious controversialism, but with a positive appreciation of traditional Judaism and of its parameters which pervades the whole. It would therefore be a pity if the readership which this book reached were to be confined to membership of the liberal and reform congregations, since the living issues to which the author draws our attention demand, on ethical grounds, address by all – not only, indeed, by both traditional and modernist Jews, but also by others, beyond the Jewish community, to whatever faith or secular moral code they may subscribe: each is called upon to consider them in the idiom of their respective authorities. What we have here is palpably the mature fruit of one who, walking uprightly and speaking truth in his heart, assuredly abides in God's tabernacle.

Raphael Loewe
September 2005

***

It will be apparent that the foregoing was composed in the knowledge that John Rayner was unlikely to see the publication of this book. An email copy of what I had written was read to him, whilst he was still able to follow it, on the evening he died. His book must now be regarded as its author's moral testament, of a stature endorsed by the exemplary manner in which he contemplated his own approaching end.

R.L.

Preface

A few years ago, an Anglo-American publishing company, Berghahn Books, published two collections of sermons of mine, *An Understanding of Judaism* (1997) and *A Jewish Understanding of the World* (1998), and a collection of lectures entitled *Jewish Religious Law: A Progressive Perspective* (1998). The present collection, mainly of more recent sermons and lectures, supplements these, and is a summation of my life as a preacher and teacher. It is hereby offered to a wider public than the relatively small audiences to which they were originally addressed.

If there is a common thread that runs through this volume, it is its emphasis on the gentler and more outward-looking values of Judaism, which are not much in evidence nowadays. For it is by cultivating and exemplifying these values that Jews can best contribute to humanity as it struggles to shake off its present troubles and yearns to find again the signposts to justice and peace, not only in the Middle East but everywhere.

My thanks are due to all those who have encouraged me in this project, especially my wife Jane and daughter Susan, who have painstakingly prepared the manuscript; Rabbi Elizabeth Tikvah Sarah, Chairperson of the Liberal Judaism Publications Committee, for her helpfulness in the early stages of this project; and a number of well-wishers who have contributed to the cost of this undertaking. They include: Dr Bernie and Vivien Bulkin, Dr Max Caplin, Jane Cohen, Professor Sidra DeKoven, Professor

Yaron Ezrahi, Ernst and Thilde Fraenkel, Bob and Ann Kirk, Robin Leigh, Sarah Jane Leigh, Tony and Pauline Margo, Trevor Moross (in memory of his mother, Lola Moross), Michael and Jenny Nathan, Anthony and Maureen Roe, Michael and Jill Salmon, Martin and Vicky Slowe, Ludwig Spiro, Professor Stephen and Alison Spiro, Anthony Steen MP, Walter and Betty Woyda, Tony and Rosemary Yablon, and especially Willie and Jo Kessler, who, in addition, have very kindly negotiated on my behalf with the publishers, Vallentine Mitchell, to whom I also wish to express my appreciation.

John D. Rayner
Autumn 2005

PART I
SERMONS

The Meaning of Mitzvah

16 January 1999

Professor Arnold M. Eisen, head of the Department of Religious Studies at Stanford University in California, has recently written a book entitled *Rethinking Modern Judaism*, which has been much talked about and highly praised. Therefore when I was asked to review the book for an Anglo-Jewish journal, I seized the opportunity with some eagerness.

To say that it didn't come up to my expectations would be something of an understatement. It is indeed, as I say in the opening sentence of my review, 'a book of the highest academic quality – erudite, cultured, stylish, magisterial'. But as I go on to say, 'it fails to deliver what its title gratuitously promises. For it offers no rethinking about the key issues of modern Judaism: the nature of God and Revelation, the authority of the Bible and Talmud, the mutual relations of Israel and Diaspora, of Judaism and other religions, and the ultimate future of the Jewish people and humanity.'

What then does the book deal with? The answer, in a word, is *observances*. And that is what I should like to discuss with you this morning. How important are observances? Well, I suppose it depends on your point of view. If you are an anthropologist, they are *enormously* important. Indeed, they are just about the only thing that is of any interest in religion. And it doesn't matter whether they are good or bad, beautiful or ugly, sensible or foolish. They are all equally grit for the anthropologist's mill; indeed, the more bizarre the better.

In recent years there has been quite an upsurge of interest in ritual. Thanks to the influence of anthropologists such as Mary Douglas, all sorts of strange rites, like those of levitical purity and impurity, are suddenly treated with solemn seriousness and without the slightest hint of a suggestion that there is anything primitive or antiquated about them.

This renewed interest in ritual has even influenced Progressive Judaism. More and more Progressive congregations are reviving previously discarded customs such as *Tashlich*, which involves going down to a river on Rosh Hashanah in order symbolically to cast away one's sins. More and more Leo Baeck College students and graduates put on *Tefillin* when they say their morning prayers. The Jewish feminists are almost desperately trying to create new rituals to celebrate lifecycle events important to women which patriarchal Judaism has neglected. And the draft new platform of the Central Conference of American Rabbis could be summed up as a plea for more ritual. Therefore Professor Eisen wrote a book about Jewish observances and called it *Rethinking Modern Judaism*. However, he doesn't discuss *particular* observances, their histories or meanings, still less their merits or demerits, which is, as I said, a non-question from an anthropological point of view. What interests him is the general level of observance in Judaism, which declined sharply in the modern period but now, in the post-modern period, is rising again. And even about that he gives no facts or figures but only general impressions. Instead, what he does – and does superbly well – is to examine how the *thinking about observances* – the understanding of their function in religion – has changed in the last two hundred years, as evidenced by the writings of leading philosophers, theologians, anthropologists and sociologists.

All of which is perfectly legitimate – except that 'observances' are not a Jewish category! What Judaism traditionally talks about is not 'observances' but '*Mitzvot*'.

The use of '*Mitzvot*' for 'observances' raises three problems which we need to consider. The first is that the term '*Mitzvot*' does not refer only to ritual behaviour. It also refers to behaviour of an entirely different kind, especially *ethical* behaviour. Therefore to use the word *Mitzvot* as if it referred only to rituals is to ignore one half of its meaning. That is the first problem.

But the mere mention of the distinction I have just made

should immediately remind us that from the point of view of the Prophets – or at least the greatest of them, like Isaiah and Jeremiah – ethical behaviour is *immeasurably more important* than ritual behaviour. Therefore, if the Prophets were right, then to use the word *Mitzvah* exclusively in the sense of ritual is not merely to ignore one half of its meaning, but actually to ignore the more important half! That is the second problem.

But then there is a third, and it has to do with the root meaning of '*Mitzvah*', which is of course 'commandment'. Now from a liberal point of view it is not too difficult to think of the ethical *Mitzvot* as being divinely commanded. We have been taught to think of God as being first and foremost a *moral* God. Therefore, when we encounter biblical injunctions such as 'you shall not kill', 'you shall not steal', 'you shall love your neighbour as yourself', 'seek peace', and so on and so forth, it seems quite natural to suppose that they emanate directly or indirectly from God.

But when it comes to laws of ritual, it isn't nearly so clear. With some of them, because they so obviously serve a good purpose, we may indeed believe that divine revelation, interacting with human interpretation, played a part in their evolution: the Sabbath, for instance, as a weekly day of rest and contemplation; the celebration of freedom at *Pesach*; and several more. But when it comes to the innumerable details of prayer and sacrifice, of purity and impurity, surely they are *human contrivances*, developed by religious leaders on the basis of ancient customs and their own perceptions of what might be spiritually helpful to the people of their time.

That very distinction is made again and again by the Prophets – God commands righteousness, God does not command ritual – for instance by Jeremiah when he says in God's name: 'On the day that I brought your ancestors out of the land of Egypt I did not speak to them or command them concerning burnt offerings and sacrifices; but this command I gave them: Obey My voice, and I will be your God, and you shall be My people, and walk only in the way that I command you' (7:22f.). And the same point was made succinctly by the late Rabbi Ignaz Maybaum of the Edgware Reform Synagogue when he wrote: 'The Thou Shalt of the Moral Law must not be spoken where ritual is concerned.'

What transpires, therefore, is that the use of the word *Mitzvot* as a synonym for acts of ritual is trebly unfortunate: because it tells only half the story, because it tells the less important half, and because it tells that part of the story to which its root meaning of 'commandment' is least applicable. It is indeed indicative of the shrinkage in meaning of the concept of Halachah or Jewish Law, which was once a grand design for human life in all its aspects, into a handful of more or less trivial ceremonies. Or, as I put it in my review, it is 'a mark of the modern degeneration of Judaism into Yiddishkeit'.

True religion is made of sterner stuff. It is first and foremost about right conduct. And that is not something vague and general. It is every bit as specific as the legislation concerning ritual, as you will see when you read a new booklet of mine entitled *Principles of Jewish Ethics*, which has just been published.

In it there is a section entitled 'The Primacy of Ethics in Judaism'. That, I submit, is a principle we must maintain, and nothing the neo-modernist, neo-traditionalist, neo-obscurantist recidivists tell us should ever deflect us from it, no matter how much anthropological jargon they throw at us.

But when all that has been said, it must still be added that 'observances' in the sense of rituals are *also* important. For though they are not an end in themselves, they do have an important function as *means*. They are bonds that bind us to our people, past, present and future; they are symbols subtly transmitting significant messages and values; and in their cumulative effect they can raise us above materialism to a higher state of consciousness in which the sense of holiness, and of the presence of God, comes more naturally. Therefore, provided we use our intelligence to discriminate between those that are and those that are not sensible and appropriate, it is probably true for all of us to say that we would do well to become less frigid and inhibited, more generously self-giving towards traditional Jewish observances.

For the benefits to be derived from them are not to be dismissed as trivial. They can make a big and beneficial difference to our lives, and it is a safe bet that God would wish us to make good use of them. In that sense it is still possible for us to say, *asher kidd'shanu b'mitzvotav v'tzivvanu*, that God has commanded us to sanctify our lives by performing those rituals which can intensify our awareness of our Jewishness and therefore also of those obligations – chiefly ethical – which being Jewish entails.

The Golden Rule

6 May 2000

Today tradition decrees that we should read the nineteenth chapter of Leviticus which already the ancient Rabbis regarded as the greatest chapter of the Torah (*Sifra* on Lev. 19:1–2).

It is a chapter full of good things, but the 'jewel in the crown' is undoubtedly verse 18, also known as the 'Golden Rule': 'You shall love your neighbour as yourself'. Let us see whether we can't sharpen our understanding of it by asking three questions about it.

First, then, is the Golden Rule unique to Judaism? And the answer is, of course: no. Not only is it found in traditions, like Christianity, which took it from Judaism, but it also features in Far Eastern religions like Confucianism and in many other literatures. But that doesn't make it any less Jewish!

For one thing, none of the other occurrences of it are quite as old as Leviticus. For another thing, its occurrence there is not an isolated instance. In one form or another it occurs again and again in Jewish literature. From the third century BCE we have the book of Tobit, in which the eponymous hero says to his son: 'What you hate, do not do to any person' (4:15). From the second century BCE we have the Testaments of the Twelve Patriarchs in which there are teachings such as 'Love God and your neighbour' (*Issachar* 5:2) and 'Love God throughout your life, and one another with a sincere heart' (Dan 5:3). From the first century BCE we have the famous story of how Hillel, the greatest of the Pharisees, said to a would-be proselyte, echoing

Tobit's advice to his son, 'What is hateful to yourself, do not do to others', and added: 'That's what the Torah is all about' (*Shab.* 31a). In the first or second century CE the greatest of all the rabbis, Akiva, said about 'Love your neighbour as yourself': *zeh k'lal gad-ol ba-torah*, that it is the greatest principle of the Torah (*Sifra* on Lev. 19:19).

So the Golden Rule is not *exclusive* to Judaism, but it is nevertheless *characteristic* of Judaism. To give an analogy, just because other peoples besides the English – the Indians, for example, love cricket, it doesn't follow that love of cricket is not an English characteristic. Or to give a different analogy, just because a particular dish – let us say, bread and butter pudding – is the *spécialité de la maison* of one restaurant, that doesn't mean that it can't also be the *spécialité de la maison* of another restaurant. So we may safely assert that 'love your neighbour as yourself' is the *spécialité de la maison* of the House of Israel.

So much, I hope, is clear, but if we now go on to ask our second question – Who is your neighbour? – things get a little bit more complicated. The word in question, *re'a*, doesn't exactly mean 'neighbour', for which Hebrew has another word. It really means 'associate' or 'fellow member' of whatever group it is that you belong to, and in the time in which it was written it meant primarily 'fellow Israelite'. Non-Israelites didn't come into the picture except in so far as they had settled among the Israelites. Such immigrants were called *gerim*, usually translated 'strangers'. And just in case anybody should think that the Golden Rule didn't apply to them, the very same chapter of Leviticus which says 'You shall love your neighbour as yourself' goes on to say: 'The strangers who live with you shall be to you like the natives among you, and you shall love them, too, as yourself' (19:34).

So far, so good. However, the Rabbis assumed, not entirely without justification, that the 'strangers' mentioned in the Bible would normally have become Jewish, and so the word *gerim* came to mean 'Jews by conversion' or 'proselytes'. This had both an advantage and a disadvantage. On the one hand it meant that all the nice things the Bible says about the treatment of strangers were applied to proselytes, so that they came to be held in high esteem. But on the other hand it meant that for strictly legal purposes the Golden Rule of Leviticus 19 was understood to refer to two categories only, born Jews and proselytes, so that unconverted non-Jews were not covered by it. Which is why the Rabbis found it necessary to make a separate provision for non-Jews, namely that when it comes to acts of practical kindness, such as supporting their poor, visiting their sick and burying their dead, we treat them in exactly the same way as fellow-Jews (*Git.* 61a).

But that is only the technical–legal side of the story. For all other purposes 'love your neighbour' was *always* understood in Judaism as applying to Jews and non-Jews alike. That is evident from Hillel's teaching, 'Be a disciple of Aaron, loving peace and pursuing peace, loving your fellow men and women', where the Hebrew word used makes it clear that it refers to human beings as such, whatever their race or religion.

And just to clinch the point, we have the famous remark of Ben Azzai that, great though the Golden Rule of Leviticus 19 undoubtedly is, there is an even greater verse in Genesis 5, beginning 'This is the book of the descendants of Adam', because it goes on to say that all human beings were created in God's image and so provides the *reason* behind the Golden Rule (Gen. R. 24:7).

And when you come to think of it, Hillel and Ben Azzai only re-emphasised a point already made many centuries earlier by the prophet Amos when he said in God's name, 'Are you not as the Ethiopians to Me, O people of Israel...?' (9:7).

If all human beings are God's children, created in God's image, and if that is the reason behind the Golden Rule, then, quite clearly, the Golden Rule applies to Jews and non-Jews alike.

And so we come to our third question: how can you do it? How can you love other people as much as you love yourself? What if they are not very lovable? What if you positively dislike the way they look or speak or behave, or have behaved badly to you? How can you love them then?

The answer, of course, is that the Golden Rule doesn't command us to feel towards others what we don't feel. It only commands us to *act* towards them on the principle that their needs, their rights and their welfare are as important as our needs, our rights, our welfare because they, no less than ourselves, are God's children. If we do that, and keep on doing it, we may in the end come to see the Divine Image in our fellow men and women, and so to feel love for them as well. And if that happens, so much the better. But whatever we feel or don't feel, that is the right way, and the Jewish way, to behave.

And in a general sort of way, we know well enough what it means. But how exactly do you put the principle into practice, say, between parent and child, brother and sister, husband and wife, teacher and pupil, doctor and patient, merchant and customer, employer and employee, police and public, judge and litigant, government and citizen, nation and nation? That is not nearly so easy, and to try to answer these more difficult questions is what the teachers of Judaism have been doing for thousands of years. To a large extent, the literature of Judaism is one gigantic commentary on the Golden Rule.

Which brings us back to Hillel. For what he told the would-be proselyte was not only the Golden Rule, and not only 'That is what the Torah is all about', but he went on to say, 'The rest is a commentary on it, *zil g'mor*, go and learn!'

Thou Shalt Not Kill

17 May 2002

What really happened at Sinai, we shall never know. We can only guess. And a reasonable guess would be that Moses assembled the people at the foot of the mountain, solemnly adjured them to enter into a Covenant with the God of their ancestors, and set before them a few of the basic rules of conduct which that Covenant entailed. If that is so, then these rules may very well have been the Ten Commandments, even if not quite in the form in which we have them now.

Let us then make that assumption and focus on one of the Ten Commandments, which must surely go back all the way to Sinai, if anything does. It is the sixth commandment, *lo tirtzach*. But what does it mean? The King James Version of 1611 translates it 'Thou shalt not kill'. But all subsequent versions have 'Thou shall not murder'.

And that is undoubtedly right, (a) because the Hebrew verb does mean 'to murder' rather than generally 'to kill', for which there are other verbs, and (b) because otherwise the Bible would contradict itself, since it sanctions both capital punishment and war. Therefore, if we understand the Hebrew correctly, there is no problem: murder is all wrong but capital punishment and war are all right. But are they? It is enough to raise the question to realise that there is room for doubt.

So far as capital punishment is concerned, already the ancient Rabbis were worried by it. Not that they rejected it. They couldn't do that because the Torah, which they believed to be divine, positively demands it for a number of grave offences. But they were deeply worried by the possibility, which can never be completely eliminated, of a wrongful conviction, because the accused either didn't commit the offence or was not in a sound state of mind at the time. Therefore some of the Rabbis went so far as to say that if they had sat on a criminal court they would never have convicted anybody of a capital offence (*Mak.* 1:10).

In other words, Jewish tradition has always accepted capital punishment in theory but sometimes expressed unease about its application in practice. We, however, since we are free to question the tradition, are also free to question whether it is right in this instance. And many of us, if not all, have come to the conclusion that it is not.

Personally, I find it nauseating that in the United States capital punishment is still so prevalent, with about 3,000 condemned people on death row at any time (Richard A. Block, 'Capital Punishment', in *Crime and Punishment*, ed. Walter Jacob and Moshe Zemer, Berghahn Books, 1999, p. 64). Conversely, I am very proud of the fact that the Central Conference of American Rabbis has consistently opposed capital punishment since 1958 (ibid., p. 65); that in this country it was abolished in 1965, thanks to the advocacy of a Jew, Sydney Silverman; and that in the State of Israel, with the sole exception of Adolf Eichmann, nobody has ever been executed.

However, let us now turn to the other subject of war. Surely killing in the course of warfare is permissible when necessary. Well, yes, according to the Bible, and hence according to Jewish tradition. But much depends on what you mean by 'necessary'. Already the book of Deuteronomy (chapter 20) lays down a number of restrictions, and the Rabbis distinguished between *milchamot mitzvah*, obligatory wars, which are essentially wars of self-defence, and *milchamot r'shut*, optional wars. So at least an attempt was made to limit the scope of legitimate war.

But in recent times the problem has assumed a new complexion. For modern warfare is so sophisticated and so horrific, so liable to kill and maim combatants and non-combatants alike on a vast scale, and even to destroy the environment for future generations, that it is hard to conceive of *any* circumstances in which it could be justified. Therefore, just as many Jews and others have come to question whether capital punishment is ever right, so they have begun to question whether war is ever right.

Even if we don't go all the way with the pacifists, at least we must surely agree that far, far greater efforts need to be made than has generally been the case in the past to resolve international conflicts by other than military means. After all, when two individuals have a dispute, they don't usually kill each other. They compromise, and if they can't agree on a compromise, they may ask a third person to arbitrate for them. Why on earth shouldn't nations do the same? Surely future generations will shake their heads in disbelief that as late as the twenty-first century nations resorted so readily to wholesale slaughter.

Surely most armed conflicts, if not all, could be avoided if both sides, or even just one of them, took the right action at the right time. Would not the American Civil War have been avoided if the Southern States had had the decency to abolish slavery when the immorality of it was first pointed out? Even the Second World War, which we think of as a righteous war if *ever* there was one, could perhaps have been avoided if the Allies had taken strong enough political and economic measures against Hitler as soon as his evil intentions became clear.

And as for the Middle East conflict, however much the Palestinians are to be blamed for it, it would still be true to say that if successive Israeli governments had heeded the United Nations and evacuated the West Bank settlements, or even just stopped building more and more of them, and offered the Palestinians real hope of achieving their national aspirations, then the level of their resentment would have been so much lower, the extremists among them would have enjoyed so much less popular support, and quite possibly the second *intifada*, like the first, would never have begun.

I have been reading a book entitled *Holy Land Unholy War* by the former Middle East correspondent of the *Daily Telegraph*, Anton La Guardia, which gives an eminently fair and balanced account of the Middle East conflict. And just this past week I came across a passage in it which is highly relevant to our theme. After making some damning remarks about the Palestinian leadership and its failure, except under strong pressure, to condemn acts of violence against Israeli civilians, he has the following paragraph:

In the cradle of monotheism, the land which devised the concept of one God and universal ethics, every atrocity has an excuse, a mitigating circumstance, an explanation in terms of a previous atrocity committed by the other side, in either the recent or distant past. When it comes to political conflict, priests, sheikhs and rabbis seem incapable of standing up for the simple principle that killing is wrong. They are little more than tribal spokesmen, defending the interests of their sides. (p. 209)

That is a damning indictment, and I am sure we all recognise how much truth there is in it. The fact is that in most times and places, the clergy – Jewish, Christian, Muslim and otherwise – have been cheerleaders for their nations at war, and made little or no attempt to exercise any objective moral discrimination. It is one of those devastating facts which from time to time make me feel ashamed to be associated with organised religion.

But let me end on a positive note. The 'Solidarity with Israel' rally in Trafalgar Square on Bank Holiday Monday ten days ago could easily have been a demonstration of the same phenomenon, and in some respects it was. But the slogan chosen by the organisers, 'Yes to Peace, No to Terrorism', struck a different note. So, from all accounts, did the atmosphere generally prevailing among the perhaps 50,000 people who crowded the square. And so did the negative reaction of most of them to Binyamin Netanyahu's strident, chauvinistic diatribe. Instead of militancy, the traditional Jewish longing for peace asserted itself. So that was reassuring.

Even more reassuring was the peace rally which took place in Tel Aviv last Saturday night, the biggest for 20 years, when 100,000 people crowded into Rabin Square. One of the chief speakers was Yossi Beilin, a former justice minister, who said: 'The main thing that killed the peace process happened here seven years ago, when Yitzhak Rabin was killed.' And he added, his voice breaking with emotion, 'I promise Yitzhak Rabin that we will finish the job.'

Perhaps, therefore, the time is coming, after all, when Jews and others will stand up 'for the simple principle that killing is wrong'. Perhaps it is not such a bad thing, after all, that the King James Version mistranslated *lo tirtzach* 'Thou shalt not kill'. Perhaps the day is not as far off as it usually seems when Isaiah's prophecy, reiterated by Micah, will come true, that they 'will beat their swords into ploughshares, and their spears into pruning hooks; nation shall not lift up sword against nation, neither shall they learn war any more' (Isa. 1:4, Micah 4:3).

The Mystery of the Cherubim

28 February 1998

A recent survey of undergraduates at an unnamed university showed that about one-third of them didn't have the first notion of English grammar. It didn't surprise me, for having received my education in an age when these things were not yet considered totally unimportant, I am one of those tiresomely old-fashioned people who wince whenever a word like 'media' or 'data' is used as a singular, which happens on average about a hundred times a day.

But if you think such disdain for grammar is only a recent phenomenon, let me disabuse you by reading to you a translation of three verses from today's *Sidra*: 'And thou shalt make two cherubims of gold, of beaten work shalt thou make them, in the two ends of the mercy seat. And make one cherub on the one end, and the other cherub on the other end, even of the mercy seat shall ye make the cherubims on the two ends thereof; toward the mercy seat shall the faces of the cherubims be' (Exod. 25:18–20).

I have been quoting from that unsurpassed masterpiece of English literature, the Authorised Version of the Bible of 1611. How is it possible that the learned professors who produced it by command of King James I didn't know that 'cherubim' is a plural and cannot be further pluralised? It is a mystery to me. But then the cherubim, even without an 's', are themselves something of a mystery.

What exactly is a cherub? The word conjures up a young child with chubby face, a beatific smile and a pair of wings. But this is only because that is how cherubim are depicted in Renaissance art, and why they are so depicted is yet another mystery! One possible reason is the influence of a passage in the Talmud which tries to explain the Hebrew word *k'ruv'* as coming from *k'ravya*, which is Aramaic for 'like a child' (*Suk.* 5b, *Chag.* 13b).

But that is not how Cherubim are depicted in the Bible! Nor are they depicted consistently. The first mention of them is in the Garden of Eden story, where they stand next to a flaming sword to prevent Adam and Eve from re-entering the Garden, and must therefore have been fierce rather than babyish in appearance (Gen. 3:24). They next appear in our *Sidra*, describing the furnishings of the Tabernacle, where, as we have just heard, they are golden figures at the two ends of the *kapporet*, which the King James Version translates 'mercy seat', but which was most probably merely a lid covering the Ark. There each cherub has one face – but we are not told what kind of a face – and two wings.

Essentially similar is the description of the Cherubim in the account of the construction of King Solomon's Temple in the First Book of Kings from which our Haftarah was taken. But there they are made of olive wood overlaid with gold, and we are given the further information that each cherub had a wingspan of 10 cubits, that is, something between 15 and 20 feet (I Kings 6:23–26).

The prophet Ezekiel, on the other hand, has a vision of what he calls *chayyot*, 'living creatures', subsequently identified as cherubim, each having four wings and four faces: a human face, the face of a lion, the face of an ox, and the face of an eagle (Ezek. 1:6,10 and ch. 10 *passim*).

What shall we make of all that? It is virtually certain that the Hebrew *k'ruv* comes from the Babylonian *kuribu*. A *kuribu* was a mythical creature, part human, part animal and part bird, and such figures have in fact been found by archaeologists, especially at the entrances of temples and palaces, all over the Near East. They were a common feature of ancient pagan mythology in that part of the world, and our ancestors learned about them from the peoples among whom they lived. The cherubim, moreover, are only one of many different types of angels who became part of Jewish folklore and are occasionally mentioned in the Bible as well as post-biblical Jewish literature.

What then is the point of these creatures? The main idea underlying them seems to be this: a king, especially an oriental king, needs to have a retinue of ministers; the greater the king, the bigger the retinue; and a divine king needs to have a superhuman retinue as numerous as the stars of heaven. Therefore the supreme King of kings, who is the Creator of the universe, must be surrounded by myriads of angels of every grade, which is just what we find in Jewish folklore.

But what do these angels do? Chiefly, they sing God's praise. Sometimes they perform particular errands, as when they visit Abraham to announce that Sarah will have a child. Sometimes they act as a bodyguard, as when they accompany Jacob on his way to Mesopotamia. Sometimes they convey human petitions to God; there are even prayers in the traditional Jewish liturgy in which they are called upon to do that.

Is there then any good reason to believe that angels exist? None whatsoever. Even Rabbi Dr Louis Jacobs takes that view, though he hedges his bets just a little by quoting the famous lines from Francis Thompson's poem,

> *The angels keep their ancient places;*
> *Turn but a stone, and start a wing!*
> *'Tis ye, 'tis your estranged faces*
> *That miss the many-splendoured thing,*

and then commenting: 'Fine poetry or halting expression of a reality? Most of us would opt solidly for the former. Yet perhaps, a very faint perhaps, a question mark is still there' (*A Jewish Theology*, p. 113).

On the other hand, Kaufmann Kohler, President of the Hebrew Union College at the beginning of the century and a great authority on angelology, did not equivocate. 'We need no intermediary beings', he wrote, 'and they all evaporate before our mental horizon like mist, pictures of the imagination without objective reality' (*Jewish Theology*, 1943 edn., p. 204). No faint 'perhaps' there!

We took the same view when we compiled our last generation of prayer books, and eliminated angels from them, which prompted the late Professor Jakob Petuchowski to write to me: 'As long as there is room for music and poetry in the Jewish service, there is also room for the seraphim and the cherubim, the whole company of angels and archangels.' And he added: 'Often, indeed, they are far less distracting, and far more conducive to true worship, than their terrestrial counterparts in the choir loft' (letter dated 9 November 1965). Of course he wrote that without having heard the LJS Choir! But we did take his point, and in our new *Siddur* angels have made a little bit of a comeback, though strictly as poetic images only.

But let me come back to the cherubim of our Torah portion. Since they are only sculpted figures, they are obviously symbolic. And what do they symbolise? To understand that, you have to know that in the Tabernacle God was believed to speak to Moses, now and then, from above the Ark and hence from above the Kapporet which covered the Ark. Therefore the cherubim at either end of the *kapporet*, symbolically supported the invisible throne of God. Hence God is often referred to in the Bible as 'enthroned above the cherubim' (for example, Ps. 99:1, I Sam. 4:4).

Finally, let us give our story one more twist. You will recall that in our Sidra the cherubim are said to be 'facing one another' (Exod. 25:20). But in another passage, in the Second Book of Chronicles, we are told that they did not look at each other but stared into the Temple (II Chron. 3:13). This discrepancy gave rise to a controversy in the Talmud which was resolved as follows: when the people do God's will, as they did in the days of the First Temple, the cherubim face each other, as a symbol of God's love for Israel; but when they fail to do God's will, as in the time of the Second Temple, when they harboured groundless hatred, then the cherubim look away from each other, as a token of God's displeasure (*BB* 99a).

But let the last word go to Rabbi Joseph Patsanovski, whose book *Pardes Yosef* was published in Russia in 1931. Commenting on the talmudic passage I have just quoted, he repeats that the cherubim face each other when the people do God's will, but then goes on to ask, what is God's will? And he answers: 'that we should care for others and not only for ourselves and our own families' ('*Itturey Torah*, Vol. 3, p. 215).

Whatever we may think of the cherubim, with or without an 's', that little bit of symbolism, derived from the biblical description of their posture, we may safely endorse.

Aspects of Progressive Judaism

Encounter with Modernity

13 December 1997

If you were to make a film of today's *Sidra*, and you had to choose for it one of those snappy, single-word titles which seem to be *de rigueur* nowadays, what would it be? My suggestion is 'Encounter'.

As a matter of fact, there are *two* encounters. First, in a dream on the bank of the river Jabbok, Jacob encounters a mysterious being who is referred to nondescriptly as *ish*, 'a man'.

Who is this *ish*, and is he good or bad? According to the Haftarah traditionally read on this Shabbat, he is 'an angel' (Hos. 12:5), a messenger of God, and therefore presumably good. And this interpretation seems to be confirmed by the sequel in which Jacob names the place Peniel, which means 'the face of God', saying 'for I have seen God face to face' (Gen. 32:31). Peniel, in other words, is the place of Jacob's encounter with God.

On the other hand, the *ish* might be an evil spirit. Why? Because the dream takes place beside a river, and at night, which suggests one of those sprites of popular folklore who hover where there is water during the hours of darkness but at daybreak vanish into thin air, as in Jacob's dream the *ish* says to him 'Let me go, for day is dawning' (Gen. 32:27). In line with this, the *Zohar* (Gen. 170a) identifies the mysterious being with Sammael, which is another name for Satan.

Paradoxically, therefore, Jacob's encounter is either with God or with Satan! And then there is a third possibility. According to the Midrash, the mysterious being is the 'prince' or 'genius' of Esau

(Gen. R. 78:3). And that makes good sense, since the prospect of meeting Esau, the brother he treated so badly so long ago and who is quite possibly still bent on vengeance, is what preys on Jacob's mind as he lies down to sleep on the bank of the Jabbok.

And that brings us to the second encounter of our Sidra, which takes place the following day, when the brothers really do meet. But is Esau good or bad, and therefore, when he kisses Jacob, is it a genuine kiss or, as some Midrashim suggest, is he really trying to bite him? Let us keep all these possibilities in mind as we leap across the chasm of time to the present.

Last Sunday, in London, under Orthodox auspices, there took place what was billed as an 'Encounter Conference' under the title 'Judaism Faces Modernity'. And what's the connection? Yes, you have guessed it! As Jacob, in his dream, encountered a mysterious being, so Judaism, for the past two hundred years, has been encountering modernity; and as the great question about Jacob's *ish* is whether he is good or bad, so the great question to be asked about modernity is whether it is good or bad.

What then is modernity? According to some sociologists, the essence of modernity is faith in reason and faith in science, and since we no longer have so much faith in reason or in science, therefore we have already left modernity behind and live in a post-modern age.

Well, that may be how the word 'modernity' is used in sociology, but it is a huge oversimplification! For one thing, thank God, we still have *some* faith in reason, for reason is what stands between civilisation and barbarism. Likewise, we still have some faith – indeed, a great deal of faith – in science. The danger of global warming, for instance, is not to be laid at the door of science. On the contrary, it is science which has alerted us to the danger, and we are heavily dependent on science to overcome it.

In any case, modernity is *not* only about reason and science. It is about all those things which significantly distinguish the modern age from the Middle Ages. They include, we must admit, some negative things, like nationalism, racism, totalitarianism, secularism, materialism, consumerism and permissiveness. But they also include many positive things, like the rediscovery of classical civilisation, the spirit of free inquiry, the toleration of diversity, individual autonomy, equality, democracy and universalism.

To this complex cluster of phenomena which constitutes modernity, what should be our attitude as Jews? There are four possibilities. First, we could sell our souls to it, or to whichever part of it appeals to us. In that spirit, many Jews at the beginning of the last century, like Heinrich Heine, converted to Christianity, with or without conviction, as a way of merging into a new society in which they could conveniently forget their Jewishness; and in the same spirit, a few generations later, many opted for Marxism as their sole ideology. It is the way of apostasy.

At the other extreme, it is possible to ignore modernity altogether, to turn our backs on it, to say to our people, 'Keep well away from it, for it is evil; avoid any encounter with it', or, as Lewis Carroll might have put it, 'Beware the Jabbok, my son'. That is the way of old-time Orthodoxy, represented at the beginning of the nineteenth century by the Chatam Sofer, known for his slogan, *chadash asur min ha-torah*, that 'anything new is *ipso facto* forbidden by the Torah', and today by the *Charedim*.

Between these two extremes there are only two possibilities. One is the way of Neo-Orthodoxy, or Modern Orthodoxy, which goes back to Samson Raphael Hirsch with his slogan, *torah 'im derech eretz*, by which he meant that one should combine traditional Jewish belief and practice with participation in European culture. And it is the spirit of the conference that was held in London last Sunday. It is a way of saying: we are not hostile to modernity; we are interested in it and want to listen to it; but on the other hand, it has nothing significant to teach us, and therefore nothing it may say is going to make any significant difference to the way we understand and practise our Judaism. It is an encounter, but a one-sided one: more like a confrontation.

Which leaves the way of Progressive Judaism. We don't sell our souls to modernity, and we don't turn our backs on it. We face it, but not in a spirit of condescension. We don't pretend that Jewish tradition has all the answers and that therefore we have nothing to learn from modernity. On the contrary, modernity has already taught us many things. It has even given us a truer understanding of how the Bible came to be written and how Judaism grew and developed. It has certainly taught us those Enlightenment values which I mentioned earlier, like individual autonomy, pluralism, democracy, equality – especially as between men and women, and universalism.

Of course the roots of these ideas can be traced, to some

extent, in Jewish sources, too. But the realisation of their full implications has come, not from traditional organised religion, whether Jewish, Christian or otherwise, but often against the opposition of traditional organised religion, from modernity, from the Enlightenment, from the spirit of reason and science. And through this realisation, Judaism, in its Progressive form, has been enriched.

Jacob had a hard struggle with his adversary, and a limp to show for it. Outwardly, he did not emerge unscathed. But inwardly, his dream was a growing experience. When he awoke, he was no longer Jacob, the schemer, but Israel, the one who knows the difference between what is divine and what is not divine. He became mature, and in his new maturity he could face Esau, and respect the good in Esau, and make peace with him.

Modernity is not all good, but neither is it all bad. And through what is good in it, God has spoken to us more clearly than through the hidebound defenders of an immutable tradition. A Judaism that respects individual autonomy, that celebrates diversity, that gives equal rights to women, that repudiates the atavistic hope for a return to priestly sacrifice, and that looks forward to a messianic age conceived universally, is a nobler, larger Judaism: outwardly modified, it is true, but inwardly more mature.

As Jacob made his peace with Esau, and as Jeremiah advised the exiles to make their peace with Babylonia (Jer. 29:1–14), so Progressive Judaism has made its peace with modernity, and is the better for it.

From our point of view, Judaism's encounter with modernity, like Jacob's encounter with his *ish*, has been a positive encounter, a give-and-take encounter, a growing experience. It has been for us a Peniel, an encounter with God.

A Response to Orthodoxy

22 July 2000

If we were asked who was our least favourite biblical character, I think we might choose the eponymous hero of today's *Sidra*: Pinchas, or Phineas, as his name is anglicised.

Why is that? Partly because he is the reputed ancestor of the priesthood, which presided over the sacrificial cult, which, to put it mildly, doesn't commend itself to us as a sensible or nice way of worshipping God. But chiefly on account of an incident at a place called Shittim related at the end of last week's *Sidra* and the beginning of today's.

The exact nature of the incident is unclear. On the one hand, there was an act of gross idolatry, immorality and indecency publicly committed by some prominent Israelite men at the instigation of some equally prominent Moabite and Midianite women. On the other hand, there was a plague. Perhaps the misbehaviour produced the plague as a divine punishment. Perhaps the plague came first, and the hideous ritual was a pagan way of trying to appease the local deity, Baal Peor, to ward it off, in which case it was singularly unsuccessful, since 24,000 people died.

In any case, Pinchas stepped forward and killed the ringleaders, whereupon the plague ceased. In other words, he acted as a zealot (Num. 25:11) – the same word used in our Haftarah when Elijah, alluding to his triumph over the prophets of Baal at Mount Carmel, says of himself, 'I have been very zealous for the Eternal One, the God of hosts' (I Kings 19:10).

And zealots – or fanatics – are not people we tend to admire.

Therefore it is not easy for us to accept the fact that for his action Pinchas is almost invariably praised both in the Bible and in subsequent Jewish literature. Of course we can tell ourselves that sometimes it is necessary to stand up for one's principles, to act resolutely, and that extreme situations call for extreme measures. Perhaps what happened at Shittim was such a situation. Perhaps the whole continuity of the monotheistic enterprise, and therefore of God's plan for humanity, was under threat. Perhaps it was a time for swift action, and for pondering the moral questions afterwards.

Perhaps, but we still hesitate, and I think we do so because what we have experienced of zealotry in modern times does not dispose us favourably towards it. There has been far too much zealotry, both political and religious.

What is especially disturbing from our point of view is that there has recently been an increase of zealotry within the Jewish community, and that some of it has been directed against non-Orthodox expressions of Judaism, and therefore against us. Two weeks ago in his sermon, Rabbi Mark Solomon referred to an attack on the Hebrew Union College in King David Street, Jerusalem, when vandals smashed its beautiful glass door and daubed the word 'Satan' next to it. It was the latest in a spate of attacks on Progressive and Conservative synagogues and kindergartens in Israel as well as women worshippers at the Western Wall, and in all cases the perpetrators are known or believed to have been Orthodox religious fanatics.

But even just to say that is to become aware of a danger: that when we hear about such incidents they may encourage in us a tendency, from which I suspect most of us are not quite immune, to harbour hostile or disdainful or otherwise negative feelings towards Orthodoxy. So let me take a few minutes to try and set the record straight if I can.

Essentially, Orthodox Judaism is Rabbinic Judaism: the kind of religion which dominated Jewish life from the destruction of the Temple until the Emancipation. To that extent, to despise Orthodox Judaism would be to despise our own past, the rock from which we were hewn.

What the Emancipation did was to expose those who took advantage of it to modernity: to all those streams of philosophical, historical, political and religious thought which had emerged in European civilisation since the close of the Middle Ages.

At this time there arose two parties in Judaism. One party, which called itself Reform or Liberal or Progressive, broadly speaking embraced modernity, said 'yes' to it, and tried to combine what seemed best in it with what seemed best in Jewish tradition. That was an honourable option.

The other party, which became known as Orthodox, broadly speaking rejected modernity, said 'no' to it, determined to carry on as before, on the ground that Judaism is not to be judged by modernity but, on the contrary, modernity is to be judged by Judaism. That was also an honourable option.

The parting of the ways between these two honourable options can be dated to the opening of the Hamburg Temple in 1818.

But because Orthodoxy was from the start in opposition to Reform and more generally in opposition to modernity – because it involved swimming against the current of the age – therefore it developed a certain intransigence, a certain back-to-the-wall defensiveness and sometimes aggressiveness, which distinguished it significantly from the more relaxed Rabbinic Judaism of pre-Emancipation times.

To be a little more specific, there developed two different kinds of Orthodoxy. One is associated with Moses Schreiber, known as the Chatam Sofer, who led the attack against the Reform movement, and whose motto is said to have been that 'everything new is forbidden by the Torah'. It therefore rejected modernity altogether and may be called 'Ultra-Orthodoxy'. In today's world it is represented by the Charedim and Chasidim who live in cultural enclaves and have little contact with the outside world.

The other tendency, known as 'Modern Orthodoxy', was founded a little later by Samson Raphael Hirsch, whose motto was *torah 'im derech eretz*. That is to say, he favoured combining the traditional Jewish way of life with participation in modern European culture, but in separate compartments, without either influencing the other. Today that kind of Orthodoxy is represented by the United Synagogue, although that is now being squeezed between the ultra-Orthodox on the one hand and the Progressives on the other.

To the immense credit of Orthodoxy in both its forms, but especially ultra-Orthodoxy, it must be said that among many of its members there are to be found levels of commitment, of dedication, of self-discipline, of piety, of observance, and of learning, which scarcely exist among us and which those of us who have not had personal experience of their way of life can hardly even imagine. That is something we should always bear in mind, and respectfully acknowledge, when we speak about Orthodoxy.

Of course it doesn't mean that we have to agree with it. On several issues – for instance, its rejection of modern Bible scholarship, its discrimination against women, and its retention of the ancient hope for the restoration of the Temple with its sacrifices – we think it is mistaken, even profoundly mistaken, and we have every right to say so, with all due politeness.

But there is one general feature of Orthodoxy which is bound to cause us concern, and that is its tendency to claim that it is the *only* authentic form of Judaism, for that can easily lead to zealotry. Happily, the overwhelming majority of Orthodox Jews are *not* zealots. At least in their personal relations with other Jews they are perfectly tolerant. But it is not always easy to be sure whether their tolerance stems from Jewish ethics or from the urbane, democratic, pluralistic, let-us-agree-to-differ ethos of Western society. In either case, let us be grateful for it.

Nevertheless, to believe that yours is the only legitimate way is the equivalent intellectually of what politically is called totalitarianism. Therefore it can easily lead to verbal aggression against non-conformists, and we have experienced plenty of that over the years, and from that it is only one step to political discrimination, and one step further still to physical violence of the kind we have seen recently in Israel. Of course it is only a tiny, unrepresentative minority who go that far; but the danger is apparent.

Unfortunately, there is not a great deal we can do about it, except to make sure that we don't over-react, and that we don't exacerbate the situation by displaying any kind of aggressiveness in return. After all, for us, because we believe in pluralism, tolerance is easy; therefore we have even less excuse for intolerance than our opponents.

Beyond that, we can only appeal to our fellow-Jews of all denominations to join us in promoting a communal atmosphere of mutual courtesy, respect and tolerance. In that connection, the election of a past chairperson of the ULPS, Tony Sacker, as a

Vice-President of the Board of Deputies is a good omen. And let us take seriously the words of the Psalmist which we sing so often as a song: 'How good it is, and how pleasant, when brothers and sisters live together in unity!' (133:1).

The Role of Progressive Judaism

29 May 1997

Last *Shabbat* I had the privilege of preaching at a special service of the Finchley Progressive Synagogue to mark the retirement of Rabbi Frank Hellner, 33 years after coming over from America to take charge of what was then a fledgling congregation. In his response, he gave a wonderful summary of what he had tried to achieve during his ministry, and then added: 'I am not retiring from Judaism; therefore, as they say, see you in *shul*.'

Since it is coming up to ten years since my retirement, I may perhaps say that I, too, have not retired from Judaism. But retirement does give one a certain perspective of distance, and after ten years of it I thought you might allow me to attempt some kind of a summation of what I have seen as my task, and therefore to deal, for once, not with specifics, whether of today's Scripture readings or of current affairs, but to reflect on this Progressive Jewish enterprise of ours in the most general terms. What essentially is it, and what is its role in the larger scheme of things?

The first point to be made is that Progressive Judaism is about *Judaism*. But let us be clear what that means. Judaism is just one strand in the rich tapestry of human civilisation. But we have a special relationship with it because it has been transmitted to us, or because we have chosen it. And in that strand we see much that is precious. It may be its philosophy. It may be its ethics. It may be its festivals and rituals. It may be its family life. It may be its sense of community. It may be its history, or its literature, or its music. Most probably, it is a combination of all of these.

In all of these aspects of our Jewish heritage there are values far too great to be squandered; values the disappearance of which would seriously impoverish ourselves, our community, and our world. Whatever may be the process by which Judaism became our heritage, it *is* our heritage, and we affirm it and feel deeply committed to its continuation.

But all that having been said, we must add: *not everything* in the total Jewish heritage commends itself to us. Along with many wonderful things, it includes just a few that are less admirable. There is, for instance, its discrimination against women. There is its intolerance of diversity and resistance to change. There is its less than fully universalistic attitude to non-Jews. There is its adherence to antiquated concepts such as miracles, resurrection, monarchy, priesthood and animal sacrifice.

The fact that we feel entitled to make such critical judgments shows that we do not regard Jewish tradition as the *sole* repository of all truth, that we subscribe also to another source of values. What is that other source? Why, for instance, do we believe in equal rights for men and women? Why do we believe in liberty and tolerance and reason and conscience and democracy and progress? Of course these values can be found, embryonically at least, in Judaism itself if we choose to look for them and to emphasise them. But they stem more obviously from Greece and Rome, from the Renaissance and the Enlightenment and the French Revolution, and the Universal Declaration of Human Rights.

There is no one word which satisfactorily embraces all these streams of thought, but since we do need to speak of them collectively, let us plump for 'Secularism'.

This is not to say that Progressive Judaism is an amalgam of the two. Essentially, its values are the values of Judaism, but *modified* by those of Secularism. It is, if you like, 90 per cent Judaism and 10 per cent Secularism. But even that way of putting it makes too sharp a distinction between them. For the values of Secularism are themselves rooted, as we have seen, in Judaism. There is, for instance, in Jewish tradition a clear tendency towards raising the status of women, which Progressive Judaism has merely carried to its logical conclusion. Again, it is hardly possible to read the Universal Declaration of Human Rights without being struck by the Hebraic spirit that pervades almost every clause of it.

Progressive Judaism is Traditional Judaism modified by what is good and true in Secularism. And not only modified but enhanced. For we believe that a Judaism which gives equal rights to women, which encourages innovation, that welcomes diversity, and whose vision of the ultimate future is a universal vision, is a more excellent Judaism than one which refuses to make these adjustments to modernity.

If what I have said is an acceptable account of where we Progressive Jews stand *vis-à-vis* Jewish Tradition on the one hand and Secularism on the other, then there follows a consequence of huge importance. For what has been going on in the Jewish world throughout the twentieth century, and with increasing vehemence as we approach the twenty-first, is nothing less than a *Kulturkampf*, a titanic struggle between two cultures, which is being played out chiefly in Israel but has its repercussions everywhere.

What are these two cultures? One is a traditional Judaism which claims that it has nothing to learn from modernity, which is determined to carry on exactly as it was before modern times: in other words Orthodox Judaism. Now there are of course different trends in Orthodox Judaism, and it would be unfair to tar them all with the same brush. There is an urbane, tolerant, democratic trend, known as Modern Orthodoxy, which we can live with very happily. But the logical conclusion to which Orthodox thinking, if consistently pursued, leads is represented in Israel by the so-called Charedim or Ultra-Orthodox. That kind of Orthodoxy is an anti-modern and anti-democratic force which, if it gained enough political power, would turn Israel into a theocratic state, a state ruled by an unreformed *Halachah*, which would unashamedly discriminate against non-Jews and against non-Orthodox Jews and against women, which would abolish the High Court as now constituted, and which would oppose territorial compromise and so make peace with the Palestinians permanently impossible.

The other culture is Secularism, which is what the majority of Israeli Jews subscribe to. That is to say, they accept modernity, democracy, pluralism, sex equality, and all that; but though they are of course in many ways consciously or unconsciously influenced by their Jewish roots, and may occasionally go to a synagogue for a Bar-Mitzvah or a wedding, they repudiate the religious component – which is to us the most important component – of their Jewish heritage, and indeed, because they tend to identify religion with what they see of the Charedim, look upon it with revulsion and contempt.

Furthermore, having repudiated their religious heritage, the Secular are always liable to fall for a chauvinistic kind of nationalism in which might is right, and the end justifies the means, and moral scruples count for nothing. Hence the strange alliance of the Ultra-Nationalists with the Ultra-Orthodox, which sustained the Likud government for so many dark years in a common determination to keep Greater Israel, to deny the Palestinians, to defy world opinion, and to resist the peace process.

The recent election in Israel was a victory of the mainstream, moderate Secular against both the Ultra-Nationalists and the Ultra-Orthodox. It was a vote for common sense, for modernity, for democracy, for pluralism, and for peace. And I am sure it was greeted by most of us with a huge sense of relief. As one Israeli memorably put it on the day of the election, 'Today we rejoin the family of nations'.

But the underlying conflict remains, and given the demographic growth as well as the increasing militancy of the Charedim, it is difficult to be sanguine about the future. Ehud Barak wishes to reunite the nation, and we hope he will succeed. But it is hard to see how there can ever be any reconciliation between the Orthodox and the Secular; they are so fundamentally and bitterly opposed to one another.

What hope then is there for the long-term future? Surely the hope lies with a Third Force which is neither religious in the sense of being anti-secular nor secular in the sense of being anti-religious, but which combines the best of both; which says to the Orthodox, 'You don't have to reject modernity; Judaism is quite capable of absorbing it, and will be the better for it', and which says to the Secular, 'You don't have to reject your religious heritage; appropriately modernised, it can still speak to us both rationally and inspiringly'.

That Third Force, or Middle Way, already exists. It is called Progressive Judaism. Sometimes its progress seems painfully slow, but it is not only making headway, it is actually gathering momentum: here in Britain, in the United States, in France, in Germany, in the former Soviet Union, and not least in Israel itself. Sooner or later it will grow exponentially. My generation will not see it, but the next, or the next but one, surely will.

At any rate, this is the measure of the importance of Progressive Judaism: that it alone can resolve the *Kulturkampf*, that it alone provides a platform on which the majority of Jews will be able, sooner or later, to reunite. And this is the task to which Rabbi Frank Hellner and I, along with many others, have dedicated our lives: quite simply to demonstrate that it is possible to combine the best of Jewish Tradition with the best of modern secular culture. I do hope you share our feeling that it is a task worthy of your allegiance.

Doing and Hearing

5 February 2000

Na'aseh v'nishma', literally 'We will do, and we will hear' (Exod. 24:7): that is the key phrase of our Torah portion. Let us focus our minds on it.

To the ancient Rabbis it was a favourite text. Faced as they were with the challenge of Christianity, which taught that God had rejected the Jewish people and made a 'New Covenant' with the Church, they often quoted it by way of self-assurance, as if to say: 'It was our ancestors who stood at Mount Sinai and accepted God's Law – so eagerly, indeed, that they promised to live by it even before they knew exactly what it entailed. And we have kept their promise, for we still live by the same Law. Therefore, whatever others may say, we are still God's people.'

In modern times, too, *na'aseh v'nishma'* has been much quoted, to show what a *practical* religion Judaism is: a religion of deed rather than creed. It is a popular point to make. For it chimes well with British pragmatism; it serves as a gentle dig at Christianity with its dogmatic theology; and in a time when many Jews are unsure of their faith, it is comforting to be able to say: 'It doesn't really matter all that much what we believe as long as we do what we are supposed to do.'

In all that there is much truth, but it does raise two or three questions which we need to consider. In the first place, what kind of 'doing' are we talking about? Usually when people speak about the Jewish way of life, it is its *observances* that they have in mind. But there is also another kind of 'doing': right conduct in the ethical sense. About that too Judaism has a great deal to say, and though we tend to think of it as just a matter of ordinary human decency, it is in fact deeply rooted as well as precisely defined in Jewish tradition.

Which, then, of these two kinds of 'doing' is the more important? The Prophets (with one or two exceptions) had no doubt about that. In their view right conduct was immeasurably more important. Our *Haftarah* provided one of many examples: '*These* are the things which you shall do: speak the truth to one another, render in your gates judgments that are true and make for peace, do not devise evil in your hearts against one another, and love no false oath' (Zech. 8:16f.).

It is true that in the welter of minute legislation, which is the Talmud, this Prophetic emphasis got somewhat lost, but Liberal Judaism has revived it, and there is no question in my mind but that it has been right to do so. And yet it has become increasingly clear to me over the years that the other side of Jewish practice cannot be neglected with impunity. For though it doesn't have the same *intrinsic* importance, it does play a special role in what one might call the dramatisation, and therefore the transmission, of Judaism. For I can't help noticing that it is in homes which not only have high moral standards but also pulsate with the rhythm of Jewish rituals, sincerely and lovingly performed, that Jewish identity and commitment are most likely to be effectively transmitted from generation to generation. Of course there is no guarantee even then; but *on the whole* I think that is the case.

About the second word *nishma'*, 'we will hear', there is an intriguing Midrash.

A king said to a servant: Look after these two precious glass goblets for me, and be very careful with them. But when the servant entered the palace, a calf standing near the gate attacked him, and one of the goblets got broken. Terrified, the servant appeared before the king, who asked him why he was trembling; but when he explained what had happened, the king, magnanimously, said to him: Now be doubly careful with the other goblet. Likewise [the Midrash continues] God said to Israel: At Sinai you filled two goblets, in that you promised to do and to hear. The first you broke when you committed the sin of the Golden Calf; now be careful that you don't break the second one also. (Exod.R. 27:9)

What we can take from that Midrash is this: we may not always do what we should; but as long as we still 'hear' – as long as we still acknowledge our Jewish obligation – so long there is hope.

To 'hear', then, is to affirm our Jewish identity, with the responsibilities it entails, and that is a lot better than nothing. But more generally, *nishma'* refers to the internal, as distinct from the external, expression of our Jewishness. It refers to thinking and learning, prayer and meditation.

What then is the relative importance of these two aspects of Judaism, *na'aseh* and *nishma'*, doing and hearing, external and internal? That question has been debated in our tradition for over 2,000 years. On the whole, as we have seen, it has tended to emphasise doing. There is, for instance, the statement in *Pirkei Avot*, 'Not the study of Torah is the main thing but its practice' (1:17). Similarly, James, the most Jewish of the New Testament writers, perhaps in allusion to *na'aseh v'nishma'*, exhorts: 'Be doers of the word, and not only hearers' (1:22).

On the other hand, the Talmud records a debate which took place in the second century in a famous house in Lydda as to which is the more important, *talmud*, study, or *ma'aseh* (action), when various views were expressed but finally all agreed with Rabbi Akiva that study is the more important, 'because study leads to action' (*Kid.* 40b).

In the end, therefore, we must say that both are, in their own way, equally important, and furthermore that much depends on the individual. Those of us who are inclined to be inward-looking and contemplative should perhaps become more active, and those of us who are inclined to be hyper-active should perhaps do more to cultivate our inner spiritual life.

But if doing is what ultimately counts, then we must ask one more question of the greatest importance: how can we know what we *should* do?

From an Orthodox point of view the answer is beautifully simple. It is all there, in the Torah. Not indeed the Written Torah only but the Oral Torah as well. But the Oral Torah only spells out what, incipiently, is already contained in the Written Torah. It develops, but only from within itself, without any fresh input from without. Since Sinai, on this view, that is, for over 3,000 years, there has been no further revelation and no real progress in humanity's understanding of right and wrong, and hence of God's will.

But of course that is exactly where we liberals differ. The Sinaitic Revelation, described so dramatically in our Torah portion (Exod. 24:1–11), is a powerful myth which has its appeal for us. But we know that not everything was revealed at that time, and even what was revealed was not necessarily understood correctly by those present, let alone by those who recorded it centuries later.

We know that there have been genuine advances all through the ages. On sacrificial worship, on priestly privilege, on democracy, on slavery, on capital punishment, on equal rights for men and women, and for heterosexuals and homosexuals, on respect for other religions, and on animal rights – on all these and many other subjects there have been, not least in modern times, changes in outlook which we see as genuine advances in humanity's understanding of the Divine Will.

For us, therefore, the question, what God wishes us to do, is not simple at all. It requires us, not only to study the texts of our own Jewish tradition, although that should always be the first step, but also to learn what we can from other sources of knowledge, and to think hard about it, and to consult our consciences. It requires us to seek answers to our questions, not with minds closed by dogmatic assumptions about the authority of ancient texts, but with minds open to all genuine insights, old and new alike.

And so for us the promise of our ancestors at Mount Sinai, *na'aseh v'nishma'* acquires an even larger meaning. It is a promise that we will endeavour to *do* what God requires of us, but also that we will endeavour without preconception to understand what it *is* that God requires of us, and to that end to *hear* – to listen to the voice of God as it speaks to us, not only from the pages of ancient scriptures, but in all sorts of ways and in all sorts of times and places; to say, with the child Samuel in the house of Eli: 'Speak, Eternal One, for your servant is listening' (I Sam. 3:9).

The Jewish Religious Union a Hundred Years On

20 October 2002

'We have met here for a solemn and sacred purpose.' With these words Claude Montefiore began his address at the first service of the Jewish Religious Union on 18 October, 1902.

This too is a solemn and sacred occasion. Solemn, because centuries are a rare occurrence on this side of St John's Wood Road. Sacred, because our purpose today, as then, is a religious one. That is to say, we want to ask ourselves how God might judge the hundred years we have come here to recall and to celebrate.

Surely God's judgment would not be *wholly* favourable. For our founders were human and fallible and children of their age, as we are of ours, and none of us can step outside our skins. The danger of conceding too much to the *Zeitgeist* – the spirit of the age – is real. But so, too, is the danger of failing to take it sufficiently seriously, for through it, perchance, the Eternal God may speak to us.

We know that in our zeal for the new we have sometimes undervalued the old; that in our emphasis on ethics we have sometimes underestimated the importance of ritual; that in our enthusiasm for the universal we have sometimes paid too little attention to the particular; that in our concern for the individual we have sometimes neglected the community. And we know, too, that sometimes we have erred in the opposite directions. Sometimes we have been slow to respond to new developments in Jewish history, such as the creation of the State of Israel, and in human thought, such as post-modernism, and sometimes we have embraced them too uncritically.

Today, in retrospect, we confess our errors, and from the One whose judgement alone matters, we ask forgiveness.

Nevertheless, there *is* cause for sober satisfaction. In many ways, the story we have come here to recall is a success story. It was not a foregone conclusion when the JRU was founded that it would be. Our detractors decried it as misconceived and predicted that it would fail, and even our founders were only cautiously optimistic. As Montefiore went on to say, 'Whether the religious services, of which the first is being held to-day, will prove, according to the stereotyped phrase, a success, we do not know. How long they may endure, we cannot tell. Humbly and reverently...we dedicate them to God.'

A hundred years later I think we may claim, equally humbly and reverently, that the venture has succeeded. At least it has stood the test of time. In Jewish tradition, it has been jocularly said, a foetus is not considered viable until it passes its law exams. Surely a religious movement may be considered viable when it passes its centenary.

Not only have we survived, but we have grown from small beginnings to a union of thirty congregations with a member-ship of ten thousand and a host of activities. And though our numbers have remained more or less static for some years, we have at least maintained ourselves in a demographically declining community and therefore continued to grow as a proportion of it.

What is more important, our Movement has succeeded in retaining or regaining the loyalty to Judaism of countless individuals and families who, without it, might have drifted beyond its gravitational pull. Far from being a force for assimilation, as its enemies used to allege, it has proved itself to be a *goder peretz*, a 'repairer of the breach' (Isa. 58:12), a restorer of the fractured or attenuated relationship between the Jewish people and their heritage. In the great majority of cases, when people have joined our synagogues, the effect on them has been to strengthen, not, Heaven forbid, to weaken their Jewish commitment.

What is perhaps even more important, our Movement has exerted a considerable influence on Anglo-Jewry as a whole, and beyond. Many of the positions it has taken have come to be accepted far beyond its borders.

Take, for instance, Bible Criticism, that is, the study of ancient Jewish history and literature by the methods of modern scholarship. A hundred years ago Claude Montefiore was virtually the only Jew in this country to take it seriously and to draw from it the inescapable conclusion that Scripture comprises both eternal truths and antiquated notions. Today only fundamentalists deny that this is true, and only obscurantists deny that it is important.

Or take the hope that at some future time the Temple with its sacrifices will be restored. This is a major motif of the traditional liturgy but one which our founders rejected in favour of the conviction that the Synagogue represents a more advanced form of worship which has permanently replaced the older form. Today prayers for the restoration of the sacrificial cult are still recited in many synagogues; in others they are modified or obscured; only in our Movement is the liberal view consistently affirmed. But if an opinion poll were conducted, surely it would show that in this matter the vast majority of Jews think as we do.

Or take the Jewish liturgy more generally. A hundred years ago it was an official dogma that Jewish worship must remain forever unchanged. Since then we have demonstrated how it is possible to combine the best of tradition with the best of modernity: to modify inherited texts when honesty so demands, to supplement them with previously unutilised gems of Jewish literature, to write new prayers and compose new music. In all these respects our example has been followed by other Progressive movements in this country and throughout the world.

Or consider the position of women. A hundred years ago they were strictly debarred from equal participation with men in Jewish worship. The JRU, from its inception, introduced mixed seating; and its first synagogue, the LJS, almost from the beginning, allowed women to preach and read. Since then we have taken other steps to grant women equality with men in synagogue worship and marriage law. In most of these respects the Reform movement has followed our example. But other branches of Anglo-Jewry are still debating whether women may sit on synagogue councils and vote in synagogue affairs.

Can there be a shadow of a doubt that in all these matters we have done what will sooner or later come to be generally seen to have been right? Surely, then, Liberal Judaism has abundantly vindicated itself. Surely we are entitled to look back on our first century as a success story.

But if that is so, we need to ask, what have been the causes of our success? For on the answer our continuing success will crucially depend. Let me suggest four causes.

First, the JRU was from the outset a *religious* movement. Its founders were religiously motivated. Claude Montefiore and Lily Montagu, especially, 'walked with God' (Gen. 6:9). God dominated their universe, and all questions, to them, were ultimately about God's will. They were not always right, but nobody who knew them, or has read their writings, can have any doubt that *this* is what drove them. Because they imbued the JRU with such a spirit, people were drawn to it.

Secondly, the JRU was, as its name also implies, a *Jewish* movement. Its founders were very zealous for Judaism. True, they believed that Judaism would grow and develop in the future, as it had in the past. But they never doubted that it was the truest and best of all religions, and that the contribution it had to make to the religion of humanity was vitally important. That is why they did what they did. As Montefiore said in his inaugural sermon (probably in allusion to the rabbinic phrase, *shev v'al ta'aseh, Eruv.* 100a), 'it would have been much easier to sit still and do nothing'.

Thirdly, the JRU was a *union*. It did not seek to impose uniformity, but accommodated a broad range of options in belief and practice, and generated a spirit of mutual understanding, respect and friendship transcending individual differences. And on the whole that spirit has endured. Of course we have had our episodes of turbulence. But we have remained a united movement. Come to our residential conferences and you will experience a spirit of camaraderie, even a family atmosphere, which is perhaps unique in Anglo-Jewry.

In all three respects, therefore, we have remained a JRU: Jewish, Religious and a Union. But pervading all of them, and inseparable from them, is a fourth quality which has from the beginning distinguished our Movement, and that is *integrity*.

Integrity is inseparable from religion, for, as the Rabbis said, *chotamo shel ha-kadosh baruch hu emet*, 'the very signature of God is truth' (*Shab.* 55a). Nobody understood that better than Claude Montefiore. As he said in a famous sermon, 'There can be no truth which is *not* Divine, there can be no falsehood which *is* Divine' (*Truth in Religion*, 1906, p. 3).

Integrity is also inseparable from Judaism. For how can we affirm Judaism unless our understanding of it is in harmony with what we believe to be true, and how can we practise it unless what we practise is in harmony with what we believe? In Judaism, as in any religion, honesty is paramount. Who may dwell on God's holy mountain? Only those, says the Psalmist, 'who speak the truth in their hearts' (15:2).

Integrity is also inseparable from unity. Precisely because we insist on the right and duty of every individual to seek the truth, we accept the diversity of perceptions which, given the diversity of human beings, is the inevitable consequence. And 'unity in diversity' is what the 'U' in JRU stands for.

Integrity was perhaps the outstanding quality of our founders. They imprinted it deeply on our Movement, and we have tried, more or less consistently, to maintain it ever since. It is our greatest asset, and if we wish our Movement to endure, we had better be careful not to fritter it away. As Rabbi Israel Mattuck said in his Induction sermon at the LJS in 1912, 'To sacrifice principle to conformity would jeopardise our cause'.

The temptation to do so is ever present: to follow fashion; to swim with the stream; to court popularity; to play to the gallery; to swallow scruples for political gain. All these temptations we must resist, fully knowing and fully accepting the cost. For integrity is not cheap. It may involve refusing a request or declining a gift. It may cause us to be misunderstood and misrepresented. It may entail accepting a lower rate of numerical growth than we should have wished. It may mean remaining a minority for a long time to come, or even forever. That too is a price we must be willing to pay, for it is better to be few and right than to be many and wrong.

An ancient rabbi taught: *Kol k'nesiyyah she-hi l'shem shamayim, sofah l'hitkayyem*, 'Any assembly that is convened for God's sake will ultimately vindicate itself' (*Avot* 4:11). In centennial retrospect, I think we may safely say that what took place in the Wharncliffe Rooms of the Great Central Hotel on 18 October 1902 was such an assembly. That is why we are here today, and if we remain faithful to that spirit there will be many more anniversaries for us and for our children and children's children to celebrate in times to come. *Ken y'hi ratzon*. Please God, and let us say: Amen.

The Open Door

11 April 1998

One of the most curious customs of the *Seder* is the opening of the door after the meal. What exactly is the point of it? Perhaps, if we explore that question, it will open for us one or two doors into a deeper understanding of this Festival.

Our point of departure – in more senses than one – is our Torah reading with its dramatic account of how our ancestors, in the middle of the night, set out from Egypt, and in particular this verse: 'It was a night of watching for the Eternal One, to bring them out of the land of Egypt; this same night is one of watching both for the Eternal One and for the children of Israel throughout their generations' (Exod. 12:42).

There are two things to be noticed about that verse. One is that in it the key word, *shimmurim*, for 'watching' seems to be used in two different senses: on the one hand, God *watches over* the Children of Israel, keeping them safe from the Tenth Plague that is devastating Egypt; on the other hand, the children of Israel *watch out* for a signal that the moment of their departure has arrived. The other is that the vigil in question was not a one-off affair, but that the Children of Israel are to observe the night of the fifteenth of Nisan in the same spirit of hopeful vigilance 'throughout their generations', from which an important inference was drawn by Rabbi Joshua, when he said: 'On that night the Israelites were redeemed in the past, and on that night they will be redeemed in the future' (*Mechilta, Bo* 14).

Rabbi Joshua's comment combined with other things to make

Pesach night one of intense messianic expectancy. But it also led to a strange custom which arose in the Middle Ages: to leave the doors of the house unlocked throughout the first night of the Festival.

We know this from three medieval sources. One is Rabbi Eleazar ben Judah of Worms, known from the title of his major work as the *Rokeach*. Another is Rabbi Abraham ben Nathan of Lunel, known as *Ha-Manhig*. And a third is Rabbi Isaac ben Moses of Vienna, known as *Or Zarua'*, whose synagogue in Vienna, incidentally, has just been excavated.

All three lived in the age of the Crusades, which makes their practice all the more remarkable. As a matter of fact, the *Rokeach* had a horrific experience in the First Crusade, when the Crusaders burst into his house, murdered his wife and children, and severely wounded him. In these circumstances, to leave the doors unlocked was an act of extraordinary bravery if not foolhardiness.

Why then did they do it? As a demonstration of faith in Rabbi Joshua's messianic interpretation of our key verse with its twofold use of the word *shimmurim*: that on this night God *watches over* us, so that we need not be afraid, and that on this night we *watch out* for a sign that the time of redemption, heralded by the prophet Elijah, has come, so that we may go out to greet him without a moment's delay (Menachem Kasher, *Haggadah Shelemah*, pp. 180, 194).

But of course it *was* a risky business, leaving the house unlocked, in view of the danger of burglary, let alone pogroms, and we may be sure that the Metropolitan Police would not have approved at all. Therefore, already in the fifteenth century Rabbi Jacob Moellin, known as the Maharil, wrote that in places of danger 'we don't rely on miracles'; and by the sixteenth century it had become customary to open the door only for a moment at the end of the *Seder*, close to the witching hour, which we should call the watching hour, of midnight (Kasher, p. 194).

So there you have the origin of the custom. It is *not*, as some Haggadahs say, a gesture of hospitality. Incidentally, one such Haggadah was published exactly a hundred years ago, in 1898, by the colourful Reverend A. A. Green of the Hampstead Synagogue. To the obvious objection, that it's a bit late to invite guests in when the meal has already been eaten, he has a ready answer, by suggesting that in ancient times the door was opened *twice*: before the meal to let them in and after the meal to see them out (p. 27); but that is a conjecture without foundation.

No, the opening of the door was never anything but a symbol of messianic expectancy: an expression of trust in God's power to redeem. But we must add that it became associated with a particular *aspect* of the messianic hope. And to understand that, we have to remember that to the dreamers of the messianic dream it was always obvious that its fulfilment depended on the removal of the one great obstacle that stood in its way, namely the domination of the world by the Roman Empire, or the Holy Roman Empire, or whichever power was oppressing the Jewish people at the time. In short, the triumph of the Jewish people must be preceded by the defeat of their enemies: by the eschatological war of the Children of Light against the Children of Darkness.

So it became customary, during the opening of the door, to utter a kind of curse against the forces of evil, and to use for that purpose appropriate damnatory verses from the Bible, of which there are not a few. The favourite one was taken from Psalm 79: 'Pour out Your wrath upon the nations that do not acknowledge You' (Ps. 79:6). But to that other verses in the same vein were added. In Southern France they recited ten such verses, in Northern France twelve, and in medieval England seventeen (Kasher, p. 177f.).

What shall we say about that practice? Is it understandable? Absolutely! Considering what our people suffered in the Middle Ages, it shows considerable restraint on their part that they did nothing worse to their enemies than recite a few imprecatory Scripture verses against them (see A. A. Green's Haggadah, p. 68f.).

Understandable, certainly. But is it commendable? About that even A. A. Green had his doubts. As he wrote, 'Whether these verses are to be said now is a question which we English Jews may indeed pause to consider' (p. 68). He, having considered it, decided to stick to the traditional text. But other Haggadahs, of a more liberal kind, omitted it. They did indeed retain the opening of the door, but instead of reciting *Sh'foch Chamat'cha*, 'Pour out Your wrath ...', they substituted something like Psalm 27, which begins: 'The Eternal One is my light and my salvation; whom shall I fear?' And now Rabbi Dr Michael Shire, the Director of the Centre for Jewish Education, has published a new, magnificently illustrated Haggadah, based on the ULPS one, in which, nevertheless, *Sh'foch Chamat'cha* is back.

There is, of course, something to be said for it. As we approach the end of the twentieth century, we must be blind if we are not painfully conscious that evil is real, and must be defeated before the messianic age can dawn. There is a need for realism, and I suppose the *Sh'foch Chamat'cha* reminds us of it.

On the other hand, the danger is very great – and never more so than in these days of Jewish chauvinism – that we may fall into the trap of seeing the world as divided into two camps: we and they, we the victims and they the oppressors, we the goodies and they the baddies, we on God's side and they 'the nations that do not acknowledge God'. But the world is not like that. The distribution of good and evil is much more complex. In the Middle East conflict, for instance, it is by no means always clear who is the victim and who is the oppressor; and even British Foreign Secretaries who try to further the peace process by talking to both sides, however clumsily they may go about it, mean well.

Besides, we don't really believe (do we?) that the messianic age will come about suddenly, through an all-out war between good and evil. That is a catastrophic view of history which we have rightly abandoned. Yes, evil has to be defeated, and that may entail fighting in the future, as it has in the past. But wars, though they may sometimes be necessary, don't make the world better: at best, they stop it from getting worse, and often they create as much evil as they destroy. Yes, evil has to be defeated, but it exists in us, Heaven help us, as well as in others; and the way to defeat it is not by military pyrotechnics but by the much more boring, much more difficult, painstaking process of strengthening the Good Inclination against the Evil Inclination, in ourselves as well as in others, and by giving up the way of confrontation and violence in favour of the way of compromise and reconciliation. That is the only kind of messianic hope that makes any sense from our Liberal Jewish point of view.

But to affirm the messianic hope, so understood, is as important as it has ever been, perhaps more so, and the opening of the door remains a powerful symbolic way of expressing it. *Pesach* night is *leyl shimmurim*, a night of watching, in both senses. It is an expression of trust in God's power to redeem and trust in human beings, that they will, sooner or later, allow that power to do its redeeming work. And what is more, to express that trust – to keep alive the messianic hope – is itself a contribution to its fulfilment. As Moses Isserles wrote in his commentary on the Arba'ah Turim, 'By virtue of this act of trust we shall be redeemed' (*Darchey Mosheh, Orach Chayyim* 480). To which we need only add, in the words of the medieval song with which we shall conclude our service, *bim'herah b'yameynu b'karov*, 'Speedily, soon, in our lifetime.' Amen.

Praying for Humanity

6 June 1998

A few weeks ago, on the last Wednesday in April, at the Grove End Road Synagogue, which is only a stone-throw from here – except that, happily, the only missiles likely to be thrown in the intervening space are cricket balls – there took place a remarkable service. Remarkable not only because it was jointly organised by four of the major branches of Orthodox Judaism, not normally renowned for co-operation; and not only because it celebrated the Fiftieth Anniversary of the State of Israel; and not only because the guest of honour was the Prince of Wales – it was apparently the first time this century that a Jewish communal service has been attended by a member of the Royal Family; but also for another reason which, though only a small detail, has wider significance.

I can't personally vouch for it because I wasn't present, but according to somebody who *was* present, and who had a letter in the correspondence column of last week's *Jewish Chronicle*, Chief Rabbi Dr Jonathan Sacks not only gave an inspiring sermon, but also recited *Kaddish*, and when he came to the end of the Aramaic-and-Hebrew text, repeated the last verse in English and added something to it, so that it read: 'May He who makes peace in His high places grant peace to us and to all Israel *and to all mankind.*'

I don't know whether this earth-shattering innovation was premeditated or impromptu, but either way we may safely assume that it was not unconnected with the presence of the royal guest. Something must have insinuated into the mind of the Chief Rabbi of the United Hebrew Congregations the thought that it would not only be quite right, in the presence of Prince Charles, to pray only for the peace of the Jewish people, comprising a mere 300,000 or half a per cent of the people whose Sovereign the Royal Prince may expect one day to become. In other words, the occasion seemed to demand such a token expression of universalism.

But then the question may be asked: should we not express our hope for peace in universal terms even in the absence of royalty? After all, there is always a chance that there may be a non-Jewish visitor present; and even when that is not the case, we should perhaps take some little cognisance of the fact that we live in a world inhabited 99.5 per cent by non-Jews.

Not only *may* that question be asked, but it *was* asked by the writer of the letter in the *Jewish Chronicle* I have already mentioned, and his answer was clear. 'A humanistic version of the *Kaddish*', he wrote, 'should not limit the divine peace-making process to Jews alone.' He expressed the opinion that 'most United Synagogue members ... would wish to pray for peace for all humanity on *all* occasions.' And the wording he suggested was *ve'al kol b'ney adam*, 'and to all human beings'.

Well, we have news for him, don't we? The news is that what he suggests, and in the precise words he suggests, has been done in the LJS and its co-affiliates for exactly 75 years. Why only 75? Because in the earlier orders of service of the Jewish Religious Union, *Kaddish* still ended, traditionally, *v'al kol Yisrael*. But in the three volumes of the Liberal Jewish Prayer Book, edited by Rabbi Israel Mattuck, which began to appear in 1923, the words *v'al kol b'ney adam* were added. That, therefore, has been our expression of the messianic note, on which *Kaddish* ends, ever since. But it has never been adopted by any other Jewish movement in the country, not even the Reform Synagogues of Great Britain.

The case for it is very simple, and it is twofold. First, peace is indivisible. So the prophet Jeremiah, in his famous letter to the Jews of Babylonia, exhorted them to seek the peace of the city to which they had been exiled, and pray to God on its behalf: 'because in its peace you will have peace' (29:7). In other words, our enlightened self-interest dictates that we should pray for the peace of the society in which we live.

But even if no Jewish self-interest were involved, it would still be appropriate that we should pray for the peace of the other 99.5 per cent because they are our fellow men and women, created like ourselves in God's image, whom we should respect and love, and whose welfare we should seek, for that reason.

But, prior to 1923, was this lofty ideal ever put into practice? Take, for instance, the oldest prayer for peace, the Priestly Benediction, which is the centrepiece of today's *Sidra*. It is true that in its preface the *Kohanim* are instructed, 'Thus shall you bless *the children of Israel*' (Num. 6.23). But we do know from various sources that many non-Israelites used to attend Temple services, even to bring their own sacrifices. So it is legitimate to wonder: when the *Kohanim* pronounced the Priestly Benediction, ending with the words, 'and give you peace', did they feel themselves to be included? We can't be sure, but we can hope so.

We do know, however, that once a year, during the festival of *Sukkot*, 70 bullocks were sacrificed in the Temple explicitly on behalf of the '70 nations' of the world (*Suk.* 55b); and on that practice the Rabbis of the Talmudic period commented: 'Although the nations hate us, we nevertheless pray for them' (Num. R. 21:24 and parallels, interpreting Psalm 109:4).

That phrase, 'although the nations hate us', is of course an apt description of what became an everyday reality in the ensuing centuries, especially for Jews living under Christian rule. In these circumstances it would hardly be reasonable to expect them to have prayed for the hostile, persecuting nations among whom they lived – at least in the here and now. That *ultimately*, in the messianic age, all would turn to God and live in peace, was of course always a Jewish hope, expressed in prayers such as the *Aleynu*.

However, even in the context of the unredeemed present, Jews did sometimes pray at any rate for the gentile sovereign who ruled over them. Hence what we know as the Prayer for the Royal Family. But the standard form of that prayer until the end of the nineteenth century was very much an expression of Jewish self-interest, in the spirit of Jeremiah's letter to the exiles. For example, in the first edition of Singer's prayer book, which dates from 1890 and therefore refers to Queen Victoria, the key phrase reads: 'May the supreme King of kings in his mercy put compassion into her heart and into the hearts of all her counsellors and nobles, *that they may deal kindly with us and with all Israel.'*

But only a few years later the then Chief Rabbi, Hermann Adler, felt that the prayer shouldn't stop there but should go on to express some concern for the welfare of Her Majesty's non-Jewish subjects as well. So he amended the phrase to read, '*that they may uphold the peace of the realm, advance the welfare of the nation,* and deal kindly and truly with all Israel.' That was in 1898, the year in which the very same change appeared in a new edition of the prayer book of the West London Synagogue, largely influenced by the Rev. Morris Joseph. It would be interesting to know whether this was a rare case of interdenominational liturgical co-operation or just of great minds thinking alike.

Even so, the prayer still *ended* on a particularistic note, with the words: 'In her days and ours may Judah be saved, and Israel dwell securely, and may the redeemer come unto Zion.' But what about England, Scotland and Wales, and other nations? Is it not to be desired that they, too, may be saved and dwell securely? That thought occurred to Hermann Adler's successor, Chief Rabbi Joseph H. Hertz, and prompted him, in 1935, when the Sovereign was King George V, to make one further change to the Prayer for the Royal Family, so that it ended: 'In his days and ours, *may the Heavenly Father spread the tabernacle of peace over all the dwellers on earth*, and may the redeemer come unto Zion.'

Therefore, when Chief Rabbi Jonathan Sacks, in the presence of Prince Charles, concluded *Kaddish* with a petition that God might grant peace `to all mankind', he followed in a tradition going back to the Prophet Jeremiah which, in recent times, has included two of his own predecessors as well as the Rev. Morris Joseph and Rabbi Israel Mattuck.

How we conclude *Kaddish* is, as I said, a mere detail, but a detail of great significance because it shows to what extent we are conscious of the fact that, as the God we worship cares for all humanity, so should we.

Our World and Welcome to It

27 March 1999

Three more shopping days till *Pesach*! I thought I would just mention that in case any of you have not yet bought the ingredients for your favourite *Charoset* recipe, but more immediately so that we may begin to focus our minds on the forthcoming festival, which is by tradition the function of *Shabbat ha-Gadol*.

If every festival has a characteristic mood – if, for instance, the mood of the High Holydays is one of solemnity and the mood of Purim one of hilarity – then the first word that springs to my mind as characterising *Pesach* is *domesticity*. I think of it chiefly, of course, on account of the *Seder*, as a *cosy* festival, even a slightly claustrophobic one if you need to squeeze a lot of people into a small space while still leaving them enough elbow room to lean to their left without making their neighbours spill their wine all over their Haggadah.

But there is another sense, too, in which *Pesach* is a cosy festival. It is all about the Jewish people: their redemption from Egyptian bondage in the past and their hoped-for future redemption, expressed in the concluding words of the *Seder*, 'Next year in Jerusalem!'

Where then does the rest of humanity come in? The short answer is: it doesn't! On the contrary, there was, already in ancient times, a policy of deliberately *excluding* non-Jews from the celebration of the Passover. 'No foreigner may eat of the paschal lamb', says the book of Exodus (12:43). And again: 'No uncircumcised person shall eat of it' (12:49).

And in the text of the Haggadah, non-Jews can hardly be said to receive a good press. They are represented primarily by Pharaoh, who is the arch villain of the story. They are especially identified, although only by innuendo, with the Roman Empire, which, in the formative period of the *Seder*, was the equivalent of Stalin's Soviet Union or Hitler's Third Reich. The *rasha*, the 'wicked son', even though the context makes it clear that he is a Jew, is paradoxically depicted in many medieval illustrated *Haggadot* as a Roman soldier. And one of the highlights of the *Seder* is the moment when the door is opened and, traditionally, the Psalm verse is recited, 'Pour out Your wrath upon the nations that do not acknowledge You...' (79:6).

All in all, it has to be said that the non-Jewish world – that is to say, the other 99-point-something per cent of the human family – does not feature positively in the forthcoming festival as traditionally celebrated. And why do I mention that? Not to criticise our ancestors who have handed the tradition down to us in that way. We all know that there were, to say the least, extenuating circumstances. The hostility by which we Jews have been surrounded during the greater part of the past 2,000 years more than explains the aloofness towards its non-Jewish environment which the Tradition, for the most part, displays.

On the contrary, what is perhaps remarkable is that, nevertheless, the record is by no means wholly negative. It is, after all, *something* that non-Jews could become Jews. As the Rabbis said, 'the gates are open at every hour, and whoever wishes to enter may enter' (Exod. R. 19:4). It *is* something that non-Jews, once converted, had exactly the same rights as other Jews, including participation in the Passover. It *is* something that non-Jews who chose not to convert were not therefore disbarred from salvation but could make themselves acceptable to God by observing the Seven Noachide Laws. It *is* something that non-Jews, if they so wished, could bring offerings to the God of Israel (Lev. 17:8, 22:18, Num. 15:15, 16, 29, Deut. 16:11, 14). It *is* something that during the harvest festival of *Sukkot* 70 sacrifices were offered in the Jewish Temple for the 70 nations of the world (*Suk.* 5:6).

Therefore non-Jews didn't fare altogether badly in Jewish tradition. Nevertheless, they were on the whole excluded from Jewish ritual, and especially – to come back to where we started – from the celebration of *Pesach*. Why then do I mention it?

Because we live in a different world from the one that shaped Jewish tradition. Not *totally* different, to be sure. Anti-Semitism is still a fact of life. Indeed, its worst barbarities occurred in the century now drawing to its close. So it would be a great mistake to live in a fool's paradise.

Nevertheless we do live in a different world: a world in which anti-Semitism, though still ominously present, is, partly because of the Holocaust, no longer respectable; a world, on the whole, of democracy and religious freedom; a world of inter-faith dialogue; a world of international travel and communication; a world of ethnic and cultural pluralism and intermingling; a world of open societies in which Jews and non-Jews live and work in close proximity, and do and will marry into each other's families.

In short, there is a sea-change in the interrelationship between Jews and non-Jews which has been going on for some generations but with increased momentum in recent years; a sea-change which has affected mainly, of course, the Diaspora but is discernible even in Israel, where intermarriage between Jews and Arabs is becoming steadily less uncommon; a sea-change which Orthodox Jewish leaders have either not noticed or refused to recognise, which at any rate they have failed to do anything about other than to bemoan it; but which Progressive Judaism *has* recognised and is trying seriously, positively and constructively to take into account and to respond to.

One example of that is the 'Outreach Movement' which seeks to make non-Jews who are married to Jews feel welcome in our synagogues. Another, which applies especially to the Liberal movement, is the creation of the possibility, for those of them who wish it, of a relationship with the Synagogue as 'Friends' or 'Associates'. Here, in the LJS, that step was taken two or three years ago. A similar step, more recently, by the Northwood and Pinner Liberal Synagogue drew forth, in last week's *Jewish Chronicle*, a scurrilous article by Norman Lebrecht which proved not only how riddled he is with prejudice but also how out of touch he is with reality.

We need no longer practise our Judaism in hermetic isolation, either fearful or defiant, from the world around us. We can practise it openly, confidently, and invite our non-Jewish friends and neighbours, especially in so far as they have married into our families, to share it with us to whatever extent they wish.

All of which has implications, among other things, for *Pesach*.

Of course I hope that the *Seder* will always retain something of its cosy and domestic quality. But it need no longer be claustro-phobic. We may invite our non-Jewish friends and relations to join us in the celebration of it. When we open the door, it should not be to call down a curse on those who don't share our faith. It should be a symbol of hospitality, as expressed in the opening formula of the *Seder*, 'Let all who are hungry come and eat', and should remind us that not only Jews are hungry.

In 1942 James Thurber published a book entitled *My World – and Welcome to It*. The open door of the *Seder* should have a similar meaning. It should be a way of saying: 'Our Jewish world – and welcome to it'.

Of course the ultimate reconciliation of Jews and Gentiles is a future hope. I have not forgotten that the open door is primarily an invitation to the prophet Elijah to announce the Messianic Age. But when we read in the *Haftarah* for *Shabbat ha-Gadol* that 'he will turn the hearts of parents to their children, and of children to their parents' (Mal. 3:24), we should not take that to mean only that he will close the 'generation gap' within the House of Israel, but also that he will turn the hearts of Jews to gentiles, and of gentiles to Jews. And if we have an opportunity, here and there, to anticipate the coming of that time a little, how can it be otherwise than God's will that we should do so?

We and They

15 July 2000

Those of you who have been to Israel will almost certainly agree with me that the view from the top of Massada across the Dead Sea towards the Moabite mountains is one of the most glorious sights on earth. Those mountains are of course named after the people who inhabited the region during the biblical period and they – the Moabites – are the villains of today's *Sidra*.

What do we know about them? They first appeared in the region in the fourteenth century, just before the time of the Exodus, when they changed their nomadic way of life to one of agriculture and cattle raising. To defend their territory, they often engaged in warfare with neighbouring peoples, including the Israelites, and were often defeated, but sometimes victorious. A rare victory of theirs over the Israelites, in the ninth century, is recorded on the famous Mesha Stone, named after their king of the time (II Kings 3:4), now in the Louvre in Paris. It is written in the same script as ancient Hebrew and shows that their language was extremely similar to Hebrew.

Religiously, they were, like everybody else in the ancient Near East except the Israelites, polytheists and idolaters. Their principal god was Chemosh (I Kings 11:7), and human sacrifice was not unknown among them. On one occasion, recorded in the Bible, their king sacrificed his firstborn son as a burnt offering (II Kings 3:27), which gives an edge to our *Haftarah*, where Micah mentions Moab and in the same breath pours scorn on sacrifices and goes on to say: 'Shall I give my firstborn for my transgression, the fruit of my body for the sin of my soul?' (6:7).

Eventually the Moabites were conquered by the Assyrians under King Sennacherib and a century or two later by the Babylonians. Then they were dispersed and disappeared from history in the same way as the Ten Tribes of Northern Israel did around the same time.

What is interesting about the Moabites to me, and I hope to you, is that what the Bible has to say about them throws a whole lot of light on how our Israelite ancestors related to adjoining peoples. To put it mildly, there was no love lost between them and the Moabites, and that in spite of the fact that they were next-door neighbours and spoke virtually the same language. There was even a tradition that they came from common Hebrew stock, for according to the Bible the Moabites' ancestor was none other than Abraham's nephew Lot. In other words, they were, so to speak, cousins.

But notice how that story of a common ancestry is told. According to the biblical account (which should be marked 'parental guidance') it went back to an unsavoury incident when Lot's two daughters got their father drunk and themselves pregnant by him, with the result that the elder daughter gave birth to Moab, ancestor of the Moabites, and the younger to Ammon, ancestor of the Ammonites (Gen. 19:30–38). Obviously, the Moabites, like the Ammonites, were already much hated when that story was written. It was a way of saying that they were a misbegotten people, a bunch of bastards.

Why were they so hated? Because of a series of hostile encounters. The first occurred at the time of the Exodus, when the Israelites, unable to enter the Promised Land from the south because it was too heavily fortified by the Canaanites, chose the second-best route, via Transjordan, with the intention of making their incursion across the Jordan from the east. But that meant going through the territory of the Moabites, so they demanded of them a guarantee of safe passage as well as provisions – in twentieth-century terms – that they should set up a series of NAAFI canteens along the route where food and drink would be freely available with the compliments of the king.

To that request the king of Moab did not respond well. In fact, he was rather less enthusiastic about it than the Catholics of Northern Ireland are about the marches of Orangemen through their areas. Knowing what a formidable reputation the Israelites had as warriors, he first panicked, then took precautionary measures. A modern ruler would have ordered a general call-up, built air-raid shelters and perhaps consulted an astrologer. King Balak summoned the greatest of the pagan prophets, Balaam, and bribed him to curse the Israelites. And though, by divine intervention, the curse was turned into a blessing, Balak's intention was ever after held against him.

To make things worse, the story went round that a group of Moabite women had seduced some of the Israelites into taking part in a debauched ritual in honour of a god of theirs called Baal-peor (Num. 25:1–5).

Bitter fighting ensued, and renewed itself from time to time in the following centuries. On one occasion, for instance, King David defeated the Moabites, then made them lie down on the ground and measured them off with a cord, a longer one for those who were to be put to death, a shorter one for those who were to be spared (II Sam. 8:1f.) – an early form of *Selektion*.

Finally, a law was promulgated forbidding Israelites to intermarry with Moabites, even if they converted to Judaism, forever. And the reason for the law is clearly stated: 'Because they did not meet you with food and water on your journey after you left Egypt, and because they hired Balaam . . . to curse you' (Deut. 23:4–7).

From the evidence so far, what shall we say about the attitude of our Israelite ancestors to their neighbouring peoples? Surely we must say that it was on a level with the attitude of most nations engaged in territorial disputes with other nations in most times and places: no worse, but also no better. And when we read that the law forbidding intermarriage with Moabites – motivated by an eternal vindictiveness – was a divine command, surely we must respond with Mel Calman's cartoon depicting God as an old man with a long beard sitting on a cloud, holding a book and shaking his head, with the caption 'I've been misquoted'. Surely this one example alone, even if there were not many more, would furnish proof positive that the fundamentalist view of the Bible as 'the Word of God' is mistaken.

In Anglo-Jewry, the first religious leader to face that fact with complete frankness was the founder of our Synagogue, Claude Montefiore. As he wrote, the Bible 'is not good because it is from God; it is from God so far as it is good' (JRU Manifesto, 1909). And the first Orthodox scholar to come to the same conclusion is Rabbi

Dr Louis Jacobs, to whom we send our best wishes on his eightieth birthday the day after tomorrow. As he says in his latest book, the Bible contains 'higher and lower, error as well as truth, the ignoble as well as the noble' (*Beyond Reasonable Doubt*, p. 51).

Clearly the evidence we have considered so far belongs to the 'lower' level, since it shows that the Israelites related to their enemies just like other nations. But that is not the end of the story! There is also *positive* evidence. Take for instance the Edomites, another people closely related to the Israelites who lived on their borders and engaged in warfare with them. What does the book of Deuteronomy say about them? 'You shall not abhor an Edomite, for he is your brother' (23:7). Or take the two mighty empires which enslaved and conquered Israel. What, according to Isaiah, does God say about them? 'Blessed be Egypt My people, and Assyria the work of My hands, and Israel My inheritance' (19:25). Surely you will not find anything like that in any other ancient literature. In these instances the Hebrew Bible is centuries and even millennia ahead of its time. They belong to the 'higher' level.

Or take the Moabites themselves. Considering the bitter hatred in which they were held, is it not astonishing that an Israelite author had the courage to write a short story with a Moabitess, Ruth, as its heroine, asserting that she was none other than the great-grandmother of David, the most beloved of Israelite kings? And even more astonishing that the book was admitted into the sacred canon of the Hebrew Bible?

But even that is not the end of the story. Because the book of Ruth *was* admitted into the canon, therefore the Rabbis decided that the intermarriage prohibition applied only to male, not to female, Moabites (*Yev.* 8:3). And only a short time later, one of the greatest of the Rabbis, Joshua ben Chananya, argued successfully against his colleagues that the law should be rescinded altogether on the ground that Sennacherib, king of Assyria, had long ago mixed up the nations, so that the descendants of the ancient Moabites are no longer identifiable (*Yad.* 4:4).

For the greater part of the last two thousand years, therefore, *all* non-Jews, regardless of their racial or national origin, have been in principle entitled to become members of the Jewish people, subject to conversion, although, as we all know, Orthodox Judaism makes that process more difficult than Progressive Judaism. And in the most recent years we have gone

one step further still, known as 'outreach', by declaring that non-Jews, even if they *don't* convert, are welcome in our community as honoured guests. And so we have come full circle from our starting point, and the universalism, which has always been inherent in Judaism, has finally been carried to its logical conclusion. I hope and believe that the God of Israel and all Humanity, who never commanded any vindictiveness against the Moabites, may be pleased with us on that account.

Israel and Palestine

The Big Issue

First day of *Pesach*, 8 April 2001

Preachers generally take their text from a chapter or verse of the Bible, or even a single word. I shall take mine from a single syllable – or, more precisely, one-and-a-half. You all know that *Pesach* is known in our tradition as *zeman cherutenu*, 'The Season of our Freedom'. Well, it is the first person plural suffix – the *enu* part of *cherutenu* – which I would like to take as my text.

Yes, *Pesach* is the season of *our* freedom. It celebrates *our* liberation from Egyptian slavery. It marks the beginning of *our* self-consciousness as a people, and of *our* unique journey through history. And therefore our focus during this festival is rightly on *our* liberation from Egyptian bondage.

But if the Exodus from Egypt is a liberation paradigm for *us*, it can also serve that purpose for other peoples, and it has done so. Almost every national liberation movement in Europe, America and Africa has invoked the Exodus, drawn inspiration from it, and used its slogans, as in the spiritual, 'Let My people go'. As Heinrich Heine famously said, 'Since the Exodus, Freedom has always spoken with a Hebrew accent' (J. L. Baron, *A Treasury of Jewish Quotations*, 311.27).

We naturally feel complimented when other liberation movements draw on our experience and borrow our language. Sometimes we have even given them a helping hand. Rabbi David Einhorn preached against slavery – and had to flee for his life from Baltimore to Philadelphia. Helen Suzman helped to pave the way for the ending of apartheid in South Africa. And

Jewish leaders, not least rabbis, accompanied Martin Luther King on his civil rights marches.

And that is as it should be. For if freedom is so precious, then we surely *must* desire it for others as well as ourselves. Then it is not enough to celebrate *cherutenu*, *our* freedom: we must seek, and actively promote, *cherutam*, their freedom as well.

But if that applies to other peoples generally, does it not have a special application to the Palestinians, whose modern history has been so intertwined with ours, and who are still awaiting their national liberation? Some people would say 'no' to that and argue as follows.

The land of Palestine, they say, doesn't actually belong to the Palestinians. They just happen to live there, and they don't *need* to, since there are plenty of other Arab countries for them to go to. The land belongs to us, the Jewish people. Nevertheless, in our generosity, we have always been willing to share it with them. The trouble is that they have not been willing to share it with us. From the beginning of the modern Zionist immigration, they resented our coming, although we had nothing but goodwill towards them, and paid their absentee landlords handsomely for every *dunam* of land we purchased. Admittedly we rejected the idea of a bi-national state in which Jews and Arabs might have enjoyed equal rights, but then so did they. And when the United Nations voted for the only possible alternative, partition, which we accepted, they rejected that as well.

From that rejection, so the narrative continues, all their troubles have stemmed. Because of it, Israel was born in war, and in that war hundreds of thousands of Arabs fled the country. But they fled of their own accord, or at the prompting of the commanders of the invading Arab armies. We didn't drive them out. On the contrary, we begged them to stay.

In the ensuing years they occasionally raided us from across the borders, and we had no choice but to hit back hard because force is the only language they understand. Then came the Six Day War, which left us in control of all of Palestine and gave us the unenviable task of ruling a huge Palestinian-Arab population. We did our best to treat them decently, but they resented us more than ever, and waged an intermittent guerrilla war against us. They even shelled our Galilean settlements from inside Lebanon, so that in 1982 we were reluctantly compelled to invade that country to root them out.

Five years later they started their *intifada*, which only ended when we magnanimously decided to hand over to them the administration of the Gaza Strip and parts of Judea and Samaria. And then came the Oslo peace process, in which we participated in good faith. But it soon became apparent that they didn't really want peace, they only wanted to drive us into the sea. And when Arik Sharon took his perfectly innocent walk on the Temple Mount, they used it as a pretext to launch their long-planned second *intifada*.

In short, the Palestinians have brought their tragedy on their own heads. We are not responsible for it. We have done nothing wrong. Our hands are clean. So runs the narrative, and I am sure we all recognise it. It is the version which the Jewish Establishment has continually disseminated and which, in the past, many of us have gone along with. But there are two things wrong with it.

In the first place, there is nothing religious about it. It is purely political. It is the sort of thing any nation in conflict with another might say in self-righteous self-justification. It is simply partisanship, untouched by any universal ethic.

In the second place, it is untrue. Well, not completely, but largely. By any natural justice, the Palestinians' claim to the land is, for different reasons, as valid as ours, and their resentment of our taking it over readily understandable. During the War of Independence, except for one isolated exception, we did *not* beg them to stay. On the contrary, we encouraged them to leave.

Nor can it truthfully be maintained that the way in which those who stayed were treated by successive Israeli governments was always benign. There have been innumerable confiscations of their land and property; demolitions of houses and collective punishments – all in plain violation of Jewish ethics; and, in defiance of the United Nations and world opinion, the creation of more and more settlements in the occupied territories. Indeed, many of the actions of successive Israeli governments must surely look to any independent observer like stages of a grand strategy to implement the 'Greater Israel' dream, which would leave the Palestinians totally dispossessed.

Similarly, there is no truth in the story that Northern Israel was subjected to constant PLO shelling from Lebanon in 1982. Apart from one minor incident, there was no such shelling but, on the contrary, an operative cease-fire. The Lebanon War, as Menachem Begin admitted, was not a war of self-defence but of 'choice', which is a euphemism for a war of aggression. It was devised, as part of his Greater Israel ideology, by Arik Sharon; and his recent walk-about on the Temple Mount was anything but innocent.

As for slogans such as 'force is the only language they understand' and 'they only want to drive us into the sea', we Jews, of *all* people, should know how wrong it is to stereotype and demonise a whole nation in that way. If we have not learnt *that* from our history, we have learnt nothing at all.

The truth, then, is that in the Jewish Arab conflict over Palestine many mistakes have been made, and many wrongs done, by *both* sides. The refusal to face that truth, and the denial of it, which has been called 'the myth of Jewish innocence', is, I believe, the besetting collective sin of our people. It is a consuming spiritual sickness which will destroy us if we do nothing about it.

We are *not* innocent. Our hands are *not* clean. We *do* have a share of responsibility for the fact that the Palestinians have not yet attained their liberation, that to their ears freedom speaks with anything *but* a Hebrew tongue.

That is the BIG ISSUE. I believe that our relationship with the Palestinians is the greatest moral test we Jews have faced in modern times, and, to put it mildly, we have not acquitted ourselves well. What can and should be done about it at this late stage is indeed another question, which the politicians will have to sort out. But of one thing we can be sure: that as long as each side only protests its own righteousness, and refuses to listen to the other, so long a just solution will not be found or, if found, the will to implement it will be lacking.

What then can we do to help? Not very much at all except for one thing. We can at least build bridges of mutual under-standing, sympathy and friendship between Jews and Palestinians living here, for instance, by attending last week's Deir Yassin remembrance, as some of us did.

Incidentally, I can now report to you that the meeting was a great success. The Peacock Theatre where it was held, which seats a thousand people, was packed, mainly with young Palestinians, who were impeccably behaved. The whole atmosphere was a model of dignity, courtesy and restraint. There was no acrimony or recrimination, not even criticism except for a poem by the Jewish poet Michael Rosen which was so relevant to my theme that I must mention it. The point it made was that while Anatoly Sharansky was a prisoner of conscience in the Soviet Union he became internationally famous for his courageous and eloquent advocacy of freedom. But when he became a member of the Israeli government he said to the Palestinians: 'Sorry, chaps, but there's not enough freedom to go round for *everybody*!'

In South Africa Nelson Mandela set up a 'Truth and Reconciliation Commission'. The title is exactly right. If there is to be reconciliation between Jews and Palestinians, then both must face the truth about themselves, acknowledge their past mistakes, take on board each other's pains and aspirations, and together resolve to make a fresh start, to build a future in which both enjoy *cherut*, freedom, and live together in the land which they both love so passionately, in dignity, friendship and peace.

Beyond Retribution

17 November 2001

'Everything's got a moral,' says the Duchess in *Alice in Wonderland*, 'if you can only find it.' Everything? Well, perhaps not everything. Much of the biblical narrative, for instance, is simply folklore. And when it comes to folklore, the ancient Israelites were not essentially different from other peoples. They enjoyed a good yarn! And the story of Esau and Jacob is certainly that. Not least the account of how Jacob tricks his brother first out of his birthright and then out of his father's blessing. Our ancestors, we may be sure, found that highly entertaining, without necessarily bothering their heads a great deal about its moral implications.

Nevertheless, like many other Bible stories, it does lend itself extraordinarily well to reflection on the moral issues it raises. And such reflection is not only a modern pastime: it has been going on all through the ages. Already in the Bible itself – in Hosea (12:3f.) and Jeremiah (9:3), for example – there are hints of disapproval of Jacob's deceitful behaviour towards his brother. Indeed, his whole life-story can be read as a series of fitting punishments on that account: how he had to flee for his life and go into exile, how there he was exploited by his uncle Laban, and how his old age was overshadowed by grief for his supposedly dead favourite son, Joseph.

But there is one particular moral issue arising out of the story which I would like to explore with you this morning, and that is the motif of hatred and revenge in the relationship between the two brothers.

Esau is understandably furious with Jacob for what he has done to him, and resolves to kill him (Gen. 27:41). That is why Jacob, on his mother's advice, flees to Mesopotamia. When, 20 years later, he returns, he fully expects Esau's anger to be unabated. So he prays to God: 'Deliver me, I beseech you, from the hand of my brother...for I am afraid of him, lest he comes and kills us all' (Gen. 32:12). And the next morning, when Esau approaches with a small army of 400 men, he naturally fears the worst. But he need not have worried. After a passage of 20 years Esau's lust for revenge has evaporated, and he embraces his brother in a scene of reconciliation as touching in its way as the reconciliation, a generation later, between Joseph and his brothers.

What then is the moral of the story? Perhaps it is that reconciliation is sweeter than revenge; that it is best to 'let bygones be bygones' and make a fresh start. At least that is one possible reading of the story.

But it is not the end of the matter. For Esau and Jacob are not only Esau and Jacob. They are also Edom and Israel, the two peoples supposedly descended from them. And between these two peoples the former enmity of their progenitors renews itself with a vengeance. This time, however, the roles are reversed. The Edomites are no longer the hard-done-by victims of an injustice: they are the culprits, the villains, the aggressors.

Already at the time of the Exodus, they showed their cruelty by refusing to allow the Israelites safe passage through their territory on their way from Egypt to the Promised Land (Num. 20). And there were other hostile encounters in later times. The worst of all occurred in 586 BCE, when the Babylonians conquered Judea and destroyed the Temple. Then, instead of coming to the defence of the Jews – their ethnic kinsfolk – they rejoiced in their calamity and actively sided with their enemies: an unspeakable act of treachery.

At least that was the Jewish understanding of the history of the relationship between the two peoples. I daresay the Edomites, if their records had been preserved, would have given a different account of it. But however that may be, the enmity that evidently existed between the two peoples transposes the story of Esau and Jacob from the personal to the international plane and raises the question: how should a nation respond when faced with the hostility of another?

To that question conventional wisdom gives a clear and simple answer: with counter-hostility. And this conventional wisdom is well represented in the Bible, not least by the prophecy of Obadiah from which we have taken our *Haftarah* this morning.

Perhaps written shortly after the Babylonian conquest, it is a bitter denunciation of the Edomites for their treacherous behaviour at that critical time. Because of that treachery, they will be brought to justice. Though they may think they are safe 'in the clefts of the rock' (1:3), they will be rooted out. Retribution is on its way and nothing can stop it. The whole philosophy is summed up in the concluding verse of our *Haftarah*: *ka-asher 'asita ye'aseh lach*, 'As you have done, it shall be done to you' (1:15).

That is the conventional wisdom: the answer to evil is counter-evil. It is the philosophy of retaliation. And by that philosophy, otherwise known as *Realpolitik*, nations of every kind have conducted themselves all through the ages.

The trouble is that it achieves nothing except to make a bad situation worse. Of that there is no plainer illustration than the modern history of the relationship between the State of Israel and the Palestinian Arabs. In fairness it must be said that the violence was begun by the Arabs already in the days of the Mandate. But that was long ago, and nowadays it hardly matters any longer who started what. Whenever an attack is launched by either side, the other strikes back, and in the case of Israel, with its immense military superiority, two or three times as hard.

It seems the right thing to do by the most elementary of all moral principles – the retaliation principle – which is as unquestionable as the laws of nature. Even if the politicians didn't believe in it, which most of them do fervently, they would have no choice, because retaliation is what the people demand. Politicians must always be tough, never soft; otherwise they would soon be turfed out of office. And even if it were not a matter of retaliation for retaliation's sake, there would still be the argument of deterrence. You've got to deter the enemy. If you don't hit back they'll only do it again.

That is the theory. But it is belied by the facts. For if your enemies hate you for what they think you have done to them, your hitting back won't change their minds. On the contrary, it will only confirm in their minds how right they were to hate you in the first place. Every act of violence or counter-violence deepens the hatred, exacerbates the anger, intensifies the hunger for revenge. And so the conflict escalates until it becomes uncontrollable except by the annihilation of one side by the other, in short, by genocide.

In the history of the Middle East conflict that has been proved over and over and over again. It has been there for every child to see. Yet it persists. Is there really no way out of it, no way of stopping the escalation, of reversing the trend? Of course there is! It is the way of restraint, of moderation, of magnanimity. And it, too, is to be found in Judaism, as in other religious traditions.

It is to be found already in the Hebrew Bible, and even in relation to the Edomites! For in the book of Deuteronomy we read: 'You shall not abhor an Edomite, for he is your brother' (23:8). Given all that we have heard about the hostility between the two peoples, isn't that amazing? There we hear a note different from *Realpolitik*, different from nationalism: a religious note!

And it is only part of a trend which runs like a golden thread – although, it must be admitted, a somewhat slender one – all through our literature. In the great chapter 19 of Leviticus, for instance, we read: 'You shall not take vengeance or bear a grudge' (19:18), and although that refers to individual behaviour, the principle is surely transferable to international relations. The book of Proverbs tells us: 'Do not say, I will do to others as they have done to me' (24:29); and again, 'If your enemy is hungry, give him bread to eat' (25:21); and it commends 'the soft answer that turns away wrath' (15:1).

And the trend continues. The Gospel teaching of 'turning the other cheek' (Matt. 6:39) is a famous example of it – somewhat extreme but completely Jewish, for Jesus never taught anything but Judaism. It was the Jewish authors of the Apocrypha and Pseudepigrapha who taught: 'Forgive your fellow human beings the wrong they have done' (*Sira* 28:2); 'Drive hatred out of your hearts ... And if anyone sins against you, speak to them words of peace' (Testament of Gad 6:1, 3). It was the Rabbis who taught: 'If others speak ill of you, do not respond in kind' (*Derech Eretz Zuta* 1:7); and 'Who is the greatest hero? The one who turns an enemy into a friend' (*ARN* 23:1).

This is the golden thread of our tradition which we need to rediscover if we are ever going to put an end to the vicious cycle of violence and counter-violence as it drags us inexorably towards catastrophe in the Middle East and throughout the world.

It doesn't mean that crime should not be punished; of course it should! It doesn't mean that nations should not defend themselves against aggression; of course they must! But it does mean forswearing retaliation, which is only a polite word for revenge. It does mean using *minimum* force to achieve what must be achieved. It does mean renouncing the language of confrontation in favour of 'the soft answer that turns away wrath'. It does mean seeking political solutions and showing magnanimity in the process.

Exactly two weeks ago, on the sixth anniversary of the assassination of Yitzchak Rabin, 80,000 Israelis gathered in Tel Aviv to demonstrate for a return to the path of sanity and peace. One huge banner, which could be seen throughout the square, read: 'Peace – the sane retaliation'. If everything has a moral, then *that* is the moral of the story of Esau and Jacob, of Edom and Israel, of the Middle East conflict, and of the whole blood-stained history of humankind. It may not be easy to find, but we had better find it soon. *Bimherah beyameynu, Amen.*

Passion and Peace

18 December 2001

A FELICITOUS JUXTAPOSITION

I don't know if the juxtaposition of passion and peace was a brainwave of the organisers of RIST or taken from an antecedent source. In either case it is felicitous because it triggers so many interesting as well as topically relevant trains of thought. Whether the particular train of thought it triggered in my mind is what the organisers intended, I have no idea, since the texts selected by Jonathan Gorsky and Joanna Weinberg only reached me two or three days ago, too late for me to rewrite what I had planned to say. I am afraid, therefore, that my paper will not be any kind of summation of what we have been studying today, but perhaps it will supplement it a little.

PASSION AS SUFFERING

Let us begin with the word 'passion'. Etymologically, it comes from a Late Latin word for 'suffering', itself connected with the Greek word 'pathos'; and that sense is preserved in the Christian term for the suffering of Jesus on the cross. It was also made use of, incidentally, by Solomon Schechter in an essay on Abraham Geiger. There, referring to his bitter controversy with Solomon Tiktin, which occurred in Breslau round about 1840,[1] he wrote with mischievous humour: 'It is the Passion Story of the Reform Gospel, with the only difference perhaps that in this case legend has it that it was Caiaphas who died of a broken heart, whilst the Saviour of Modernity came out triumphant from his Via Dolorosa.'[2]

PASSION AS LUST

Much more commonly in recent times the word 'passion' has been used to refer to the self-regarding drives of human nature, such as the yearning for power and pleasure. In that sense it has been jocularly said that 'The natural man has only two primal passions, to get and beget'.[3] Both of these, the acquisitive urge and the sex urge, are included in the Rabbinic concept of the famous saying that 'but for the *yetzer ha-ra'* a man would not build a house, marry, beget children, or engage in business'.[4] More often than not, the *yetzer ha-ra'* refers to the sex drive, which the Rabbis, anticipating Freud, evidently regarded as the most powerful. Thus the Talmud rules that a Jew, even if he is a *kohen*, may have sexual relations with *yefat toar*, a beautiful girl captured in war, on the ground that *lo dibirah torah ela k'neged ha-yetzer*, 'the Torah makes allowance for the human sex drive'.[5] That, too, is the sense of 'passion' in expressions such as *crime de passion*.

PASSION AS ZEAL OR ZEALOTRY

But more commonly than either 'suffering' or 'lust', the word 'passion' nowadays connotes 'strong feeling'. To feel passionately is to feel strongly. The feeling may be of a desirable kind, in which case another word for it would be 'enthusiasm' or, in Chasidic language, *hitlahavut*. Or the feeling may be of an undesirable kind, in which case another word for it would be 'fanaticism'. The distinction may also be illustrated by the two related words, 'zeal' and 'zealotry', which we tend to use in a positive and a negative sense respectively – 'zeal' is good; 'zealotry' is bad. The opposite of zeal is apathy, or indifference; the opposite of zealotry is tolerance, or moderation.

That passion in the sense of 'zeal' or 'enthusiasm' is a good thing, is a point worth emphasising in a RIST context. For a rabbi lacking that quality would hardly be effective and a sermon lacking it would surely fall flat. So one of the best bits of advice to be given to anybody who aspires to be a good preacher would be: Above all, preach with passion, for if it is not apparent to the congregation that you feel passionately about the topic of your sermon, they certainly won't.

On the other hand, passion in the sense of 'zealotry' or 'fanaticism' is not only a bad thing but one of the chief evils of our time and, in particular, the greatest obstacle to peace.

The same duality represented in English by 'zeal' versus 'zealotry' is to be found in Hebrew in the various usages of the root *qna*. The most famous occurrence of it is in the Decalogue, when it speaks of the Deity as *el qana*, a 'jealous' or 'zealous' God.[6] The sense there is one of righteous indignation, carrying heavy penalties, incurred by any derogation from God's authority or defiance of God's will. Similarly, God's *qin'ah* occurs in Deuteronomy in parallel with the word *af* for 'anger'[7] and *esh okhela*, 'a devouring fire'.[8]

ABRAHAM

Turning now to the human level, let us ask ourselves who in the history of Judaism displayed conspicuously the quality of *qin'ah*? One person who comes to mind is Abraham, not so much from the biblical account of his life as from the later legend of how he smashed his father's idols.[9] Was that an act of zeal or zealotry, of enthusiasm or fanaticism? Were our ancestors altogether too intolerant towards idolatry, and did they mistakenly impute such intolerance to God, perhaps even in the Second Commandment to which we have just referred? There is at least a hint to that effect in the legend about the old fire-worshipper whom Abraham drove out of his house, whereupon God rebuked him, saying: 'I have borne with that ignorant man for 70 years: could you not have patiently suffered him one night?' (See *Siddur Lev Chadash*, p. 314).

MOSES

A more obvious exemplar of the quality of *qin'ah* is, however, *Mosheh Rabbenu*. His killing of the Egyptian taskmaster who has been beating a Hebrew slave[10] was clearly an act of passion, and so was his breaking of the tablets following the sin of the golden calf.[11] Similarly, the Tosefta depicts Moses as an uncompromising champion of right, whose motto is *yiqov ha-din et ha-har*, 'Let justice split the mountain', unlike his brother Aaron, whom it depicts as a compromiser for the sake of peace.[12] Some of you will recall the use Achad Ha'am made of that passage in his celebrated but deeply flawed essay *Kohen w'habi*, where he contrasts the idealism of the prophet with the realism, or pragmatism, of the priest.[13]

PHINEAS

But if one character more than any other in the Torah exemplifies the quality of *qin'ah*, it is Phineas, Aaron's grandson, who, when the Israelites at Shittim committed the sin of worshipping Baal-Peor, which involved some kind of sacred prostitution, summarily executed the chief culprits.[14] For this action God praises him, saying: 'Phineas, the son of Eleazar, the son of Aaron the priest, has turned back My wrath from the children of Israel, *b'qan'o et qin'ati b'tokham*, in that he was zealous on My behalf among them, *v'lo kiliti et b'ney yisrael b'qin'ati*, so that I did not destroy the children of Israel in My zeal.'[15]

Notice also the reward Phineas receives for his zeal. 'Therefore,' says God, 'I hereby grant him My covenant of peace. It shall be for him and for his descendants after him a covenant of perpetual priesthood, *takhat asher qine lelohaw*, because he was zealous for his God, and made atonement for the children of Israel.'[16] Especially noteworthy is the juxtaposition of *qin'ah*, zeal, with *shalom*, peace. This is very unusual but perhaps harbours the truth that sometimes it is necessary to take stern measures for the sake of peace.

For his zealous action Phineas is furthermore praised once in Psalm 106, which says *watekhasheb lo litz'dakah*, that 'it was reckoned to him as righteousness',[17] once in Ben Sira,[18] and frequently in Rabbinic Literature.

ELIJAH

If Phineas had a reincarnation a few centuries later, it was surely Elijah, who demonstrated his passion in his contest with the prophets of Baal at Mount Carmel.[19] Subsequently at Mount Horeb he says of himself: *qan'o qin'eti*, 'I have been very zealous for the Eternal One, the God of hosts …'.[20] Needless to say, Elijah's zeal is praised in the subsequent literature.

INTERLUDE: A DISSENTING VIEW

Considering the glowing praise bestowed on both Phineas and Elijah in the classical sources, it is all the more remarkable to find a dissenting voice within the tradition. It comes from the great Chasidic master Menachem Mendel of Kotsk (1787–1859), and is a comment on the passage in Numbers 27 where Moses prays that 'the Eternal One, the God of the spirits of all flesh' may appoint a worthy successor after his death.[21] Already Rashi had commented that the way Moses referred to God implied that he wished for a successor who would be tolerant of individual differences.[22] This prompts the Kotsker to remark: 'When Moses saw how important Phineas had become, he feared that he might be chosen as the next leader. Therefore Moses begged of God that Israel's leader should be one who would be patient with every individual, that is to say, one who would be *manhig savlan w'lo manhig kanna'i*, a tolerant leader, and not a zealot' like Phineas.[23]

Similarly, another Chasidic commentator on the same verse refers to Elijah's experience at Mount Horeb, when he discovered that God was not in the wind, nor in the earthquake, nor in the fire, but in the still, small voice,[24] and remarks: 'By this means God sought to make him understand that godliness is not transmitted *'al y'day shalhevet qin'ah*, by the flames of zealotry, nor does the spirit of religion enter the human heart through the fulminations of the fanatic, but only through the still small voice of gentle, kind and pleasant speech, only through words of sweet reason and good sense.'[25]

MATTATHIAS

In post-biblical times Mattathias comes to mind as manifesting the spirit of passion or zeal. In the First Book of Maccabees we read: 'Then Mattathias cried out in the town with a loud voice: Let everyone who is zealous for the law [here Abraham Kahana's

Hebrew translation has *kol ha-am'qan'e l'torah*] and stands by the Covenant follow me!'[26] But it is interesting that Jewish tradition did not glorify the military exploits of Mattathias and his sons but emphasised instead the miracle of the oil,[27] and by way of *Haftarah* for the Sabbath in Chanukkah chose the Zechariah prophecy with the punch-line, *lo b'khayil w'lo b'koach ki im b'ruchi*, 'Not by might, nor by power, but by My spirit, says the God of hosts'.[28]

THE ZEALOTS

A century or two later we hear of the Zealots, in Hebrew *qanaim*, whose very name refers to the quality we are considering. They instigated the disastrous revolt against Roman rule, which resulted in the loss of the last vestiges of Jewish sovereignty as well as the destruction of the Temple in 70 CE. They also terrorised and massacred any number of fellow Jews who did not share their fanaticism. It was lucky that Yochanan ben Zakkai managed to escape from Jerusalem to found the academy of Yavneh, and it is a sobering rhetorical question whether he or the Zealots did more for the cause of Judaism and Jewish survival.

BAR KOCHBA

The intense nationalism of the Zealots resurfaced less than a century later with Bar Kochba. The name has been familiar to me since my childhood in Nazi Germany, when I joined a Jewish sports club named after him. I assumed then that he had always been considered a Jewish hero. It was only many years later that I discovered that, on the contrary, Rabbinic literature generally regarded him as a villain because of the great catastrophe he brought upon the Jewish people, and it was only the Zionist movement which transformed him into a hero.

That point was brought home to me when I read a book published in 1983 by Yehoshafat Harkabi, then Professor of International Relations and Middle Eastern Studies and a former head of Israel's Military Intelligence. The book, *The Bar Kokhba Syndrome: Risk and Realism in International Politics*, is essential reading for our subject.

According to Harkabi, the Bar Kochba Rebellion led to 'the most severe politico-military disaster in Jewish history'.[29] He estimates that up to 90 per cent of the population of Judea may have been wiped out.[30] He also points out that only the Jews of Galilee, because they did not take part in the rebellion, escaped unharmed, and that it was there, at places like Usha and Tiberias, that Jewish life and learning continued, and Judaism was perpetuated. 'It seems to me', he writes, 'that it is no exaggeration to claim that the survival of the Jewish people is due to the moderation of the Jews of the Galilee.'[31]

SHIM'ON BAR YOCHAI

Among the many rabbis of the talmudic period, the one who stands out as a personification of the quality of passion or *qin'ah* in the sense of zealotry or fanaticism is of course Akiva's disciple Shim'on bar Yochai. It was he who taught that one who walks in the countryside studying Mishnah and stops to admire a beautiful tree is considered by Scripture *k'ilu mitchayev b'nafsho*, as if he were guilty of spiritual suicide.[32] He combined an almost insane megalomania[33] with an implacable hatred against the Romans and indeed against non-Jews generally. He is, for instance, the author of the counsel, *tov she-ba-goyim harog*, which, decency dictates, must be left untranslated.[34] Best known about him is the story of how, with his son, he hid in a cave for 12 years (I don't think it was called Tora Bora but he certainly studied Torah there) because the Romans had condemned him to death for criticising their regime. When they finally emerged and saw a fellow Jew sowing and ploughing, instead of fighting against the Romans, they were so enraged that the fury in their eyes caused everything they gazed upon to go up in smoke. (And if looks could kill that might well be a true story.) Whereupon a *Bat Kol* (supernatural voice) said to them in God's name: *l'hachariv 'olami y'tzatem*, 'Have you come out to destroy My world?', and added: *chizru lim'aratkhem*, 'Go back to your cave!'[35]

It would seem, therefore, that the same God who rebuked Abraham for throwing out an idolatrous guest; and who taught Elijah that the Divine Presence is in the still small voice; and who decreed that Moses should be succeeded by somebody a bit more tolerant than Phineas; and who inspired the Rabbis to arrange that the Maccabean military victory should be celebrated by telling the fairy-tale of the oil and reading Zechariah's prophecy that the right way is not by might, nor by power, but by the Divine spirit; did not altogether approve of fanaticism, Shim'on bar Yochai style.

MODERN ZEALOTS

If we now skip many centuries and ask ourselves who are the zealots of modern Jewish history, the answer is obvious. They are Vladimir Jabotinsky and his latter-day disciples Menachem Begin, Binyamin Netanyahu and Ariel Sharon. Harkabi's book was written in the aftermath of the 1982 Lebanon War, which was not only a disaster in every way but foreseeably so because motivated by what Harkabi called the Bar Kochba Syndrome, that is, the pursuit of an ideological goal in defiance of hard political facts and rational calculations. It was of course the brainchild of Ariel Sharon, the very man in charge of Israel's destiny today, and there is reason to think that the policies he is pursuing are similarly irrational – that the same Bar Kochba Syndrome is at work – and likely to lead to even more disastrous consequences.

I know that many people see Israel as merely responding to suicide bombings and other terrorist attacks from the Palestinian side and so doing what any government must to protect its citizens. But I am afraid the reality is more complicated and more sinister. Of course security is a major consideration. But it is doubtful whether reprisals deter; the evidence suggests, rather, that they provoke counter-violence, and there is even reason to fear that that may be, in part, their purpose. After all, it has always been a dogma of the Revisionist ideology to which Sharon subscribes that the whole of Palestine belongs to the Jewish people. That is why he invaded Lebanon in 1982, to destroy the PLO and so prevent a peace settlement which would inevitably have involved the creation of a sovereign Palestinian state alongside Israel. The fact that his helicopter gunships are targeting not only Hamas but also, if not chiefly, the Palestinian Authority, strongly suggests that he still has the same purpose in mind.

At any rate, it seems clear to me that zealotry of the kind that is currently dominant in Israel, and the policies which it inspires, can never lead towards peace, but only away from it, and therefore sooner or later to catastrophe. In these circumstances, I would maintain, to proclaim solidarity with Israel is not to strengthen its security but to aid and abet its self-destruction.

THE DILEMMA

The trouble is that in the Middle East, as throughout the world, the forces of nationalism, of fundamentalism, of passion in the sense of zealotry and fanaticism, are immensely powerful and enticing, whereas the contrary forces, of reason, of restraint and moderation and compromise, are relatively weak and even in retreat.

In this there is nothing new. I remember from the early days of the Cold War a radio interview with Bertrand Russell in which he was asked: 'Why do you think it is that the Soviet Communists are so much more enthusiastic about their Communism than we Westerners are about our Western democracy?' And he answered: 'There is nothing strange in that. It is always easier to arouse passion for a crazy idea than for a sane one.' He went on to illustrate his point with the Flat Earth Society whose members, he said, are so much more enthusiastic about their belief that the earth is flat than the rest of us are about our belief that the earth is round.

This, then, is the great dilemma, so memorably expressed by W. B. Yeats when he wrote:

> Turning and turning in the widening gyre
> The falcon cannot hear the falconer;
> Things fall apart; the centre cannot hold;
> Mere anarchy is loosed upon the world,
> The blood-dimmed tide is loosed, and everywhere
> The ceremony of innocence is drowned;
> The best lack all conviction, while the worst
> Are full of passionate intensity.[36]

THE CHALLENGE

The challenge therefore is to strengthen the constructive forces of reason, restraint, moderation, compromise and reconciliation against the destructive forces of mendacious propaganda, fundamentalism, chauvinism, intransigence and confrontation. The challenge is to arouse in ourselves and in those we can influence a passion – a *qin'ah*, in the sense of zeal, not zealotry – for truth, for justice and for peace, sufficiently powerful to match and overcome the forces arrayed against them. For it is on these that, according to Rabban Simeon ben Gamaliel, the continuation of civilisation depends.[37]

It is noteworthy that just these three values are emphasised in our tradition with particular insistence. *Dab'ru emet*, 'Speak the truth to one another', says Zechariah.[38] Who may dwell in God's tent, asks the Psalmist. Only *dover emet bil'vavo* , 'one who speaks truth in their heart'.[39] *Chotamo shel ha-kadosh baruch hu emet*, 'The very signature of God is truth', added the Rabbis.[40] In regard to the Middle East conflict, which is of particular concern to us, we have a positive duty to ascertain the truth, and it is ascertainable. It has been told with commendable honesty by historians like Benny Morris and Avi Shlaim; it differs from the 'official story'; and we are no longer entitled to ignore it.

Tzedek tzedek tirdof, 'Justice, justice shall you pursue', says the Deuteronomist.[41] 'The sword enters the world', said the Rabbis, *''al 'inui ha-din w'al 'iwut ha-din*, because of justice delayed and justice denied'.[42] Justice demands that the Palestinians be enabled to establish a contiguous state alongside Israel where they can exercise self-determination and live in dignity and prosperity; and it is illusory to think that security for Israel can be purchased at any cheaper price.

Above all, there needs to be a passionate devotion to the cause of peace. *Shalom shalom, la-rachok w'la-karov*, 'Peace, peace, to the far and to the near', says Deutero-Isaiah.[43] Again that repetition. *Bakesh shalom w'rod'fehu*, 'Seek peace, and pursue it', says the Psalmist.[44] 'Be of the disciples of Aaron, *ohev shalom w'rodef shalom*, loving peace, and pursuing peace', Hillel adds.[45] Peace will come about in the Middle East, as elsewhere, only if we love above the values of nationalism such as territory and pride.

REALISM AND IDEALISM

Is that realism or idealism? Here I come back to Achad Ha'am's essay with its differentiation between the idealism of the prophet and the realism of the priest. I think that is a profound misunderstanding because it leaves out a vital teaching of the Prophets, which is that what is morally right, though it may seem politically inexpedient at the time, will ultimately prove to have been expedient, after all. Therefore the teaching of the Prophets, although of course idealistic, is also long-term realistic. And it is for this combination of idealism and realism that we need a commitment full of 'passionate intensity'.

Passion and peace sound like opposites because so many of the causes that arouse passion – fundamentalism and nationalism particularly, especially when combined – militate against peace. But passion *for* peace is also possible. It is in fact, or ought to be, the Jewish *spécialité de la maison*. And our task as rabbis is to cultivate it, first in ourselves and secondly in those whose minds our rabbinate enables us to influence.

NOTES

1. For a detailed account, see David Philipson, *The Reform Movement in Judaism*, Ch. III.
2. Schechter, *Studies in Judaism*, Third Series, p. 53.
3. Sir William Osler (1849–1919), *Science and Immortality* (1904), Ch. 2, quoted in *The Oxford Dictionary of Quotations*, 4th edn. (1992), p. 502.
4. Genesis Rabbah 9:7.
5. *Kiddushin* 21b; *Mishneh Torah, Hilchot Melachim* 8:4.
6. Exodus 20:5, Deuteronomy 5:9.
7. Deuteronomy 29:19.
8. Deuteronomy 4:24.
9. Genesis Rabbah 38:13.
10. Exodus 2:11f.
11. Exodus 32:19.
12. *Tosefta, Sanhedrin* 1:2, quoting Malachi 2:6.
13. *Kol Kitvey Achad Ha'am*, Dvir, 1949, p. 90ff.
14. Numbers 25:1–15.
15. Numbers 25:11.
16. Numbers 25:12f.
17. Psalm 106:31.
18. Ben Sira 45:23.
19. I Kings 18.
20. I Kings 19:10.
21. Numbers 27:16.
22. Ad loc., based on *Yalkut Shim'oni*, §776.
23. A. J. Greenberg, *Itturey Torah*, Vol. V, p. 176.
24. I Kings 19:11f.
25. *'Itturey Torah*, loc. cit.
26. I Maccabees 2:27.
27. *Shabbat* 21b.
28. Zechariah 4:6.

29. Yehoshafat Harkabi, *The Bar Kokhba Syndrome* (1983), p. 27.
30. Ibid., p. 46.
31. Ibid., p. 39.
32. *Avot* 3:17.
33. See *Sanhedrin* 97b.
34. *Mechilta B'shallach* 1 to Exod. 14:7.
35. *Shabbat* 33b; cf. *J. Shevuot* 9; *Pesikta de-Rav Kahana* 11:16; Genesis Rabbah 79:6; Ecclesiastes Rabbah 10:8.
36. From 'The Second Coming', 1921.
37. *Avot* 1:18.
38. Zechariah 8:16.
39. Psalm 15:2.
40. *Shabbat* 55a.
41. Deuteronomy 16:20.
42. *Avot* 5:8.
43. Isaiah 57:19.
44. Psalm 34:15.
45. *Avot* 1:12.

Ashamnu: We Have Sinned

Erev Yom Kippur 2003

There was once a preacher who, no matter what his subject, always managed to come up with the ideal quotation to clinch his point. How did he do it? By following the example of a certain archer who would always shoot his arrow first, then walk up to the target and draw a series of concentric circles round the point where it had landed. In other words, he chose his text first, then built his sermon round it.

Tonight let us do the same and take as our text – because it is uniquely characteristic of the liturgy of *Yom Kippur* – the 'shorter confession' beginning with the Hebrew word *Ashamnu* which you will find on page 197 of our beautiful new prayer book. It is, as you will see, an alphabetic acrostic, which is a symbolic way of saying that we have committed every sin in the book, from A to Z. And that, of course, is rather shocking. Have we *really* done all these things? Surely not! How then can we truthfully say that we have?

That depends on what is meant by 'we'. It could mean 'we as individuals' or 'we the Jewish people' or 'we the human family'. In fact, it means all three. The point of the *Ashamnu*, then, is not that each of us is guilty on every count, Heaven forbid, but that we take responsibility for what is done by others within the group to which we belong. And how can that be? Jewish tradition tells us.

There is, for instance, the talmudic teaching, *Kol yisrael 'arevin zeh ba-zeh*, that 'all Jews are answerable for one another' (*Shevu'ot*

39a), the idea being that at Mount Sinai our ancestors pledged themselves *as a people* – that is, as a collective continuum in space and time – to live by God's Law, and that, in doing so, they stood surety for all future generations. In other words, being Jewish, as well as a privilege, is also a burden, and by becoming members of the Jewish people, whether by birth or conversion, we take on ourselves the burden of the trust our ancestors placed in us.

Even so, it still seems unfair. How can we reasonably be held responsible for what others do or don't do? But here another talmudic principle comes into play: *Kol mi she-efshar limchot*, 'Whoever is in a position to dissuade a member of his family from committing a sin but fails to do so is punished along with his family – of his city, along with his city – of the whole world, along with the whole world' (*Shab.* 54b).

The implication is that we all contribute in some way, however slight, to the ethos of the group to which we belong, and therefore must accept a share of responsibility, however small, for the modes of behaviour which it promotes or tolerates. It is a sobering thought.

If we think of ourselves only as individuals, what has been our chief failing? Perhaps we have been too self-absorbed or self-indulgent or unforgiving, or insufficiently courteous and considerate towards one another. There are many possibilities for us to ponder during the next 22 hours.

If we think of ourselves as citizens, we must wonder how we may have contributed to the yob culture that is bringing shame on our national life, or to the widening gap between rich and poor, or whether we were right to go to war in Iraq, and whether we could have avoided it by pursuing a more ethical foreign policy years ago.

If we think of the world as a whole, we are bound to reflect – especially after the recent heat-wave – whether, by the relentless destruction of the environment through the shameless pursuit of national and commercial self-interest – in which we are all complicit – we have not already pronounced the doom of future generations.

But this evening let us focus our attention, not on any of these but on the one collectivity that is directly responsible for our being here tonight: the Jewish people. Let us, in other words, take *Ashamnu* to mean that we, the Jewish people, have sinned. But have we?

Two years ago, the *Jewish Quarterly* published an article entitled 'Have We Sinned?' It never answered the question, but clearly implied that the answer is 'No, not to any significant extent, at least not where the Middle East is concerned'. And that seems to be the general attitude of our people at the present time. Let me describe it to you as it comes over to me.

As individuals, we Jews are like everybody else. We may be less prone to drunkenness, we may be more prominent in certain professions, and we may have produced more Nobel Prize winners than any other people; but we don't boast about these things. For we know that fundamentally we are no different from the rest of humanity. *As individuals*, to quote from the prayer immediately preceding the *Ashamnu*, 'we are not so arrogant and stiff-necked as to say before God that we are perfect and have not sinned' (ibid.).

But *as a people* we are not so much sinners as sinned against. All through our history we have been misunderstood, maligned and persecuted, yet we have maintained our dignity and our creativity. Even from the ashes of the Holocaust we rose again and created one of the miracles of modern times – the State of Israel – which ought to be the admiration of humanity but which, instead, is constantly subjected to physical and verbal attack. As individuals we may have all kinds of faults, but as a people we have nothing to be ashamed of or to apologise for. That is the common perception, and there is more than a little truth in it. However, tonight is not a time for self-congratulation, but for taking an unblinkered look at the truth, however uncomfortable it may be.

What then *is* the truth? Let us take our cue from the prayer of the hero of the book of Daniel, which is one of the sources of the *Ashamnu*. 'Eternal, great and awesome God ... We have sinned, we have done wrong, ... We have not listened to Your servants the prophets, who spoke in Your name...' (9:4ff.). Do .we recognise ourselves in that confession? We should! For we have largely forsaken our Prophetic heritage.

If the Prophets taught anything, it is that our overriding loyalty belongs to God. But in modern times religion has retreated in the collective Jewish consciousness. In Israel the great majority consider themselves 'secular', and even in Britain, as a recent survey of the Institute of Jewish Policy Research has shown, the same holds true for around 50 per cent. By any standard, that amounts to a wholesale abandonment of the religious commitment which was the driving force of Jewish existence for over 2,000 years. Most Jews have come tacitly to accept the viewpoint of secular Zionism, that we are a nation like other nations, with a national language, Hebrew, and a national home, Israel, and a national culture in which religion is only an optional element. In short, it is no longer God but the Jewish people that stands at the apex of our hierarchy of loyalties. The Prophets would have called that idolatry.

Furthermore, in dethroning God we have diminished ourselves. The Prophets loved their people with a passionate love, but they also exhorted them to be 'a light to the nations' (Isa. 49:6) and reprimanded them when they failed to live up to that challenge. Today this universalistic vision of our role in history has all but vanished. Instead, we have become an ethnic minority among ethnic minorities. As a people, we have become inward-looking and self-righteous.

This self-righteousness – which stands in the way of repentance like an impenetrable barrier – manifests itself in many ways, but most obviously in relation to the Middle East conflict. Whenever Israel is criticised, we immediately cry anti-Semitism. There is indeed an alarming resurgence of anti-Semitism, and some criticisms of Israel – though by no means all – are motivated by it or tinged with it. So we like to think that we are hard done by, that the whole world is against us, and there is, alas, much that feeds our victim mentality. Our memories of the Holocaust are still raw, and every suicide bombing of Israeli civilians hurts us almost like a physical pain because the dead and injured are our kith and kin. What happened yesterday in Haifa weighs on our hearts and minds so heavily that we can hardly bear to think or speak of it. Therefore, too, whatever we can do to assure our people there of our sympathy and solidarity in this terrible time of agony, anxiety and insecurity, we should do.

Nevertheless, we, the Jewish people, are not innocent where the Middle East conflict is concerned. Through the Zionist movement which we have embraced, and through successive Israeli governments which our fellow Jews have elected, and through their policies which we have defended or condoned, we have a share of responsibility – not all of it, perhaps not most of it, but certainly some of it – for the causation, exacerbation and perpetuation of the conflict, and for the failure of numerous peace initiatives, including the Oslo Process and now the Roadmap.

All that, in our self-righteousness, we deny, as, in our paranoia, we are blind to the positive evidence of good-will towards us, such as the new respect for Judaism in interfaith dialogue, or the fact that the United Nations and most of its member states have consistently upheld the right of the State of Israel to exist in peace and security within internationally recognised borders.

And because we see the world as negatively disposed towards us, therefore we, in our turn, take little positive interest in it. The Prophetic view, that we have a redemptive role to play in human history, has gone out of the window. No wonder that so many of our young people abandon Judaism in search of spirituality or social idealism elsewhere.

The time is long overdue for a revival of the universalism that is inherent in Judaism. Instead of indulging in self-pity and shouting conspiracy, instead of representing one more strident militaristic nationalism among other strident militaristic nationalisms, instead of demonstrating expertise in the manufacture of fighter aircraft and cluster bombs (designed to kill and maim as many innocent bystanders as possible), let us set to the world an example of humility and restraint, of tolerance and magnanimity, of respect for international law and for the rights of other peoples as well as our own. Let us be builders, not of walls of separation, but of bridges of understanding across racial, national and religious boundaries.

Surely that, as taught by the Prophets, is our true role in history: the role which alone accords with our genius and which alone is commensurate with the heavy price we have paid for our survival. Surely that is the standard by which God judges us and by which we must judge ourselves. Therefore, when we recite the *Ashamnu*, let us confess how far we have fallen short of God's expectations, not only as individuals, and not only as a species, but also as a people. Let us re-engage in the struggle of all humanity for a world of freedom and justice, love and compassion, reconciliation and peace, and so prove ourselves worthy of our heritage. Amen.

The Future of Humanity

Values

Yom Kippur 1999

As we look back on the past year – and the past century – many salient facts stand out, and they are not all bad. Human knowledge has grown, science has advanced, technology has made life easier. Health has improved, infant mortality has fallen, life expectancy has risen. In Britain the number of centenarians has jumped in 50 years from 250 to 9,000. Literacy and education, once confined to a few, have become general, and the transmission of information worldwide is now virtually instantaneous. Democracy, after some setbacks, is reasserting itself almost everywhere; and various forms of international co-operation are bringing security and prosperity to millions. This catalogue, which could easily be prolonged, is one of enormous gains and, whatever else there is to be said, we should never lose sight of them or cease to be thankful for them.

Nevertheless, in this penitential season it is the negative side of the record that demands our attention, and it is very alarming. Again let me give only a few random examples. In spite of innumerable warnings and international agreements, industrial pollution, deforestation and other human activities are still damaging our environment and changing our climate in potentially disastrous ways. Radioactive materials leaking from our power stations, buried in our seabeds and circling the earth as debris from disintegrated spacecraft, pose a constant threat. Old racial, national and religious tensions continue to simmer, and every now and then, in places like Rwanda, Kosovo and

East Timor, erupt into conflicts of unimaginable savagery.

Even here in Britain, vandalism and hooliganism, theft and burglary, road rage, racial attacks, child abuse, rape and murder, feature almost daily in the news bulletins, and several of these have actually increased in recent years. It is no longer safe to leave property unguarded, or for women to go out alone at night, or for children to walk unaccompanied to school. Nurses are attacked by patients, and teachers by pupils. The drug merchants and pornographers ply their trades, and the media unremittingly portray more and yet more adultery and violence. The number of children living in poverty, we are told, has trebled in the last 30 years to five million; 15,000 crimes are committed by children every day; one in three 14-year-olds has tried drugs; and teenage pregnancies are the highest in Europe.

Why are these things happening? There are many theories, and they all have some validity, but there is, I suggest, one underlying cause, and that has to do with *values*.

Now the word 'value' is used in different senses. There is, for instance, a commercial sense, as when we speak of the value of a property or a piece of jewellery. There is an aesthetic sense, which is best distinguished from the commercial one when we remember Oscar Wilde's definition of a cynic as one 'who knows the price of everything and the value of nothing' (*Lady Windermere's Fan*, Act 3). But of course I mean neither of these. I mean moral or ethical values, the values that govern human behaviour.

Where then do these values come from? In part they are innate, for being created in the image of God, we have an inborn capacity to discern between right and wrong. But only to a limited extent. Deposit a group of newborn babies on a desert island and they, if they survive, will develop a code of conduct, but it will be a very primitive one. In the main, we don't make up our own moral values; we learn them from our parents and teachers, and they from theirs. Moral values are culturally transmitted from generation to generation.

And if we push the question further back and ask where they came from in the first place, I think we must answer: largely from religion. That statement, admittedly, requires two qualifications. One is that the values religion has inculcated have not always been good. They have included bigotry and zealotry, and these remain powerful components in some of the bloody conflicts that rage around the world today. It is a fact which those of us who are professionally associated with organised religion must acknowledge with shame.

The other qualification is that religion is not the *only* source of moral values. There are also humanistic philosophies, political parties, professional associations and trade unions which have their own codes of conduct. But historically speaking, they don't begin to compare with the magnitude of the influence which the religions have exerted in the course of the centuries on society's perception of right and wrong. Religion, for good and ill, has been, historically, the chief generator of moral values.

But if that is so, then the decline of religion in modern times is an amply sufficient explanation of the moral condition of our society. Of course I am referring mainly to the Western world, and therefore to Christianity. Britain is no longer a Christian country as it once was. The average Briton doesn't go to church, doesn't subscribe to Christian doctrines, and looks upon bishops and clergy as amiable eccentrics.

And what has filled the void? Nothing much at all except materialism, consumerism, hedonism, and football fanaticism. We live in a pagan society! Indeed, considering that, it may seem surprising that most people still behave as decently as they do, that there is still so much kindness and compassion around. But of course moral values don't disappear overnight. Norms persist, and people go on drinking from the stream long after they have ceased to acknowledge its source. The decline is gradual, but the symptoms are unmistakable.

This is a very serious state of affairs, for it confirms what we know, that moral values are not self-sustaining, self-perpetuating. They need to be nurtured; otherwise they become atrophied or at least attenuated. Then people are liable to say: 'Yes, I believe that life is sacred, but my enemy's life is not nearly as sacred as mine. Yes, I believe in helping my neighbour, but not while I am busy with myself. Yes, I believe in sheltering refugees, but not in my back yard. Yes, I believe in conserving the environment, stopping the arms trade, and reducing television violence, but not if it means losing my profits. Yes, I believe in animal welfare, but not to the extent of doing without a fur coat or spoiling the fun of traditional country sports.' Civilisation is a tender plant which, if deprived of the oxygen of shared moral values, will eventually disintegrate. In biblical language, 'righteousness exalts a nation' (Prov. 14:34) and 'where there is no vision, a people perishes' (Prov. 29:18).

The 'value vacuum' in contemporary British society has prompted several people to propose a national commission which would attempt to formulate a code of conduct acceptable to people of all religions and of none. I did so many years ago (*A Jewish Understanding of the World*, p. 166). The Archbishop of Canterbury and Chief Rabbi Dr Jonathan Sacks have done so more recently. Similarly motivated was John Major's 'Back to Basics' call, and now Tony Blair has launched yet another such campaign, saying: 'We need to find a new national moral purpose for this new generation' (*Observer*, 5 September 1999). But nothing much ever came of any of these initiatives, and I fear that nothing much will. Nor are parents and teachers seemingly able to do much to reverse the trend, for most of them are just as confused as the young.

In these circumstances, it is more than ever incumbent on religion, to the extent to which it still can, to resume its traditional role as supplier of moral values. But what kind of religion is best fitted to perform that role? There is a kind which lives in the past, which denies modern knowledge and defies modern thought, which is dogmatic and intolerant. That kind of religion is a potent source of moral certainty to its devotees, but it cuts little ice with the majority of people; and the values it teaches, though mainly benign, are in other ways malignant. For it preserves old prejudices and injustices, and feeds old animosities, and so exacerbates the ills it should cure.

No, what is needed is the kind of religion that combines what is best in tradition with what is best in modernity, and in a Jewish context that means Liberal Judaism. Happily, after a lean period, in which it has merely held its own, our Movement seems to be growing again, and as it approaches its centenary, I think it is more united and self-confident than it has been since I first became associated with it half-a-century ago.

But I don't wish to be party-political, triumphalist or complacent. That would be out of keeping with the spirit of this penitential season. Let me therefore confess that Liberal Judaism is not perfect, it has yet to be perfected, it has much to learn from others, not excluding the Orthodox, and its rhetoric is not always matched by its performance. Too often, our protestation that we place ethics above ritual is only an excuse for taking all our obligations, *including* our ethical ones, less seriously than we should.

What I want to suggest to you nevertheless is this: that if we wish to draw strength from this penitential season not only to nourish our personal spiritual growth, but also to exert a positive influence on the value-starved, neo-pagan moral waste-land of British society as it stumbles towards the threshold of a new century and a new millennium, then Liberal Judaism, taken seriously, is a means ready-to-hand by which we may hope to do that. Let others make their contributions; let this be ours.

Leadership

22 February 2003

The story of the Golden Calf raises many intriguing questions, but the one I should like to focus on, because it will lead us into a more general topic, is the role of Aaron.

Here is the elder brother of Moses and chief negotiator in securing the release of our ancestors from Egyptian bondage, the founding father of the priesthood and, as such, the presiding officer of the national cult. He, more than almost anybody should surely be a role model.

And so he has indeed been regarded. Already Ben Sira, in his well-known celebration of ancient heroes, beginning, 'Let us now praise famous men', after disposing of Moses in just five verses, devotes no fewer than 17 to Aaron (45:6–22). Likewise Hillel, the greatest of the Pharisees, holds him up for emulation in his maxim, 'Be a disciple of Aaron, loving peace and pursuing peace, loving your fellow men and women, and drawing them near to the Torah' (*Avot* 1:12).

And yet in the episode of the Golden Calf the role Aaron plays does not seem admirable at all! Admittedly, he does not *initiate* that flagrant breach of the Covenant which later generations looked back on with horror as the worst ever collective sin of the Jewish people. It is the people who, having lost hope that Moses is ever going to come down again from Mount Sinai, demand of Aaron, 'Come, make us a god' (Ex. 32:1). Nevertheless he responds to their demand with alacrity. In the very next verse he institutes a collection of golden rings for the purpose.

How can that be? According to Rashi (ad loc., from Tanchuma, *Ki Tissa*, 19), it was really a delaying tactic! For Aaron reckoned – wrongly, as it turned out – that the women would be reluctant to part with their jewellery, and therefore hope that, while they were still thinking about it, Moses would reappear.

Is that a plausible interpretation? Perhaps. At any rate, let us give Aaron the benefit of the doubt. But as soon as the golden rings have been collected, he immediately melts them down and moulds them into a golden calf. Another case, it seems, of indecent hurry. Moreover, the people have not specified what form the idol should take. It is apparently Aaron's idea that it should take the form of a calf.

But that is not surprising, for the Hebrew word for it, *egel*, is masculine. So we are really talking about a young bull, and a young bull was throughout the ancient Near East a symbol of virility and therefore much used in the graphic representation of deities. Therefore Aaron might very well have *assumed* that when the people demanded a man-made god, that was the kind of thing they had in mind.

There is also another possibility. We know from the First Book of Kings that following the death of King Solomon, the ten northern tribes rebelled against his son and successor Rehoboam, and established a separate kingdom under their own king, Jeroboam. He, however, was understandably worried that the continuing pull of the Jerusalem Temple would undermine the loyalty of his subjects. So he built for them two rival temples, at Bethel and Dan, and in each of them he set up a golden bull. Although these bulls were of course meant to represent the God of Israel, they nevertheless amount to idolatry in the eyes of the narrator, who, through a nameless prophet, denounces Jeroboam, just as he is about to consecrate the Bethel temple, and predicts its future destruction (12:25–13:6).

As a matter of fact, there are some remarkable similarities between the two stories which have led some scholars to conjecture that the Exodus story may have been inspired by the historical event related in Kings, and may date only from that time, in which case the unfavourable judgment of Jeroboam must be retrospectively applied to Aaron as well.

At any rate, it is Aaron who fashions the Golden Calf, and furthermore builds an altar in front of it, although only after the people have proclaimed, as Jeroboam proclaimed at Bethel, and in almost identical words, 'This is your god, O Israel, who brought you up out of the land of Egypt' (32:4) – that is to say, after it has become clear that the people regard the Golden Calf as an effigy of the God of Israel rather than some other deity.

But no sooner is the altar finished than Aaron announces: 'Tomorrow shall be a festival of the Eternal One' (32:5). Once again, Aaron seems to be in a hurry, and yet it is also possible to take the opposite view, as Rashi duly does. 'Tomorrow', after all, means 'not today'. Here, too, Rashi suggests, Aaron is playing for time, hoping that before the next day dawns Moses will at last reappear and put a stop to the whole sorry business. Convinced? Even if you are not, let us once more give Aaron the benefit of the doubt. Let us assume that he meant well.

But of course to say that somebody means well is the classic example of damning with faint praise. Even if our story doesn't show Aaron in the worst light, it surely doesn't show him in a good light. At best, he is weak. When the people propose the most monstrous breach of their Covenant with God, only days after they have solemnly promised, 'All that the Eternal One has spoken we will do and we will heed' (Ex. 24:7), he makes no attempt to stand up to them, but immediately gives in to them. Even if it is his secret hope that Moses will show up in the nick of time to pull the chestnuts out of the fire, it doesn't speak well for his strength of character or courage.

Therefore, in spite of all the attempts which our Tradition understandably makes to exonerate him, Aaron represents a model of leadership which is less than commendable. And that – leadership – is the general topic which I thought we might, for a few more moments, consider this morning.

In particular, I wanted to draw your attention to an interesting distinction which was made by Achad Ha-Am, the Zionist philosopher and Hebrew essayist. In two of his essays ('Moses' and 'Priest and Prophet') he distinguishes between the sort of leadership represented by a prophet like Moses and the sort represented by a priest like Aaron.

The source of this distinction is a passage in the Talmud (*San.* 6b) where the question under discussion is whether, once a dispute has been decided in a law court, it is still permissible for the parties to seek a compromise through arbitration. One view is: no, rather 'Let justice split the mountain' – in other words, justice must be done under all circumstances. And this is said to have been Moses' motto, whereas Aaron, it goes on to say, loved peace, and pursued peace, and made peace between people.

Taking his cue from this passage, Achad Ha-Am maintains that a leader in the prophetic tradition is essentially an idealist, who demands what he believes to be right and brooks no compromise, whereas a leader in the priestly tradition is a realist and, as such, prepared to make concessions in order to obtain the best possible results in the circumstances.

Of course that is an oversimplification. Most idealists are also, to some extent, realists. Although they stick to their principles, they do make allowances for reality and are prepared, if necessary, to make haste slowly. Conversely, most realists are also idealists; although they practise the art of the possible, they do have *some* conception of the better state of affairs which they hope will ultimately be attained. So the distinction is not a hard-and-fast one.

But it is also an oversimplification in another sense: it assumes that the leader's aims, whether short-term or long-term, are good. But what if the leader has no aims worth mentioning but merely goes along with the whims of the people? And what if the leader's aims are actually evil? It seems therefore that we need to reckon with *four*, not two, tendencies in leadership: bad, neutral, pragmatic and visionary. Let us try them out for size as we contemplate the contemporary scene.

There is, alas, no lack of evil leaders in the present-day world. The worst, of course, are dictators like Saddam Hussein and Robert Mugabe. But even among democratic leaders, some are motivated by ideologies that are at least partially evil, who prize territory above peace, or national prosperity above global conservation, and who have few if any scruples about the means they employ to further their ends. And among them I feel bound to include Ariel Sharon and George W. Bush.

The great majority of leaders, I should think, are of the neutral, spineless kind. They have no strong convictions of their own, or at least none for which they would risk their popularity. So, like Aaron – if you take our *Sidra* at face value and don't accept Rashi's excuses for him – they simply give the people what they want.

Unfortunately, that seems to me to describe, with few exceptions, the Jewish communal leadership both in Israel and in the Diaspora. By and large, the present mood of our people is one of self-pity and self-righteousness, especially in relation to Israel's conflict with the Palestinians, and most of our leaders don't question or challenge that mood in any way but, on the contrary, pander to it and even exploit it, especially for fundraising purposes.

As for priestly leadership in Achad Ha-Am's sense, that is, pragmatists, that describes a good many of the leaders of the major political parties in the UK and other Western democracies. That is to say, they have more or less decent moral values, but they pay close attention to the means by which, in practice, these values may be slowly implemented without forfeiting the goodwill of their constituents, who want both low taxation and high-quality public services, both unfettered competition and social justice, and other such contradictions.

Finally, we have in the past had leaders of the prophetic kind: men and women of broad vision, personal integrity and moral authority, whose sights have been set, not on the next election or even the next generation but on the future of humanity as a whole, who by their influence have elevated the attitudes of millions and shaped the course of history for good. We have had visionary leaders like Mahatma Gandhi and Winston Churchill and Martin Luther King and Nelson Mandela and Vaclav Havel. But they seem to be a dying breed.

We need them badly. Let us hope and pray that we shall not have to wait too much longer before Moses comes down from the mountain.

Survival

Rosh Hashanah 2000

No blessing is ever recited more feelingly than the one in which we praise god *Shehecheyanu v'kiyy'manu v'higgi'anu la-z'man ha-zeh*, who has kept us alive, sustained us and enabled us to reach this season; and never more so than at the beginning of a new year.

We have survived: we individually, we the Jewish people, we the human race. We have indeed suffered losses, and they make us sad; but we have survived. We have even survived the millennium. There has been no Armageddon and no Second Coming, either of Yeshua ben Yosef of Nazareth or of Menachem Schneerson of New York. To all appearances, 'the world follows its habitual course' as the Rabbis used to say (*AZ* 54b). Therefore we can look to the future with confidence and say, in the words of the pop song: 'We will survive, we will survive, we will survive!'

But even as we say that, we wonder. We wonder because of the natural disasters which seem to be happening with increasing frequency all over the world: the hurricanes, tidal waves, floods, earthquakes and forest fires, causing devastation and loss of life on a vast scale.

We wonder, too, because some of these are due to human activity: the destruction of rain forests; the poisoning of rivers, lakes and seas; the emission of CFC gases into the atmosphere; the consequent global warming, melting of ice caps, rise of sea levels, ever more disastrous droughts, and the irreversible extinction of innumerable species of animals and plants.

We wonder, perhaps most of all, because of the terrible misdeeds daily perpetrated by human beings and nations against one another: the acts of war and genocide, terrorism and torture, persecution and discrimination, bribery and corruption, murder, rape and child abuse.

To be fair, in some areas there has been progress. Governments and industries *are* slowly becoming more environmentally conscious; some international conflicts have been resolved or are edging towards resolution; life expectancy is rising; and the new cybernetic and genetic technologies, even though they hold frightening dangers, also raise dazzling hopes.

All things considered, though, it is hard to disagree with the assessment of a Conservative MP that 'the future of mankind looks bleak unless decisive action is taken urgently' (Sir Sydney Chapman, MP for Chipping Barnet, Millennium Message).

With a bit of luck, we and our children and grandchildren will live out our natural spans, but further down the line, who can be sure? Sixty-five million years ago the dinosaurs, which have recently been brought so vividly to our cinema and television screens, became extinct, apparently because the earth was hit by a gigantic asteroid. How do we know that the human species is not also destined sooner or later to become extinct through some cosmic catastrophe or, more likely, self-destruction?

To that depressing question there are three possible answers. The first is the traditional one: that God is in charge and will not let it happen. There is indeed an ancient legend to the effect that God created and destroyed several worlds before creating ours (Gen. R. 3:7, 9:2). But, say the traditionalists, that won't happen to ours because after the Flood God gave a solemn promise, symbolised by the rainbow, never again to destroy humanity (Gen. 8:21); and for the fundamentalists, who believe that the Bible is quite literally the word of God, that must be very comforting. But as for us, who know that the Bible is only a record of what our ancestors *believed*, how can we be sure that it wasn't wishful thinking on their part?

Besides, the very assumption that everything is under God's control is open to question. It is indeed commonly believed, and it was never stated more categorically than by Rabbi Chanina when he said: 'Nobody bruises their finger here on earth unless it was so decreed in heaven' (Rabbi Chanina, *Chul.* 7b). But it runs into difficulty as soon as we bring into play the fact of human free will.

That it *is* a fact, Judaism has nearly always taught. Indeed, it was the same Rabbi Chanina who, from the opening verse of our Torah portion, 'And now, O Israel, what does the Lord your God require of you, but to revere the Lord your God …' (Deut. 10:12), deduced the principle that 'everything is in the hand of God except the fear of God' (*Ber.* 33b). In other words, *everything else* is predetermined, but whether or not we do God's will depends on us. In this one area – which is the most important of all – we are free to choose, and to that extent God has presumably relinquished control over human destiny.

But because the Rabbis were reluctant to question God's omnipotence, therefore they clung to both horns of the dilemma. Yes, they said, human free will is a fact, but so too is divine providence. That is the paradox Rabbi Chanina affirmed, as also did Rabbi Akiva when he taught, 'Everything is foreseen, yet free will is given' (*Avot* 3:16).

The only trouble is that divine providence becomes increasingly difficult to maintain when we contemplate the horrendous things human beings do with their free will to one another. Here the traditional explanation is that those who do these things are unwitting instruments of God's punitive justice. Thus about the Assyrians, who destroyed the Kingdom of Israel, the prophet Isaiah said that they were 'the rod of God's anger' (10:5). Similarly, said the Rabbis, the First Temple was destroyed by way of divine punishment for the people's sins of idolatry, immorality and murder, and the Second Temple because they had been guilty of groundless hatred towards one another (*Yoma* 9b).

But as the Jewish people, under Christendom, suffered more and more persecutions, often because of their very loyalty to their faith, so the traditional theory wore thin, and with the Holocaust it finally snapped. Nobody has dared to suggest that the Six Million deserved their fate – nobody, that is, except anti-Semites and, a few weeks ago, the former Sephardi Chief Rabbi of Israel, Ovadiah Yossef. He, in one of the most stupid and offensive remarks ever made, suggested that the Holocaust victims were 'reincarnations of the souls of sinners' (*Jewish Chronicle*, 11 August 2000).

Of course that obscene suggestion was immediately rejected

by almost everybody, but even those who rejected it, like Chief Rabbi Dr Jonathan Sacks, could only bring themselves to say that 'the Holocaust remains a mystery' (ibid.), the implication being that in some mysterious way, completely beyond our understanding, it was God's will that it should happen. I find that utterly unacceptable. To me it seems plain that when murder, let alone mass murder, is committed, what happens is not in any sense whatsoever attributable to God's will but a ghastly violation of it. To me the Holocaust is proof positive that God does not intervene in human history. It is the *reductio ad absurdum* of the traditional belief in an interventionist God.

But if we can't accept the traditional view that our future is guaranteed by God, can we endorse the humanist view that it is guaranteed by humanity itself? On the face of it, that is even harder to believe. For history suggests that, on the contrary, we are hell-bent on self-destruction.

If, then, we are forced to reject *both* views – that God will intervene to save us and that humanity is capable of saving itself – is there any hope at all? I think there is, and I find a basis for it in a talmudic statement which reads: 'Whoever wishes to pollute himself with sin will find all the gates open before him, and whoever desires to attain the highest purity will find all the forces of goodness ready to help him' (*Yoma* 38b). Please consider with me the tremendous implications of the asymmetry of that statement.

If we are inclined to act selfishly or cruelly, all the gates are open. There is nothing to stop us. The wickedness of which human beings are capable knows no limits. If ever that needed proving, the Holocaust provided the ultimate demonstration. So that part of the talmudic statement is certainly true.

But if we decide to act rightly – to speak the truth even to our disadvantage, to stand up for the rights of others, to make sacrifices for those in need, to do the generous thing – then not only are the gates open but 'the forces of goodness are ready to help us'. That is to say, there is a power that emanates from God – Matthew Arnold's 'power, not ourselves, that makes for righteousness' (from an 1873 essay entitled 'Literature and Dogma') – which is constantly ready to reinforce our good impulses. And that, too, accords with human experience.

So the answer to our question is neither the traditional one nor the humanist one but a third which takes something from both. On the one hand the 'Good Inclination', although often weak, is nevertheless a fundamental part of our human make-up, not less than the 'Evil Inclination', perhaps more so. To that extent the humanists are right. On the other hand, although God doesn't *intervene* in human history, God is nevertheless *active* in human history. To that extent the traditionalists are right. But God's activity in human history is that of a Teacher, not a Dictator. God guides, persuades, cajoles us, exerts a constant pressure on us to do what is right, but never compels us. And it is the divine–human partnership, resulting from our response to God's teaching and God's reinforcement of our response, which gives us ground for hope that, in spite of all the contrary indications, we shall survive.

Even so, there is no guarantee. There can't be because, although God's part in the process is assured, the human part is not. It depends on all the innumerable free choices human beings will make in time to come.

And therefore one last thought. What if the hope is not fulfilled? What if humanity does, after all, destroy itself a few generations or a few millennia hence? What if this world, like the legendary ones that preceded it, turns out to have been another unsuccessful experiment on the part of the Creator? And what if we knew that that was going to happen? Would that empty human life of all meaning? Would that compel us to give up all purposeful endeavour and say, 'Let us eat and drink, for tomorrow we die' (Isa. 22:13)? *Of course* not, any more than our life as individuals is meaningless because it is of limited duration.

Of course the future of humanity is important, and *of course* we each have a responsibility for it. But it is not *everything*. There is another dimension, which transcends the past-present-future continuum, and from that point of view whatever has intrinsic value also has eternal value. Nor do we have to choose between the two perspectives, for they don't contradict each other. Truth and justice, love and compassion, are more than lofty ideals. On them depends the future of humanity. They are the very conditions of our collective survival. But they are also eternal values.

Therefore, as we enter a new year, let us make two resolutions which, in their practical implications, are really one and the same. Let us resolve so to conduct ourselves that we may make our contribution to the survival of humanity; and let us also resolve so to conduct ourselves that even if the story of human civilisation on Planet Earth should prove, after all, to have been only an episode in the history of God's universe, our lives will still have had eternal value.

Road Map to the Messianic Age

Pesach, 19 April 2003

What is the magic of *Pesach* that grips us anew every year? I think the answer lies in the way it moves back and forth between the ancient past and the ultimate future, the tension it creates between realism and idealism. On the one hand it reminds us of the world as it has been and is – a world of slavery and oppression, though periodically also of liberation and reconstruction. On the other hand it looks forward to a better world, of universal freedom and enduring peace.

The question is: how do we get from here to there? To which it is tempting to reply, with the Irishman who was asked for directions by a tourist, 'If I were you, I wouldn't start from here.' The trouble is: we do have to start from here. So what is the road map from this imperfect world to the perfect world of the messianic future? To that question there are three possible answers.

The first is the *military* answer: that it lies within our power radically to improve the world, if only we will muster the courage and the resolution to fight and conquer the tyrants, the terrorists, the rogue regimes, the axis of evil. Then all will be well. It will be the dawning of the messianic age, also known as Pax Americana or the New American Century.

It is a view which can find some support in Jewish tradition. The liberation of our ancestors involved the drowning of the Egyptians and the death of their firstborn – it is always the innocent children who suffer most in war. In the Song at the Sea of Reeds, alluding to that same episode, God is described as 'a man of war' (Ex. 15:3). There are militaristic overtones in the traditional Jewish liturgy, as when the Ark is opened and the congregation sings, with great gusto: 'Rise up, Eternal One, let Your enemies be scattered, and those who hate You flee before You.' And the traditional Haggadah pleads with God: 'Pour out Your wrath upon the nations that do not acknowledge You' (Psalm 79:6).

War *is* sometimes necessary. Whether that applies to the war that has just ended is indeed a matter of ongoing debate. That it has brought to the people of Iraq a freedom they have not known for 20 years, is clear, and cause for rejoicing. Nor is it negated by the fact that it has involved much suffering. Many of us, in celebrating the *Seder* this year, must have been struck by the topicality of the passage in our Haggadah that reads: 'No liberation is easy. As evil takes its toll, so does the fight against it. As tyranny brings death and terror to its victims, so the struggle to overthrow it claims its casualties. In the upheaval … innocent and guilty [alike] will suffer. There is no redemption without pain' (p. 19).

We may even express satisfaction that considerable care was taken to minimise civilian casualties. But questions remain. Was it necessary to use cluster bombs, which have exactly the opposite purpose? Why were the Coalition forces so ill prepared to deal with the predictable aftermath of their victory – the looting and the lawlessness, the catastrophic shortage of water, food and medicine? How can we feel entirely comfortable about a war that was planned long ago by an alliance of right-wing American neo-conservatives, Christian fundamentalists and supporters of Sharon, dedicated to the most illiberal policies both domestically and internationally, and launched in defiance of the United Nations and world opinion? And what will be the long-term consequences for Iraq, for the Middle East, for East–West relations, and for the world?

Only time will tell, but of this we may be sure: that the war will not solve all problems. Wars never do. The brave new world they promise never comes to pass. At the very least, *military* processes need to be accompanied by *political* ones. So far as Israel is concerned, nobody questions its right and its duty to defend its people against terrorism. There are indeed questions to be asked about some of the *methods* it employs. But the more fundamental objection to the policies of the Sharon government is that it has failed to hold out to the Palestinians any hope of realising their aspirations by political means. If it had done so, the level of terrorism would surely have been much lower.

At any rate, the second road map to the messianic age is the *political* one. That is, the creation of a world order that ensures a fair distribution of the earth's resources; economic and environmental co-operation; an all-out effort to stamp out poverty, starvation and disease; the promotion of democracy; and respect for international law. Great strides have been made in these respects in recent times, and one of the worries many people feel about the Iraq war is that it has set them back in favour of a new era marked by the domination of a single superpower.

The war has, however, acquainted us with the geography of a country most of us have never visited. It is a geography we should be familiar with from our Jewish history. Not only did the Patriarchs come from Mesopotamia, the land of the Tigris and Euphrates, indeed from the very city, Ur, where the American-sponsored meeting of Iraqi politicians took place earlier this week. And not only did Ezekiel prophesy there during the Babylonian Exile, as our *Haftarah* has reminded us. But during the greater part of the first millennium of the Common Era it was numerically and intellectually the chief centre of the Jewish world.

That phase began in the third century, when two outstanding Jewish teachers lived there: Samuel and Rav. Samuel was born in Nehardea on the Euphrates, only about 50 miles southwest of Baghdad, where he founded a rabbinic academy. He was wealthy and renowned for his knowledge of medicine and astronomy, but what matters for our purpose is his interest in politics. For example, he was the author of the maxim *dina d'malchuta dina*, that it is religiously incumbent on Jews to observe the law of the government of the land in which they live (*BK* 113b). He is also represented in the Haggadah as the author of the passage beginning 'We were slaves to Pharaoh in Egypt', which emphasises the *political* aspect of liberation. And he is said to have taught that the only difference between the present time and the messianic age is that in the messianic age Israel will no longer be subjugated by foreign empires (*Ber.* 34b). We may be sure, therefore, that Samuel would have favoured the *political* road map from the nasty present to the splendid future.

His great friend and rival was Rav, who founded an even more famous academy about 100 miles further down the Euphrates, at Sura. He was tall and handsome, he had a fine voice and a special interest in liturgy. Some of the most beautiful *Rosh Chodesh* and *Rosh Hashanah* prayers are attributed to him, and they tend to have a universalistic ring. One of them begins: 'Eternal God, teach all Your works to stand in awe before You, and let all creatures tremble at your presence.' His influence, too, is stamped on the Haggadah, for he wrote the passage 'In the beginning our ancestors were idol worshippers, but now we have learnt to worship the true God...'. That is to say, he emphasised the *spiritual* rather than the political dimension of liberation. Furthermore, it was he who taught: 'All the predicted ends of the world have been and gone, and now everything depends on repentance and good deeds' (San. 97b). Rav, therefore, may be regarded as an advocate of the third road to the messianic age: the *spiritual and moral* road.

And that is the one which should commend itself to us if we take our religious heritage seriously. War may sometimes be necessary, but it is the role of religious leaders to question it as long as there is any doubt about it, as the Archbishop of Canterbury, to his credit, has done. Political programmes for improving the world are of great importance, and religious people should contribute constructively to them, but remain critical of them. For political history is strewn with false Utopias, and all of them have foundered on the rock of human selfishness. *There is neither a military nor a political shortcut to the messianic age.* Ultimately everything depends, as Rav taught, on repentance and good deeds – on the attitudes of individual human beings. And to influence them – to teach us to honour and respect, to cherish and love, our fellow men and women, created in God's image – that must always be the *primary* task of religion. If we fail in that, everything else is doomed to failure; if we succeed, everything becomes possible – even the fulfilment of the messianic hope which is the *leitmotif* of this festival of *Pesach*.

PART II
LECTURES

Hebraism: Our Common Heritage and Hope

21 November 2002

LILY MONTAGU

I have listened to many of these annual Lily Montagu Lectures in the course of the years but never dreamt that I might one day be invited to deliver one myself. It is a daunting task, and I am duly daunted. But as one of the dwindling number who knew and worked with Lily Montagu, I welcome the opportunity which this lecture gives me to pay a reverential and affectionate tribute to her.

Of all the people I have known, she was the most other-worldly, for she lived with a constant sense of God's presence. Novalis would surely have called her, as he called Spinoza, 'God-intoxicated'. Yet she was also remarkably this-worldly, in the sense that she lived under a constant compulsion to devote every moment of her time and every ounce of her energy to the service of God by doing practical things like visiting the sick, running clubs and founding synagogues. This year, in particular, marks the centenary of the Jewish Religious Union, later renamed Union of Liberal and Progressive Synagogues, which she founded in 1902.

Her purpose then was to challenge her fellow Jews to rediscover and reactivate their ancestral heritage in the stark simplicity and austere demands of its fundamental religious and moral teachings. It was, we might say, a 'back-to-basics' exercise.

COMMON GROUND

'Back to basics' also sums up what I want to attempt in this lecture, which is to explore what we, as Jews and Christians, at the most basic level, have in common. But I must add two qualifications.

First, when I speak of Jews and Christians I don't mean to exclude Muslims. On the contrary, everything I have to say about the common ground applies to them as well. It is only the terms of reference of the Society sponsoring this lecture which impose the limitation.

Secondly, I need to confess that my choice of topic reflects a change of mind on my part. Let me explain. *Common Ground* is the title of the journal of the Council of Christians and Jews, and expresses well the emphasis which has characterised that national organisation ever since its foundation, largely in response to the menace of anti-Semitism, in 1942. But for many years I felt that, though it is indeed important for Jews and Christians to recognise and stress what they have in common, it is equally if not more important that they should understand and respect their differences.

Just that has been the distinctive emphasis since its inception of the London Society of Jews and Christians. For it was founded in 1927, 15 years before the Council of Christians and Jews, for which it helped to pave the way, 'to increase religious understanding, and to promote goodwill and co-operation between Jews and Christians, *with mutual respect for differences of faith and practice*'.

When I say that I have changed my mind, I don't mean that I no longer subscribe to that aim. *Of course* respect for differences is hugely important. It is the precondition of decent inter-faith relations. Nevertheless, just as in 1942 it was of paramount importance that Jews and Christians should stand together against anti-Semitism, so our time requires that we should again lay foremost emphasis on what unites us. For, as has been pointed out – among others by Chief Rabbi Dr Jonathan Sacks in his recent book *The Dignity of Difference* – we live in an age of two conflicting tendencies. On the one hand it is an age of globalisation, which calls for unity. On the other hand, the different faith communities, and even the different streams within them, are asserting their distinctive identities with a new stridency, triumphalism and intolerance.

Because this 'new tribalism', as it has been called, is a potentially destructive force, there is again an urgent need to highlight those teachings of the great religions which are capable of uniting rather than dividing humanity, and perhaps even to question the emphasis traditionally placed on the differences. In that context I propose to make some critical remarks about aspects both of Judaism and of Christianity which, I hope, will not cause offence.

HEBRAISM

If what Jews and Christians have in common can be summed up in one word, that word is surely Hebraism: that is to say, the religion – or more generally the world view and value system – of the Hebrew Bible.

That term has been used by a number of writers, usually in contrast with Hellenism, and is perhaps especially associated with Matthew Arnold, who, in 1869, wrote: 'Hebraism and Hellenism – between these two points of influence moves our world.'[1]

More recent writers have tended to warn against overstating that dichotomy. Writing in 1951, the American Jewish theologian Will Herberg contrasted Hebraism with what he chose to call the 'Greco-Oriental religions'. But though, he wrote, they are 'often diametrically opposed', it should not be thought that they occur 'in pure form'. Rather, 'every existing religion would probably show...a varying mixture of elements stemming from both sources'.[2]

Similarly, the great American Jewish preacher, scholar and Zionist leader, Abba Hillel Silver wrote in 1956: 'There is no unbridgeable gulf between the culture of the Greeks and the culture of the Jews. They are not in polar opposition. Both have antecedents in the Eastern Mediterranean culture which emerged in the second millennium before the common era when both the Greeks and the Hebrews made their appearance on the stage of history. There *is* a marked difference of emphasis.'[3]

Of course the problem with speaking of Hebraism at all is one of definition. Since the Hebrew Bible was written by many different authors over a period of about 1,000 years, to pretend that it always speaks with the same voice would be ridiculous – which does not prevent the fundamentalists from doing precisely that. To anybody unblinded by dogmatism it is obvious that the Hebrew Bible contains a great variety of tendencies: priestly and prophetic, pro-monarchic and anti-monarchic, particularistic and universalistic, simplistic and sophisticated, sensitive and insensitive, optimistic and pessimistic – to mention only a few. How, then, is it possible out of such diversity to distil a single coherent philosophy and label it 'Hebraism'?

I submit that it can be done provided that we are prepared to make a judgement as to what is more and what is less prevalent and enduring, intrinsically important and self-consistent, and provided that we are alert to trends showing movement in a discernible direction. Of course developments are not necessarily always positive. There is retrogression as well as advance; and I am sufficiently attuned to the currently fashionable thinking known as post-modernism to concede that in all this there is an inescapable subjective element. But I still maintain that the procedure is not *entirely* subjective.

Even so, I readily admit that we are dealing with a topic in which complete objectivity is unattainable. Historiography is not an exact science. In some ways it is more like an art such as portrait painting. In the end one can only ask those who know the subject of the portrait whether or not the artist has succeeded in conveying the essence of his or her personality.

With these qualifications, let me now try to draw a portrait of six aspects of Hebraism which seem to me fundamental to it, and consider in each case how it has fared in the subsequent history of Judaism and Christianity.

1. MONOTHEISM IN THE HEBREW BIBLE

The essence of Hebraism is of course its monotheism: its assertion that the universe is the creation of a single God, which was surely the greatest breakthrough in the history of religion. Needless to say, it was not accomplished overnight, and the critical historian can detect successive stages of its development associated with, for instance, Abraham, Moses and Amos. But the general direction of the development is unmistakable, and round about 600 BCE it was complete.

The details don't matter for our purpose. It is sufficient to recall Deuteronomy: 'Know then this day and take it to heart: the

Eternal One is God in the heavens above and on the earth below; there is no other' (4:30). And Deutero-Isaiah: 'I am the Eternal One, and there is no other; besides Me there is no God' (45:5).

The importance of this breakthrough can hardly be exaggerated. Just as the number one has unique mathematical properties, so monotheism is different *in kind* from polytheism. The single God of Hebraism is not *more* powerful than the many gods of paganism: He – and I say 'He' because Hebraism did conceive God in masculine language – is all-powerful. He does not have *more* control over nature but complete control. He does not demand *a larger share* of the devotion of His worshippers but all of it.

The biblical writers were aware of the gulf. Indeed, they exaggerated it. They made little effort to understand paganism, never suspected that it might harbour its own spiritual insights, and that even idolatry might be directed, not to the idols themselves but to the concepts they symbolise. Instead, they condemned polytheism and all its works without qualification, heaped ridicule on it, and called for its extermination.[4]

This intolerance of Hebraism towards the non-Hebraic religions of the ancient Near-East is one of its less pleasing features and stands in need of much modification in the light of the modern, sympathetic study of comparative religion. Karen Armstrong, for instance, has written: 'There were profound similarities between the monotheistic and other visions of reality. It seems that when human beings contemplate the absolute, they have very similar ideas and experiences.'[5]

I think we should all welcome such insights, not only pragmatically, because they facilitate religious co-existence in today's multi-cultural societies, but also intrinsically, as showing a truer understanding of the 'varieties of religious experience'[6] than the ancient Israelite writers could manage. But though it is a necessary corrective, it does not gainsay the immensity of the step forward in the history of religion which Hebrew monotheism represents.

Monotheism in Judaism and Christianity

Let us now consider how it has fared in the two enduring religious traditions which sprang from Hebraism in antiquity – Pharisaic-Rabbinic Judaism in the second century BCE, and Christianity in the first century CE. (Let us, by the way, bear in mind that, whereas

Judaism grew directly out of Hebraism, Christianity grew out of Hebraism plus Pharisaic-Rabbinic Judaism. And let me also explain that when, in the rest of this lecture, I refer to Judaism without qualification, I shall mean the Pharisaic-Rabbinic tradition, which, in contemporary Judaism, is somewhat rigidly represented by the Orthodox tendency and in varying degrees modified by the Progressive and Conservative tendencies.)

In Judaism the monotheistic principle has been consistently maintained and even reinforced. A major factor in this was the Pharisees' selection of the *Shema'* – the Deuteronomy passage beginning 'Hear, O Israel, the Eternal One is our God, the Eternal God is One' (6:4–9) – as a daily declaration of faith. Another is the story of how Rabbi Akiva, when tortured to death by the Romans, recited the *Shema'* with his last breath.[7] It is therefore safe to say that in the last two thousand years any Jew, asked to explain what Judaism was essentially all about, would almost certainly have answered: 'The Unity of God'.

Christianity, too, has been unwavering in its commitment to monotheism; but, unlike Judaism and Islam, has needed to reconcile it with its doctrine of the Trinity. The very ingenuity which Christian theologians have brought to that task testifies both to its inherent difficulty and to their determination to remain faithful to Hebraism.[8] Whereas Eastern Orthodox Christians have tended to regard the Trinity as a mystery unamenable to reason, 'for many Western Christians', according to Karen Armstrong, it is 'simply baffling'.[9]

The purpose of these remarks is not to challenge the doctrine of the Trinity, which would be impertinent. Obviously, Christians are entitled to affirm it with whatever degree of conviction it holds for them. For though it is not a doctrine rooted in Hebraism, it is no part of my thesis to suggest that Hebraism contains all truth. But I think it is legitimate to point out that the more Christians emphasise the unity rather than the trinity of God, the more they speak a language which non-Christians can understand, and which is therefore potentially unifying rather than divisive.

2. TRANSCENDENCE AND IMMANENCE IN THE HEBREW BIBLE

A corollary of God's unity is His transcendence. For as Creator of the universe He is necessarily different from the universe He has created, as an artist is different from the canvas on which he or she paints. Therefore God is not to be identified with nature or any of its constituent elements, whether mineral, vegetable, animal or human. Precisely the rejection of any such identification is what distinguishes Hebraism from Paganism.

Although that principle is not stated in the Hebrew Bible as a philosophical proposition, it is often implied. For instance, in Deutero-Isaiah's repeated rhetorical question, 'To whom then will you liken God?' (40:18, 25; 46:5), and in his declaration, 'For My thoughts are not your thoughts, neither are your ways My ways, says the Eternal One. For as the heavens are higher than the earth, so are My ways higher than your ways, and My thoughts than your thoughts' (55:8f.).

Admittedly, there are occasional references to angels and other mythical beings who occupy an intermediate position between humanity and God. But they have a somewhat nebulous identity. They belong to folklore rather than official religion, apparently answering to a popularly felt need to bridge the gulf between God and humanity. In serious Hebraic theology that gulf is bridged, not by angels, but by the fact that, alongside God's transcendence, it also affirms His immanence. His presence can be experienced by human beings. He watches over them, leads them like a shepherd, admonishes them, and listens to their prayers. He is active in human history. He guides the destinies of the nations, enters into a covenant with Abraham, and reveals His law to his descendants at Mount Sinai.

Transcendence and Immanence in Judaism and Christianity

Now let us consider how this twofold doctrine has fared in Judaism and Christianity.

In Judaism the emphasis on God's transcendence is strongly maintained. Admittedly, there are some surprisingly anthropomorphic references to God in Rabbinic Literature, but they are generally followed by the disclaimer *kivyachol*, which is perhaps best translated *per impossibile*. Maimonides, the pre-eminent Jewish philosopher of the Middle Ages, is very insistent that all such expressions are to be understood as metaphors and nothing more.[10]

An excellent summary of Judaism's twofold emphasis is the synagogue hymn *Adon olam*, which begins by describing God in the most transcendental terms imaginable, as pre-existing the universe and continuing to exist when it has ceased to be. But then, in a dramatic switch, it continues: 'And He is *my* God, and my living Redeemer...Into His hand I entrust my spirit, both when I sleep and when I wake, and with my spirit, my body also: the Eternal One is with me, I will not fear.'[11]

Christianity, too, has maintained the dual emphasis, but developed the concept of God's immanence in a novel way, by teaching that God 'became flesh' in Jesus of Nazareth. Like the Trinity, this doctrine of the Incarnation has no basis in Hebraism[12] – and is not to be dismissed on that account. But it does create difficulties, as the complexity of the attempts to justify it, on the part of the Church Fathers and ever since, would seem to indicate. Some Christians may therefore be drawn to the suggestion made by Geza Vermes that the term 'Son of God' was originally meant in the sense of adoption, which does not imply divinity, and should be so understood.[13] But though most Christians will no doubt continue to affirm the traditional belief in Jesus as both human and divine, it is, I think, fair to point out that the more they emphasise his humanity, the more non-Christians will feel comfortable with their language.

3. ETHICAL EMPHASIS IN THE HEBREW BIBLE

Next to God's unity and transcendence-and-immanence, what Hebraism chiefly emphasises is His morality. It is an *ethical* monotheism. And that means two things. On the one hand, God's nature is intrinsically moral. Ethical qualities such as righteousness, justice, truth, faithfulness, loving kindness and compassion are regularly attributed to God in the Hebrew Bible. On the other hand these same qualities are what God first and foremost demands of those who would worship Him.

But here a qualification is necessary. When I said 'first and foremost' I was referring to the teaching of the Prophets. In reference to the greatest of them – Amos, Hosea, Isaiah, Micah, Jeremiah and Deutero-Isaiah – I could even have said 'exclusively', for they seem to be saying that *only* right conduct is pleasing to God. Hosea's declaration that God desires 'love and not sacrifice, and the knowledge of God rather than burnt offerings' (6:6) is only one of many such prophecies.[14]

But that is not the view of all the biblical writers, or even all the

Prophets. In the Pentateuch, although there is indeed great stress on moral injunctions such as those included in the Ten Commandments (Exod. 20 and Deut. 5) and 'you shall love your neighbour as yourself' (Lev. 19:18), there is equal emphasis on matters such as observance of the Sabbath and Festivals, ritual purity, the dietary laws, and the sacrificial cult. Indeed, the two types of commandments jostle with each other without any seeming awareness of the fundamental distinction between them.

If I nevertheless choose to regard the Prophetic view that only right conduct is pleasing to God as characteristic of Hebraism, I do so because it distinguishes Hebraism from Paganism in a way in which emphasis on ritual does not. On the contrary, most of the rituals of the ancient Hebrews were little more than monotheistic adaptations of practices current before their time among the Canaanites and other Near-Eastern peoples. It is the ethical emphasis which makes Hebraism distinctive.

Ethical Emphasis in Judaism and Christianity

To what extent have Judaism and Christianity remained faithful to this ethical emphasis?

So far as Judaism is concerned, the answer has to distinguish between its legal side, known as *Halachah*, and its homiletical side, known as *Aggadah*. On the halachic side, the Pharisees and Rabbis saw it as their task to construct a system of precepts governing every aspect of life, and for this purpose interpreted the biblical legislation – which is to be found almost exclusively in the Pentateuch – in the way lawyers interpret a constitution. Therefore whatever the Pentateuch expressed in the imperative was equally grist for their jurisprudential mill; and since the Pentateuch doesn't differentiate between ethical and ritual matters, the Rabbinic *Halachah* doesn't either. That is to my mind a major weakness of Judaism which can easily lead to an excessive emphasis on ritual, and has often done so.

On the aggadic side, however, the Pharisees and Rabbis continued the ethical emphasis of the Prophets. When they were asked to explain in a nutshell what the Torah was all about, they nearly always did so in ethical terms, by quoting or alluding to such verses as 'You shall love your neighbour as yourself' (Lev. 19:18).[15] And when they drew up the 'Great Confession' to be recited on the Day of Atonement, they included in it only transgressions against the Moral Law, not against the Ritual Law.[16]

Jesus clearly stood in the Prophetic tradition, but was influenced, additionally, by the Pharisaic Aggadah. For both reasons he emphasised almost exclusively the ethical side of God's demands. Most of his parables make an ethical point, and so do many of the beatitudes of the Sermon on the Mount: 'Blessed are those who hunger and thirst after righteousness... the merciful... the peacemakers' and so forth (Matt. 5:5–9). And to the extent to which his influence has prevailed, the same ethical emphasis has characterised Christianity. If there is one qualification to be made, it is that in some of its phases Christianity has tended to emphasise right belief as much as, if not more than, right conduct. Hence the prolonged debate about 'Justification by Faith' *versus* 'Justification by Works'.

Perhaps it would be a fair summary to say that, historically, both traditions, Jewish and Christian, have remained largely, but not always completely, faithful to the ethical emphasis of Hebraism at its best.

Furthermore, in their ethical teachings Judaism and Christianity are closer to each other than in anything else – more so, for instance, than in their respective theologies, sacred calendars and liturgies. This therefore is the area *par excellence* in which they can and should co-operate.

4. HUMAN NATURE IN THE HEBREW BIBLE

Another striking feature of Hebraism is its high estimation of human nature. That note is struck already in the Creation Story with its claim that God created man 'in His own image' and gave him dominion over all the earth (Gen. 1:27f.), echoed in Psalm 8 with its assertion that God made him 'little less than divine' and 'put all things under his feet' (v. 6f.).

The same high regard for humanity in general and for individual human beings in particular is maintained throughout the Hebrew Bible. It is reflected in the humaneness of biblical legislation for the protection of human life, liberty and property; in the ability of human beings to communicate with God in prayer, and to respond to God's demands; and in their possession of free will, enabling them to choose between good and evil.

That human beings are nevertheless prone to sin is readily acknowledged. 'There is not a righteous man on earth who does good and never sins', says Ecclesiastes (7:20). And sometimes the human condition is depicted as hopeless. In the prologue to the Flood Story the biblical writer devastatingly remarks: 'God saw that the wickedness of humankind was great in the earth, and that every inclination of the thoughts of their hearts was only evil continually' and even that He 'regretted having created humankind' (Gen. 6:5f.).

But such expressions of despair are exceptional. As a general rule, the conviction is maintained that human beings are capable of fulfilling their high potential; that they can choose good over evil and life over death (Deut. 30:19); that it is not impossible for them to live as God desires. 'For this commandment which I command you this day is not too hard for you,' says the Deuteronomist (30:11). And when human beings break the divine law, the possibility of repenting and so gaining God's forgiveness is always available. In the words of the prophet Malachi, God says: 'Return to Me, and I will return to You' (3:7).

Human Nature in Judaism and Christianity

That, in brief, is the Hebraic view of human nature, and in Judaism it is both maintained and reinforced. Rabbi Akiva, for instance, taught: 'How privileged we are to have been created in God's image; how much more privileged still to have been made aware that we were created in God's image.'[17] A daily morning prayer, which goes back to the Talmud, begins: 'My God, the soul You have given me is pure. For You have created it and formed it and breathed it into me.'[18] Any tendency towards determinism is counterbalanced by a robust affirmation of freedom of choice. As Rabbi Akiva stated the paradox, 'Everything is foreseen, yet free will is given.'[19]

The destruction of the Temple, and the cessation of sin offerings and other sacrifices, led to greater emphasis than ever on prayer, and on inner repentance as the sole prerequisite of atonement. According to the Rabbis, God says to Israel: 'Open for me one gate of repentance by as little as the point of a needle, and I will open for you gates wide enough for carriages and coaches to pass through.'[20]

In Christianity, too, the Hebraic view of the preciousness of every human being has been upheld and, through it, has largely influenced Western civilisation, although the contribution of secular humanism should not be underestimated. Jesus himself set a wonderful example of caring for individuals, especially despised and vulnerable members of society, and his example has inspired Christians all through the ages, down to Albert Schweitzer and Mother Teresa in recent times.

At the same time, Christianity, more than Judaism, has stressed the dark, malevolent and rebellious side of human nature. While Judaism has tended to see sin as a weakness to be overcome, Christianity has seen it as a sickness to be cured. Furthermore, in view of the horrendous nature of the manifestations of evil we have witnessed in the twentieth century and are still witnessing today, there is much to be said for the Christian view, and it may well be that Judaism has something to learn from Christianity in that respect.

There has even been a tendency in Christianity to regard the Devil, not as a figure of folklore, but as a real evil force existing independently of God and humanity. As to that, I am inclined to agree with Joseph Conrad's invocation of Occam's razor when he wrote: 'The belief in a supernatural source of evil is not necessary; men alone are quite capable of every wickedness.'[21]

There has also been in Christianity a tendency to regard the human propensity to sin as a kind of hereditary disease going back to the 'original sin' of Adam and Eve, and this doctrine has been much used to lend urgency to Christianity's appeal to unbelievers to avail themselves of the means of salvation which it alone offers.

The right to hold such a belief is of course entirely to be respected, but it can hardly be expected to commend itself to non-Christians, and therefore to make for unity. The Apostle Paul was right when he referred to it as 'a stumbling block to Jews and foolishness to Gentiles' (I Cor. 1:23). Therefore the recent tendency in both the Catholic and Protestant Churches to back away from such exclusive claims is greatly to be welcomed.

Surely it is sufficient to acknowledge that evil is indeed the number one problem of humanity, which for that very reason requires the combined strength of all religious and moral forces to combat it. If we do that, and if we also acknowledge that the greatest antidote against evil is the goodness which, being created in God's image, also resides in human nature, then we are on solid Hebraic ground and can unite with all who share our values to work towards that end.

5. UNIVERSALISM IN THE HEBREW BIBLE

A fifth major feature of the Hebrew Bible is its universalism. Of course, there is plenty of particularism in it, too. Much of it is positively preoccupied with God's relationship with one people, almost to the exclusion of the rest of humanity. Nevertheless, it *is* a striking fact that it begins, not with the national epic of the Israelites, but with the creation of the world and the pre-history of humanity. It is noteworthy that the God of the Israelites is actively involved with other nations. As He brought them from Egypt, so He brought the Philistines from Caphtor and the Aramaeans from Kir (Amos 9:6). He condemns other nations, not only for their sins against Israel, but for their sins against one another (Amos 1:2–2:1). He has pity on 'Nineveh, that great city' (Jonah 4:11). He says to Israel: 'Are you not like the Ethiopians to Me?' (Amos 9:7). He even proclaims, in this order: 'Blessed be Egypt My people, and Assyria My handiwork, and Israel My inheritance' (Isa. 19:25). In the particularism of the Hebrew Bible there is nothing remarkable. It is its prophetic universalism which makes it unique among ancient literatures and gives it enduring worth.

Universalism in Judaism and Christianity

In Judaism this universalism is maintained. It finds expression, for instance, in the legend of how God rebukes the angels for singing His praise while His creatures, the Egyptians, are drowning in the Red Sea.[22] Likewise in the Rabbinic teaching that the righteous of other nations have a share in the world to come,[23] and in the related doctrine that by observing the so-called 'Seven Laws of the Children of Noah', Gentiles can gain God's acceptance.[24] But also in the fact that Gentiles who wished to embrace Judaism, with all the obligations which that entailed, were free to do so. As the Rabbis said, 'The gates are open at all times, and whoever wishes to enter may enter'.[25] Nevertheless it has to be admitted that in the course of the centuries, largely as a result of persecution, Judaism became increasingly particularistic, until the Progressive movement revived the universalistic spirit of earlier times.

Christianity was from its inception outspokenly universalistic. Although Jesus himself seems to have been ambivalent on the subject (cf. Mark 13:19. Matt. 10:5, 15:24), there can be no doubting Paul's universalism. One verse from his Epistle to the Galatians sums up his attitude: 'There is no longer Jew or Greek, there is no longer slave or free, there is no longer male and female; for you are all one in Christ Jesus' (3:28). With that motto, the Church abolished all ethnic boundaries. As Karen Armstrong has pointed out, 'Christianity had all the advantages that had once made Judaism such an attractive faith without the disadvantages of circumcision and an alien Law.' As a result the Church became 'almost a microcosm of the [Roman] empire itself: . . . multi-racial, catholic, international, ecumenical'.[26] Only two things have at times marred this splendid universalism of the Christian Church. One is its anti-Semitism,[27] a subject on which I do not wish to dwell but which I can hardly leave unmentioned. The other is its teaching that 'there is no salvation outside the Church'.

Thus, if Judaism has sometimes tended to be ethnically exclusive, Christianity has sometimes tended to be theologically intolerant. Which of these tendencies is the more to be regretted, can perhaps be debated, but both alike run counter to what is required of religion in the global age.

6. MESSIANISM IN THE HEBREW BIBLE

The sixth and final major aspect of Hebraism which requires our attention is, in a word, Messianism. Here I am alluding to the fact, often pointed out, that the Hebrew Bible has a linear rather than a cyclical view of human history. That is to say, it looks forward to a future time when all that is now wrong with the world will come right.

This hope expresses itself in two ways: national and universal. The national hope is closely associated with the monarchy. It is that in the more or less near future a king will sit on the throne of David who will lack all the vices and possess all the virtues of past kings, who will in fact prove to be an ideal ruler, and under whose leadership the Israelite nation will therefore flourish both politically and spiritually as never before.

The universal hope does not generally have anything to do with the monarchy. It envisages a golden age in the ultimate or eschatological future when all will be united in the worship of the One God, and 'they will beat their swords into ploughshares, and their spears into pruning-hooks; nation will not lift up sword against nation, and never again train for war' (Isa. 2:4; Micah 4:3).

Sometimes, but rarely, the two hopes are combined. Then the national restoration of the Israelite people is seen as a prelude to the redemption of all humanity. The outstanding example of that is the eleventh chapter of Isaiah, which begins by describing the righteous qualities of the future Davidic king and goes on to paint an idyllic picture of a world at peace, when wild and domestic animals will pasture side by side, and concludes: 'They will not hurt or destroy in all My holy mountain, for the earth will be full of the knowledge of the Eternal One as the waters cover the bed of the sea' (11:1–9).

Of these two forms of the hope, which has a better claim to be regarded as one of the permanent values of Hebraism? Surely the universal, for even apart from the fact that the national one lost most of its significance when the Davidic monarchy came to an end, the universal one is clearly the more inspiring, the more coherent with the other permanent values of Hebraism, and the more universally meaningful.

Messianism in Judaism and Christianity

Nevertheless, in Judaism both forms of the hope were maintained and combined – the national one by virtue of the expectation that one day the national existence of the Jewish people in its ancient land would be restored under a restored Davidic monarchy. This expectation, moreover, was only part of a more general back-to-square one eschatology. That is to say, as it was in the beginning, so it shall be in the end: Monarchy, Temple, Sacrifices, Priesthood, Ritual Purity, and all the ancient legislation pertaining to these, will be reinstated. I find that an atavistic way of seeing the future, one of the least inspiring aspects of Judaism, of little significance for non-Jews, and therefore certainly not to be regarded as one of the permanent values of Hebraism. Whereas of course the universalistic vision of a golden age for all humanity, which Judaism has also maintained and emphasised, remains as valid as ever.

But now I must add that in Judaism these two future hopes combined with a third: that of the Messiah. You will have noticed that I have not used that word up to this point. That is because *in an eschatological context* it does not occur in the Hebrew Bible. And if that surprises you to the point of incredulity, let me quote to you H. L. Ginsberg, one of the greatest Bible scholars of modern times. In his *Encyclopaedia Judaica* article on our subject he wrote: 'This is a strictly postbiblical concept'.[28]

What he meant is not that the word Messiah does not occur in the Hebrew Bible – it does occur about 20 times, but never in the eschatological sense which it acquired later. In that sense the concept is a creation of the apocalyptic movement, and though there are indeed traces of apocalypse in the Hebrew Bible, especially in Zechariah and Daniel, it came into prominence during what Christians call the intertestamental period.

But it seems to me that the apocalyptists were – not to mince words – charlatans. They imitated the prophets while lacking prophetic inspiration. They predicted the future, which is not what true prophecy was all about. They did so by misinterpreting Scripture as a collection of oracles, which it is not. More generally, they pretended to a knowledge of the ultimate future which is not humanly attainable. Therefore, not only is it inherently unlikely that the sort of transformation of humanity which the Messiah is supposed to bring about could be accomplished by one individual, but there is actually no good reason for believing in a Messiah in the first place, any more than in the other outlandish fantasies of the apocalyptists. And therefore, too, I have been using the word Messianism only metaphorically, as a portmanteau term for all kinds of eschatological expectations, not necessarily involving a personal Messiah.

If the Pharisees made a mistake in going along with the apocalyptic concept of a personal Messiah, Christianity took it over. But then Christianity gave the term, in its Greek translation *christos*, a very different meaning. In Christianity it came to mean a superhuman Saviour from sin and from death. And that is a concept which, once again, has no basis in Hebraism but must be evaluated on its own merits.

Obviously, most Christians will continue to believe in the

Messiahship of Jesus in that sense, just as most Jews will continue to believe in a Messiah yet to come in the traditional Jewish sense; and nobody should question their right to do so. But if the question is asked, which of these concepts belongs to the permanent values of Hebraism, or which of them is capable of uniting humanity, I must answer: neither.

What does remain, however, is the universal hope which both our traditions share: that ultimately God will be vindicated and humanity redeemed. And whether that happens through the First Coming of the Jewish Messiah or the Second Coming of the Christian Messiah, or simply through the victory of good over evil in human society as a whole, is of little consequence. What matters is the end product. The hope that that will ultimately come about does indeed belong to the permanent values of Hebraism, and is indeed capable of uniting, not only Jews and Christians, but also Muslims and many other branches of the human family.

CONCLUSION

I have tried to identify six major aspects of Hebraism which seem to me to have the double virtue of permanent validity and potentially universal appeal. In singling them out I do not mean to dismiss the many other aspects either of Judaism or of Christianity. I am not arguing for eclecticism. On the contrary, I think it positively desirable that both Judaism and Christianity, and all the varieties of each as well as of Islam and all the other major religions, will continue to exist and flourish for an indefinite time to come. But if it is a matter of the utmost importance that our respective religious traditions, over and above satisfying the many different needs of their own adherents, should also make a positive contribution to the cultivation of *a global spirituality and a global ethic*, then the permanent values of Hebraism are what we should above all emphasise. In that sense, Hebraism is both our common heritage and our common hope.

NOTES

1. *Culture and Anarchy*, Ch. 4, p. 110.
2. *Judaism and Modern Man*.

3. *Where Judaism Differed*, p. 30.
4, See, for example, Deut. 7:1–5; I Kings 18:20–39; Isa. 44:9–20; Psalm 115:4–8.
5. *A History of God*, Mandarin Paperbacks, 1994, p. 124.
6. The title of William James's classic work.
7. Babylonian Talmud, *Berachot* 61b.
8. For a recent example, see Marcus Braybrooke, *The Explorer's Guide to Christianity*, 1998, p. 67: 'Just as no human being can live fully in isolation from other people...so the interior nature of God is relational'.
9. *A History of God*, p. 138.
10. *Mishneh Torah, Hilchot Yesodey Torah* 1:8–12; Guide of the Perplexed, Part I, Chs. 46f.
11. For example, *Siddur Lev Chadash*, p. 525.
12. Hans Küng's argument to the contrary in his *Judaism*, p. 382f., does not seem to me convincing.
13. *Jesus the Jew*, Ch. 8.
14. For example, Amos 5:21–24, Isa. 1:11–17, Micah 6:6–8, Jer. 7:21–23, Isa. 58:2–7.
15. For instance, Hillel the Elder (*Shab.* 31a), and Rabbi Akiva (*Sifra* 89b).
16. See, for instance, *Service of the Synagogue*, 18th edn., Routledge & Kegan Paul, Day of Atonement, Vol. 1, pp. 8–10.
17. *Avot* 3:14.
18. For example, *Siddur Lev Chadash*, p. 113; Ber. 60b.
19. *Avot* 3:16.
20. Songs of Songs Rabbah 5:2.
21. Nicolas Bentley and Evan Esar, *The Treasury of Humorous Quotations*, p. 61.
22. *Meg.* 10b.
23. *Tosefta Sanh.* 13:2.
24. *Sanh.* 56a, 105a.
25. Exod. Rabbah 19:4.
26. *A History of God*, p. 125.
27. Hans Küng wrote: 'There can hardly be any dispute that already in the New Testament there is an anti-Judaism which was to have devastating consequences in later times', *Judaism*, p. 354; see also Samuel Sandmel, *Anti-Semitism in the New Testament*.
28. Vol. 11, p. 1407.

A Jewish View of Jesus

2 February 1999

INTRODUCTION

Judaism and Christianity are two tantalisingly similar yet different religions. That is what makes their interrelationship both interesting and sensitive.

The most obvious difference between them is their divergent perceptions of Jesus. In Christianity he occupies centre stage. In Judaism he occupies no place at all. From a Christian point of view he is the greatest and best human being who ever was, and even an incarnation of God. From a Jewish point of view he was only one of the great and good, and no more divine than any other human being.

I think it is important that Christians should understand why Jews cannot go along with their perception of Jesus, but also that Jews should have as positive a perception of him as their own faith permits. It is with both purposes in mind that I venture to sketch a Jewish view of Jesus – with emphasis on the indefinite article since there are of course many Jewish views which, though perhaps broadly similar, are by no means identical.

But let me make it clear that my concern is only with the Jesus of history, not the Christ of Church doctrine. What Christianity has taught about Jesus – that he was the Son of God, that he was miraculously conceived and miraculously resurrected, that his death was an atoning sacrifice for the sins of humanity, and that he is the Second Person of a Trinity, co-eternal with God the

Father and the Holy Spirit – all these teachings lie outside Judaism and are incompatible with it.

Before modern times, the historical Jesus and the theological Christ were generally deemed to be inseparable, and since Jews were bound to reject the one, they naturally tended to think negatively – or not at all – about both. That some leading Jewish thinkers of the Middle Ages, like Maimonides, nevertheless referred positively to Jesus, as preparing the way for the messianic age, is due, not to their appraisal of his person but to their perception that Christianity has, as a matter of historical fact, purveyed many of the religious and moral values of Hebraism to a previously pagan civilisation.

What enabled the distinction between the Jesus of history and the Christ of Church doctrine to be made was the rise of Bible Criticism, which has shown that the Gospels reflect the evolving theology of the Church some considerable time after the life of their hero.

Not everybody accepted these findings immediately. Christian scholars who engaged in Old Testament criticism were sometimes reluctant to apply the same methods to the New. Of S. R. Driver, for instance, it was said that when he lectured on the Old Testament he was Professor Driver, but when he lectured on the New Testament he was Canon Driver. On the Jewish side, since Orthodoxy rejected modern scholarship as applied to the Hebrew Bible, it could not easily admit its validity as applied to the New Testament, and therefore it has been left mainly to non-Orthodox (that is, Progressive, Conservative and Secular) Jews to take advantage of the new methods in order to attempt a reconstruction of the historical Jesus. Today, however, it is pretty generally accepted that it is legitimate to use the tools of critical scholarship to try to get at the truth about Jesus of Nazareth.

I have said 'try' in order to indicate that it is not an enterprise in which certainty is attainable. For Jesus did not write anything, nor was anything written about him in his lifetime; and the Gospels, which are virtually our only source of information, have at least four disadvantages as sources of historiography. First, they are relatively late – even the earliest was written a full generation after the events it recounts. Secondly, they say next to nothing about the greater part of Jesus' life but concentrate almost exclusively on his public ministry, which lasted only a year or two. Third, there are discrepancies between them. And fourth, they are tendentious, in that they adulate their hero and make little attempt to be fair to those whom they perceive as having been his enemies.

In these circumstances, one has to treat the Gospel evidence with caution, and weigh it against the testimony of other sources, Jewish and Roman, not indeed about the person of Jesus, on which they are silent, but about the religious and political realities of the time. Such an investigation can only yield probability, and is inevitably subjective – what seems probable to one person may seem improbable to another. Therefore I can only present the balance of probabilities as it seems to me, and I want to do so in the form of seven propositions: that Jesus was real, that he was human, that he was Jewish, that he was a faith-healer, that he was a preacher, that he was a prophet, and that he was a would-be messiah.

1. HE WAS REAL

Although there is much in the Gospels that is mythological, exaggerated or propagandistic, nevertheless I believe that they are essentially factual documents rather than works of fiction, and therefore Jesus was a real person. I believe that for three reasons. First, because the story the Gospels tell, shorn of its improbabilities, is inherently credible and accords well with what we know from other sources about the religious and political circumstances of the time. Secondly, because we don't have only one Gospel but several, of which at least two (Mark and the non-Marcan source of Matthew and Luke, known as 'Q') are independent of each other. Thirdly, because they contain bits of information about Jesus which run counter to the *Tendenz* of the Gospel writers and which they are therefore unlikely to have invented.

2. HE WAS HUMAN

Secondly, I believe that Jesus was human. That may seem an unnecessary point to make, since it is implied in the proposition that he was a historical person and since, from a Jewish point of view, there is in any case no other possibility. But the matter is not quite so simple.

For one thing, we do encounter in the Hebrew Bible and subsequent Jewish literature references to superhuman beings of various kinds such as 'sons of God' (e.g., Gen. 6:2), angels and demons. But these are figures of popular mythology, and the general thrust of Hebraism was towards a theology in which they have no real existence but serve only as poetic images. In its most highly developed form, I would contend, Hebraism recognises no intermediate order of existence between God and humanity.

From such a point of view, therefore, the Christian belief that Jesus was both human and divine is ruled out *ab initio*. But because Christianity makes that claim, it is perhaps necessary to indicate how Jews would respond to the reasons that are commonly adduced in support of it.

One is the story of the Virgin Birth. But Jews, like a number of Christian scholars, would regard that as a mythological element in the narrative, found also in other ancient mythologies, which is not to be taken historically. As for the 'Immanuel' verse which the Gospel of Matthew (1:23) quotes as a proof-text from Isaiah (7:14), it has long been conceded by all serious scholars that it does not refer to a virgin but to a young woman, and is in any case a prophecy about the immediate, not the distant future. In addition, there is evidence within the Gospel account itself that the Virgin Birth legend arose relatively late, for it preserves fragments of an earlier tradition which knew nothing of it. (See Mark 6:3, Matt. 1:16 and commentaries.)

Similarly, the story of the Resurrection would be regarded by Jews as belonging to the mythological part of the Gospel narrative.

Another argument one sometimes hears is that Jesus claimed to be divine and that, since he was evidently not insane, the claim must be true. But nowadays all serious New Testament scholars agree that Jesus made no such claim. Indeed, some of them even doubt whether he made the much lowlier claim to be the Messiah.

It is nevertheless true that according to the Gospels Jesus made some rather grand claims for himself. But these passages are not necessarily all authentic. For instance, the often quoted verse, 'I am the way, the truth, and the life; no one comes to the Father except through me', occurs only in John (14:6), the latest of the four Gospels, and it seems to me quite inconceivable that if Jesus had made such a sensational statement, and one so congenial to the propagandistic purpose of the Evangelists, it would have gone unmentioned by Mark, Matthew and Luke. As for the expression 'Son of Man', which Jesus probably did use about himself, and even the expression 'Son of God', which others used about him, they can be explained, as Geza Vermes has shown, without stepping outside the parameters of contemporary Judaism; and we shall come back to that point.

Finally, it is sometimes alleged that the sheer perfection of Jesus points to his divinity. But even the premise of that argument, let alone the inference, does not seem to me sustainable. For one thing, we know almost nothing about the greater part of his life. For another, he actually disclaimed perfection. When, for instance, a stranger addressed him as 'Good Master', he replied: 'Why do you call me good? No one is good except God alone' (Mark 10:18; see also Matt. 13:32).

Furthermore, the Gospel narrative, written to extol Jesus, shows him to have had some human weaknesses. For instance, he did not always practise what he preached. He preached against anger and abuse (Matt. 5:22), but was vituperative towards the Pharisees (Matt. 23). He preached 'resist not evil' (Matt. 5:39) but used violence against the merchants and money-changers in the Temple (Mark 11:15f.). And his courage, though great, sometimes deserted him. At Gethsemane, we are told, 'horror and dismay came over him' and he prayed, 'Take this cup from me' (Mark 14:34, 36); and on the cross he exclaimed: 'My God, my God, why have You forsaken me?' (Mark 15:34).

Jesus was a great and good man, even very great and very good. But to go further than that and say that he was perfect is to go both beyond and against the evidence, which shows that he was fully, and fallibly, human. So, at any rate, it seems from a non-Christian point of view.

3. HE WAS A JEW

My third proposition is that Jesus was a Jew – and I mean that not in some senses or in most senses but in every sense. He was born of Jewish parents. He was given a Jewish name. He was circumcised on his eighth day (Luke 2:21). He received a Jewish education, probably from Pharisaic teachers in Nazareth. At the age of twelve, according to one of the Gospels, his parents took him to the Temple in Jerusalem, where they went for Passover every year (Luke 2:41f.). He often went to synagogue in his hometown Nazareth, Capernaum and other places (Mark 1:21, 1:39, 6:2. etc.). The prayers he prayed were Jewish prayers. The festivals he celebrated were Jewish festivals. The company he kept was Jewish company. When asked to heal the daughter of a Phoenician woman, he said, 'I was sent only to the lost sheep of the house of Israel' (Matt. 15:24; cf. Mark 5:19). He even advised his disciples, 'Do not take the road to gentile lands, and do not enter any Samaritan town' (Matt. 10:5). Above all, the religious beliefs and values Jesus affirmed and taught were those of Judaism and not of any other religion. In short, he was Jewish through and through, and the idea of founding a new and different religion, I feel sure, never crossed his mind.

It may indeed be objected that some of the things Jesus is said to have taught strike one as uncharacteristic of, if not at variance with, what one assumes to have been the normative Judaism of his time. But to that objection there are two good answers. For one thing, not everything that is put into the mouth of Jesus by the Evangelists was actually said by him. Some of it is a reflection of attitudes that prevailed in the Christian Church towards the end of the first century. I have already mentioned the saying from John's Gospel, 'I am the way, the truth, and the life...', as a case in point. Much of the vilification of the Pharisees in Matthew 23 is probably to be explained in the same way. And there is general agreement among New Testament scholars that the passage at the end of Matthew's Gospel, where Jesus charges his disciples, 'Go therefore and make disciples of all nations, baptising them in the name of the Father and of the Son and of the Holy Spirit' (28:19), is a late interpolation.

But the other point to be made is that the Judaism of first-century Palestine was not monolithic but comprised a number of different streams: a fact of which the Dead Sea Scrolls have made us more aware than ever. The question, therefore, needs to be asked, with which of these streams Jesus should be identified. Most probably the answer is: with none; he was too much of a loner. Certainly the Sadducees can be ruled out. For they were priestly and aristocratic, whereas Jesus was neither; they were closely associated with the Temple, whereas he was ambivalent towards it; and they denied, whereas he affirmed, the resurrection of the dead (Mark 12:18–27).

Jesus and the Pharisees

On the other hand Jesus clearly had much in common with the Pharisees. Like them, as we have just seen, he believed in the resurrection. He employed the kind of Bible exegesis, and told the kind of parables, familiar to us from Pharisaic literature. The Paternoster prayer which he taught his disciples (Matt. 6:9–11) is a string of characteristically Pharisaic phrases. And when asked which was the greatest commandment, he singled out precisely the two which one would have expected a Pharisaic teacher to single out, namely, from Deuteronomy, 'Hear, O Israel, the Eternal One is our God, the Eternal God is One; and you shall love the Eternal One your God with all your heart and with all your soul...' (6:4f.), and from Leviticus, 'You shall love your neighbour as yourself' (19:18).

Incidentally, the changes that story undergoes as it is told in Mark (12:28–34), retold in Matthew (22:34–40) and then again in Luke (10:25–37) – whereas John disdains to mention it – show a clear progression from warmth to coldness to animosity in the relationship between Jesus and the Pharisees, and allows us, by extrapolating the trend backwards, to surmise that in reality their relationship was even friendlier than the earliest Gospel tradition suggests, and therefore also that the denunciations of the Pharisees in Matthew 23 owe less to Jesus and more to the hostility of the Church in the Evangelist's time.

Jesus and the Law

But did not Jesus adopt a negative attitude to the Law which was the pride and joy of the Pharisees? Only up to a point. He certainly did not reject the Law. On the contrary, he lived by its precepts. He even affirmed it, and not only the Written Law, but the Oral Law as well. Two passages are especially relevant here, and they are again of the 'telltale' kind which the Gospel writers would have been unlikely to invent. Jesus said: 'Do not think that I have come to abolish the law or the prophets; I have not come to abolish but to fulfil...Therefore, whoever breaks one of the least of these commandments, and teaches others to do the same, will be called least in the kingdom of Heaven...' (Matt. 5:17–19). And even more significantly: 'The scribes and the Pharisees sit on Moses' seat; therefore do what they teach you and follow it...' (Matt. 23:2).

It is true that Jesus performed acts of healing on the Sabbath, but that was quite permissible when it was a matter of saving life, and even otherwise if it was done, as Jesus did it, by mere speech (Matt. 12:9–14). It is also true that he allowed his disciples to eat without first washing their hands, but there is no suggestion that he did so himself (Mark 7:1–8).

The only instance in which Jesus seems to question the obligatory character of the Law is a passage in which he makes light of the Dietary Laws by saying that it is not what enters the body, but what comes out of it, that defiles, at which point the Gospel text adds: 'Thus he declared all foods clean' (Mark 7:19). But that parenthetical comment almost certainly expresses the view of the Evangelist rather than of Jesus himself, and may even be a mistranslation (see Geza Vermes, *Jesus the Jew*, London, 1973, p. 29).

On the subject of divorce, the Gospels preserve two discrepant traditions: that Jesus would allow it only on the ground of adultery (Matt. 5:32, 19:9), in which case he agreed with the school of Shammai (Mishnah, *Git.* 9:10), and that he would disallow it altogether (Mark 10:11, Luke 16:18), in which case he advocated what the Rabbis called *middat chasidut*, a higher degree of piety than the Law strictly required.

In fact, much of the teaching of Jesus needs to be understood in the light of that principle. That is especially true of the Sermon on the Mount, which we will discuss presently. Meanwhile it must suffice to say that Jesus' attitude to the Law was generally positive, but combined with a certain disdain for the hair-splitting legalism to which the Pharisees were no doubt inclined, as it has characterised the legal mind in all ages. With these qualifications, then, we may re-affirm what we said previously: that Jesus had much in common with the Pharisees.

Jesus and the Essenes

But we must add that he also had much in common with the Essenes, who in turn are generally identified with the Qumran community. For like them, he practised celibacy and asceticism, tended towards communism, and believed in the imminence of the messianic age, and the urgency of the need to repent in preparation for it. 'Repent, for the kingdom of Heaven is at hand' (Matt. 4:17) was, after all, the burden of his message. (See also Mark 13:24–27.) In addition, the Essenes were much given to faith-healing – indeed, it is possible that their name derives from an Aramaic word meaning 'to heal', as their counterparts in Egypt were known as Therapeutae – and faith-healing played a large part in Jesus' ministry.

Jesus and the Zealots

Even with the Zealots Jesus had more in common than is generally supposed. Not only was one of his disciples, Simon, a member of that group (Mark 3:18, Matt. 10:4, Luke 6:15), but several of the teachings attributed to Jesus in the Gospels strike an activistic and even militaristic note distinctly reminiscent of the Zealots. For example: 'You must not think that I have come to bring peace to the earth; I have not come to bring peace, but a sword' (Matt. 10:34); 'I have come to set fire to the earth, and how I wish it were already kindled' (Luke 12:49); and 'whoever has no sword, let him sell his cloak to buy one' (Luke 20:36). These are surely among the 'telltale' passages whose authenticity is not to be doubted.

4. HE WAS A FAITH-HEALER

My fourth proposition is that Jesus was a faith-healer. I could have said, more generally, a wonder-worker, but that would imply a belief in miracles which I do not hold. For I would regard all stories of the suspension or violation of the laws of nature as products of folkloristic imagination, whether they occur in the Hebrew Bible, the New Testament, the Talmud, or anywhere else.

In that way I would discount, for instance, the stories of Jesus walking on the lake (Mark 6:48) and the miracle of the loaves and fishes (Mark 6:38–44). But faith-healing is another matter, since it is explicable in terms of the influence of the mind on psychosomatic conditions, and well enough attested.

Furthermore, the vast majority of the miracle stories told about Jesus are in fact of the faith-healing kind. As Geza Vermes points out, 'Compared with the massive insistence of the Synoptists on the healing of mental and physical disease, other miracles assigned to Jesus are numerically insignificant' (*Jesus the Jew*, p. 26).

I find these stories essentially credible, even though some allowance must still be made for exaggeration, and though one may doubt the theory underlying the healing acts, for Jesus evidently believed that the sick were in many cases possessed by an evil spirit which had to be exorcised.

Certainly Jesus' activity as a faith-healer does not place him outside Judaism, for similar powers are ascribed to men of exceptional piety in the Hebrew Bible (especially Elijah and Elisha) and in Rabbinic literature.

It should also be added that in an age which believed implicitly in faith-healing, as in miracles generally, that belief would itself have been a factor contributing to the effectiveness of such therapy.

5. HE WAS A PREACHER

My fifth proposition is that Jesus was a preacher. That is indeed obvious, but I mean it in a particular sense. It is often said that Jesus was a rabbi, but that is doubly wrong. First, it is anachronistic, for the term was not yet used as a title, but only as a mode of address, in his time. Secondly, a rabbi was essentially a Halachist – an expert interpreter of Jewish Law, and there is little indication in the Gospels that Jesus had much knowledge of, or interest in, the legal side of Judaism.

On the other hand, many rabbis were also masters of Aggadah – of homiletics. Some even specialised in that side of Judaism, and with them Jesus may appropriately be compared. He was, moreover, a charismatic, popular, itinerant preacher. Like some of the Pharisees, he conveyed his teachings largely through parables especially about father and son, master and servant, farmer and tenant, king and subject – as well as terse aphorisms, in simple language and with vivid, homely illustrations. Some of his teachings, like some of Hillel's, are cryptic. Some are obscure. Some may have been confused in transmission. But the majority are clear, go straight to the heart of the relationship between person and person, and between

God and humanity, hit home, and belong to the gems of religious literature. There is no reason why Jews should not appreciate them. If Jesus had not been appropriated by Christianity, they would no doubt have found their way into Jewish writings such as the 'Ethics of the Fathers' and Midrash. For their content is thoroughly Jewish and in particular, as has been pointed out, Pharisaic.

There are indeed many close parallels between the teachings of Jesus and those found in Pharisaic–Rabbinic literature. Here are just a few examples. Jesus taught: 'You of little faith! Do not worry, saying, What will we eat? or What will we drink? or What will we wear?' (Matt. 6:30f.). Rabbi Eleazar taught: 'One who has enough to eat for today and says, What will I eat tomorrow? is a person of little faith' (*Mechilta* to Exod. 16:4).

Jesus taught: 'The Sabbath was made for humans, not humans for the Sabbath' (Mark 2:27). Rabbi Simon ben Menasia taught: 'The Sabbath is entrusted to you, you are not entrusted to the Sabbath' (*Mechilta* to Exod. 31:13).

Jesus taught: 'There will be greater joy in heaven over one sinner who repents than over ninety-nine righteous people who do not need to repent' (Luke 15:7). Rabbi Abbahu taught: 'Where those who have repented stand, the perfectly righteous are not permitted to stand' (*Ber.* 34b).

Jesus taught: 'Be perfect, as your heavenly Father is perfect' (Matt. 5:48). The Rabbis stressed the biblical injunction, 'You shall be holy, for I the Eternal One your God am holy' (Lev. 19:2; Lev.R. 24:4), and taught: 'As God is called merciful, gracious and righteous, so you should be merciful, gracious and righteous' (*Sifrey* Deut. to Deut. 11:22).

That saying of Jesus, 'Be perfect, as your heavenly Father is perfect', comes from the Sermon on the Mount, which, with its recurring formula, 'You have heard X but I tell you Y', is commonly taken to indicate that Jesus did, after all, seek to establish a new religion. But that is a misunderstanding, for the contrast he draws is not between an old religion (Judaism) and a new religion (Christianity) but between an incorrect and a correct interpretation of Scripture within the same religion, Judaism; and with his view of the correct interpretation, most Jewish teachers, not least Pharisees, would have agreed. Indeed, it is likely that the rejected interpretations were meant to be hypothetical rather than actual.

It may be safely asserted, then, that the teachings of Jesus are mainly aggadic rather than halachic; that they all fall comfortably within the parameters of the several varieties of Judaism that existed in first-century Palestine; and that many of them have particular affinities with Pharisaic teachings.

But to say that is not to say that all his teachings are acceptable from a modern Jewish point of view. Many Jews today would be inclined to reject, for instance, his belief in evil spirits as the cause of sickness (see above), his teachings about the 'sheep' and the 'goats', and the torments to be inflicted in hell on the wicked and on those who reject the true teaching (e.g., Mark 9:43–48, Matt. 7:13f., 13:49f., 25:32, 25:41).

However, in two respects the homilies of Jesus did differ from the general character of Pharisaic and Rabbinic preaching: that they often represent an extremist stance, and that they were delivered with a strong assertion of personal authority. To account for these features, we need to bring into play two more affirmations about Jesus.

6. HE WAS A PROPHET

My penultimate point is that he was a prophet. That affirmation will cause raised eyebrows among some Jews, but only, I think, because they take the traditional, fundamentalist view that a prophet is an infallible transmitter of divine messages, so that he can never be mistaken, and that prophecy ceased after Haggai, Zechariah and Malachi. However, from a non-fundamentalist point of view neither of these assertions need be granted. From such a point of view, the prophets were human and fallible (Zechariah, for instance, was mistaken in believing that Zerubbabel would reign over a restored Davidic monarchy) and the distinction between prophetic and post-prophetic books, as indeed between canonical and non-canonical writings, is not absolute.

There is in any case evidence that a kind of prophecy (not necessarily known by that name) continued after the closure of the canon; in particular, a tradition that seemingly modelled itself on Elijah and Elisha and that is represented in Rabbinic Judaism by characters like Choni ha-Me'aggel and Chanina ben Dosa: charismatic, ascetic, itinerant preachers, wonder-workers and faith-healers whose extraordinary piety endowed their prayers with extraordinary power. All of them came, like Elijah and Elisha, from Galilee, and all of them were popularly believed to have been specially commissioned or 'adopted' by God. That Jesus fits well into this category, of Galilean *Chasidim* (pietists) is the main thesis of Geza Vermes' seminal book, *Jesus the Jew*. It may also, as he points out, help to explain the epithet 'Son of God', which was perhaps originally applied to Jesus in the sense of 'adoption' and only later understood by a Gentile Church in the sense of divine kinship.

However that may be, it can hardly be denied that Jesus spoke in a prophetic manner, and that he made the impression of a prophet on his audiences. His teaching, we are told, caused astonishment because he spoke 'as one having authority, and not as the scribes' (Mark 1:22) – that is, not only as an interpreter of Scripture or tradition, but from personal religious experience and conviction. Some people thought he was Elijah come back to life, and some said: 'He is a prophet, like one of the prophets of old' (Mark 6:15; see also Matt. 21:11).

The fact that he was a prophet explains the critical posture he adopted towards the accepted wisdom of the contemporary religious establishment; Amos and Hosea would surely have been similarly critical of Pharisaic legalism if it had existed in their time. It also goes a long way towards explaining the authority with which he spoke. As the prophets of old would declaim, 'Thus says the Eternal One', so Jesus often declaimed, 'I say to you', meaning 'I say to you in God's name'. Yet the omission of that qualifying phrase suggests an even higher degree of authority than one would normally expect of a prophet. Perhaps it was simply due to his sense of self-importance (one of his less attractive traits from a non-Christian point of view), which would have been further inflated if the last of my seven propositions is true: that he was a would-be messiah.

7. HE WAS A WOULD-BE MESSIAH

Whether Jesus actually claimed to be the Messiah is nowadays disputed among Christian scholars; but I suspect that some of them like to deny it because the concept of a Jewish national liberation movement leader does not sit well with the image of a universal saviour. (See Hugh Schonfield, *For Christ's Sake*, London, 1975.)

One thing is certain, however: that Jesus regarded the messianic age as imminent. In other words, he believed that the old world order was coming to an end, soon to be superseded by a new world order known in Hebrew as *malchut shamayim* and commonly translated 'Kingdom of Heaven' but really meaning the rule of God. That is the message he took from John the Baptist, and it dominated his thinking for the rest of his life. In theological jargon, he believed himself to be living in the age of realised, or about-to-be-realised, eschatology.

This fact alone explains the exaggerated or extremist tendencies in some of his teachings: about turning the other cheek (Matt. 5:39), about giving away one's possessions (Mark 10:21; see also 10:25), about giving priority to discipleship rather than father and mother, son and daughter (Matt. 10:37f.), about cutting off hands and tearing out eyes (Mark 9:43–48). These teachings, which would seem extravagant in ordinary times, might well seem less so if one believed that the world was about to end.

What is also clear is that, as the leader of a messianic movement, Jesus soon came to be regarded as the central actor in the eschatological drama that was supposedly about to unfold, in other words, as the Messiah; that the point was repeatedly put to him, and that he did not deny it; and it is therefore likely that at some stage between his baptism and his triumphal entry into Jerusalem, he came to believe it himself. And if he never said so openly and explicitly, that is easily explained by the fact that to do so would have been to invite instant arrest by the Roman authorities; for however he or his followers might have understood the role of the Messiah, it clearly involved the overthrow of Roman rule, if not by political insurrection, then by divine intervention, or perhaps a combination of both (see Acts 1:6). The explanation, that is, lies in what has been called the 'concealed Messiahship'. As Mark tells us, 'he did not speak to them [the crowds] except in parables; but privately to his disciples he explained everything' (4:34).

When he asked his disciples who the people thought he was, 'Peter replied: "You are the Messiah". And he sternly ordered them not to tell anyone about him' (Mark 8:27–30). When he entered Jerusalem, he did so deliberately on a young donkey so as to enact a messianic prophecy (Zech. 9:9), and the people shouted: 'Blessed is the coming kingdom of our ancestor David' (Mark 11:1–10). When the High Priest asked him, 'Are you the Messiah?', he answered: 'I am' (Mark 14:61f.). When Pilate asked him, 'Are you the king of the Jews?', he replied, more guardedly: 'You say so' (Mark 15:2). And the inscription on the cross read: 'The King of the Jews' (Mark 15:26).

In addition to all that, only the assumption that Jesus claimed to be the Messiah, or allowed himself to be so proclaimed, can explain satisfactorily his arrest, trial and crucifixion. (That is the considered opinion of any number of scholars, including Paul Winter, Geza Vermes, Hyam Maccoby and Ellis Rivkin.)

The theory that Jesus was a would-be messiah is so amply supported by the evidence of the Gospels, and explains so many things, that it seems to me beyond all reasonable doubt. Among other things, it explains the personal authority, greater even than that of a prophet, with which he spoke.

It should hardly be necessary to add that, if Jesus did make such a claim, it would not have made him less Jewish but, if possible, more so. For if there are degrees of Jewishness, the Messiah is surely the most Jewish Jew of all!

At the same time it seems to me that the claim, if Jesus made it, was mistaken. For one thing, there is, to my mind, considerable doubt whether the very concept of a Messiah was not a mistake: a figment of the imagination of the Apocalyptists, who were surely charlatan prophets.

For another thing, although there were several different conceptions of the Messiah in first-century Palestine, and although Jesus may have had his own conception, not quite identical with any of them, nevertheless all of them surely involved a radical change in the condition of the Jewish people and of humanity; and that did not take place. The Roman empire remained in place. The Davidic kingdom was not re-established. The Jewish people were still oppressed, and even more so after 70 CE. Sin and crime, violence and cruelty, folly and ignorance, prejudice and superstition, intolerance and persecution, political and religious wars: all these continued. Indeed, it is for this very reason that the early Christians spoke of a 'Second Coming' which has never taken place.

It may also be surmised that the manifest failure of Jesus to fulfil any one of the Jewish people's messianic expectations is what induced the Christian Church to invest the Greek translation *christos* of the Hebrew *mashiach* with a connotation far removed from what Jews, of the first or any subsequent century, understood by the Messiah: a connotation that has few if any roots in Hebraism and is closer to the divine saviour of the mystery cults. (If it were recognised that what Jews mean by 'Messiah' and what Christians mean by 'Christ' are quite different concepts, much misunderstanding between them might be avoided.)

CONCLUSION

This, then, is how I see Jesus, and how he may well be seen by many Jews: as a historical person, fully and fallibly human, Jewish through and through, a successful faith-healer, a wonderful preacher, a prophet in the tradition of Elijah and Elisha, and a would-be messianic redeemer of his people and of humanity.

I know how inadequate such a perception must seem to Christians, and how disappointing it must be from their point of view that Jews cannot go along with their perception of who he was, and of the world-shaking significance of his life and death. But that is how it is, and Jews and Christians must respect each other in spite of the difference. A gap does remain between the Christian and Jewish perceptions of Jesus. It is a big gap, and nothing good is achieved by making light of it. With that gap we must live. Whether one day it will be closed, and how, is something none of us can know. But this is only a particular instance of a general phenomenon: that different people, looking at the same evidence with equal knowledge, intelligence and sincerity, sometimes come to surprisingly different conclusions.

But let us once more remind ourselves that, in spite of these and other differences, Jews and Christians do have an enormous amount in common, and though the common ground does not include the Christology of Christianity, it does include most of the teachings of Jesus which are, after all, an exposition, and a noble one, of Judaism. In a strange way, therefore, the person of Jesus, who is so differently perceived by Jews and Christians, is also, through his teachings, what binds and will always bind them closely together.

Appendix: Some Books by Jews about Jesus
(chronologically arranged)

Montefiore, Claude G.: *The Synoptic Gospels*, 2 volumes, 1909, Revised Edition 1927.

Montefiore, Claude G.: *Some Elements of the Religious Teaching of Jesus according to the Synoptic Gospels*, 1910.

Abrahams, Israel: *Studies in Pharisaism and the Gospels*, 2 volumes, 1917 and 1924, Combined Edition, 1967.

Klausner, J.: *Jesus of Nazareth: His Life, Times and Teaching*, 1925.

Montefiore, Claude G.: *Rabbinic Literature and Gospel Teachings*, 1930.

Sandmel, Samuel: *A Jewish Understanding of the New Testament*, 1957.

Winter, Paul: *On the Trial of Jesus*, 1961.

Sandmel, Samuel: *We Jews and Jesus*, 1965.

Schonfield, Hugh: *The Passover Plot*, 1965

Maccoby, Hyam: *Revolution in Judea*, 1973.

Vermes, Geza: *Jesus the Jew: A Historian's Reading of the Gospels*, 1973.

Jacob, Walter: *Christianity through Jewish Eyes, The Quest for Common Ground*, 1974.

Schonfield, Hugh: *The Pentecost Revolution*, 1974.

Sandmel, Samuel: *Anti-Semitism in the New Testament?*, 1978.

Vermes, Geza: *Jesus and the World of Judaism*, 1983.

Rivkin, Ellis: *What Crucified Jesus?*, 1984.

Vermes, Geza: *The Religion of Jesus the Jew*, 1993.

The Truth About the Pharisees: The Evidence of the New Testament

28 January 1997

Anyone at all familiar with the New Testament knows that it contains many disparaging remarks about the Pharisees, mostly put into the mouth of Jesus. Here is a sample selection according to the New Revised Standard Version: 'Isaiah prophesied rightly about you hypocrites, as it is written, "The people honour me with their lips, but their hearts are far from me..." For you abandon the commandment of God and hold to human tradition' (Mark 7:6–8). 'You brood of vipers! Who warned you to flee from the wrath to come?' (Matt. 3:7). 'You brood of vipers! How can you speak good things, when you are evil?' (Matt. 12:34). 'Let them alone; they are blind guides of the blind. And if one blind person guides another, both will fall into a pit' (Matt. 15:14). 'But woe to you, scribes and Pharisees, hypocrites! For you lock people out of the kingdom of heaven... Woe to you, scribes and Pharisees, hypocrites! For you cross sea and land to make a single convert, and you make the new convert twice as much a child of hell as yourselves... Woe to you, scribes and Pharisees, hypocrites! For you tithe mint, dill, and cumin, and have neglected the weightier matters of the law: justice, mercy and faith. It is these you ought to have practised without neglecting the others. You blind guides! You strain out a gnat but swallow a camel!... Woe to you, scribes and Pharisees, hypocrites! For you are like whitewashed tombs, which on the outside look beautiful, but inside they are full of the bones of the dead and of all kinds of filth. So you also on the outside look righteous to others, but inside you are full of hypocrisy and lawlessness' (Matt. 23:13–15, 23–24, 27–28).

There are more passages in the same vein. Some of them are directed explicitly against the Pharisees, some against 'the hypocrites', by which the Pharisees are evidently intended. Often the Pharisees are linked with the 'scribes', sometimes with other groups like the 'elders', the 'chief priests' and the Herodians.

And as Jesus is portrayed as having hated the Pharisees, so the Pharisees are portrayed as having hated him. 'Jews of every stripe – Pharisees, scribes, priests, Herodians, Herod Antipas, the Sadducees, the High Priest, the Sanhedrin, and abruptly in the passion narrative, the crowds – are virtually of a single mind in hating Jesus' (Samuel Sandmel, *Antisemitism in the New Testament?*, Philadelphia, 1978, p. 46). Worst of all, the Pharisees are said to have been among those who plotted Jesus' death. Mark, for instance, reports that, after watching Jesus cure the man with a withered hand on the Sabbath, 'The Pharisees went out and immediately conspired with the Herodians against him, how to destroy him' (3:6).

Admittedly, that is not the whole of the story. Jesus does concede the authority of the Pharisees. In one important passage he says to the crowds and his disciples: 'The scribes and Pharisees sit in Moses' seat; therefore do whatever they teach you and follow it; but do not do as they do' (Matt. 23:2–3). Just occasionally Jesus commends them for their correct understanding of what God requires. Three times Jesus is invited into the home of a Pharisee (e.g., Luke 7:37; James Parkes, *Jesus, Paul and the Jews*, London, 1936, p. 91). Luke also reports that once the Pharisees warned Jesus against Herod, who intended to kill him (13:31). And according to Acts, Rabban Gamaliel, the leading Pharisee of the time, intervened on behalf of Peter and the Apostles when they were brought to trial (5:34), as did a group of Pharisees on behalf of Paul (23:9).

These exceptions are very significant, but they hardly alter the fact that in the Gospel story the Pharisees are the chief villains. The question must, however, be asked: how reliable is the New Testament as a source of information about the Pharisees? There are two reasons for caution. The first is that the Gospels were written a generation or two after the Crucifixion and reflect the animosity towards the Jews of the Church of that time, some of which the Evangelists retroject in the form of anti-Pharisaism into the lifetime of Jesus; and there is some evidence that the actual relationship between Jesus and the Pharisees was less hostile on both sides than the Evangelists suggest. The other reason for caution is that, nevertheless, the New Testament is, editorially, a hostile witness.

THE EVIDENCE OF JOSEPHUS

Where then is the truth about the Pharisees to be found? The ideal source would be an impartial historian of the time. Unfortunately, such a source does not exist, although Josephus comes close to it; for on the one hand he was a Jew, but on the other hand he was not a Pharisee, and in any case he was a remarkably accurate historian. Here is what we glean from him.

The Pharisees, he says, are considered the most accurate interpreters of the laws; they are the leading sect; they believe in free will but also in divine providence; they believe in immortality; they are affectionate to each other and cultivate harmonious relations with the community (*The Jewish War*, trsl. H.St.J. Thackeray, The Loeb Classical Library, Boston, MA, 1976, II, 162–166; cf. *Jewish Antiquities*, ditto, XIII, 171); they are naturally lenient in the matter of punishments (*Jewish Antiquities*, XIII, 294); they are transmitters of the Oral Tradition, which the Sadducees reject; unlike the Sadducees, who enjoy the confidence only of the wealthy, the Pharisees have the support of the masses (*Jewish Antiquities*, XIII, 297–98); they live simply, not indulging in luxury; they respect their elders; they believe in reward and punishment after death; they are extremely influential among the townsfolk; all prayers and worship rituals are performed according to their exposition, this being 'the great tribute that the inhabitants of the cities, by practising the highest ideals both in their way of living and in their discourse, have paid to the excellence of the Pharisees (*Jewish Antiquities*, XVIII, 12–15).

From Josephus we also learn that when James, the brother of Jesus, was arrested by a Sadducean high priest, it was 'those of the inhabitants of the city who were considered the most fair-minded and who were strict in observance of the law', by which phrase the Pharisees are evidently meant, who interceded with

King Agrippa on his behalf (*Jewish Antiquities*, XX, 201–3).

Josephus, therefore, gives us a rather positive picture of the Pharisees to set against the negative one of the Gospels.

THE EVIDENCE OF RABBINIC LITERATURE

The only other source of information would be, if it existed, the literature of the Pharisees themselves. But unfortunately they, like Jesus, did not write anything. For they were essentially expounders of an Oral Tradition which, to keep it distinct from Scripture, was not supposed to be written down. But that counsel of perfection could not be maintained indefinitely. By about the year 200 CE, the Oral Tradition had become so extensive that it could no longer be retained in people's memories alone. It was then that the recording of what is known as Rabbinic Literature began: Mishnah, Midrash, Talmud, etc.

So the question is: how reliable is Rabbinic Literature, dating from the third century onwards, as a source of information about the Pharisees of the time of Jesus about 200 years earlier? There is also a related question: to what extent is Rabbinic Judaism a continuation of Pharisaic Judaism? My answer to both these questions is positive. I believe that the transmitters of the Oral Tradition transmitted it, though not with perfect accuracy, nevertheless punctiliously and on the whole reliably; and I also believe that there is a high degree of continuity between the religion of the Pharisees, as reflected in the oral traditions going back to the time before the Roman War, and the religion of the Rabbis as reflected in the traditions and writings of subsequent generations.

In short, I believe that Rabbinic Literature *can* be used as a generally sound source of information about the Pharisees, and in the rest of this chapter I shall single out a few areas of Pharisaic activity and teaching which seem to me reliably attested by it.

The Origin and Name of the Pharisees

But first a few words about the origin and name of the Pharisees. They are first mentioned (by Josephus, Ant. XIII, 171) during the reign of the Hasmonean ruler John Hyrcanus (135–105 BCE), and it is therefore agreed by all scholars that they emerged shortly after the Maccabean Rebellion of 168–165 BCE.

The name Pharisees, which in Hebrew is *p'rushim*, means 'those who separate themselves' or 'keep themselves aloof'. Accordingly, generations of Christian scholars have maintained that their chief distinguishing characteristic was a tendency to avoid contact with the common people (*'am ha-aretz*) for fear of being contaminated by their inattention to the laws of ritual purity, a view which goes nicely with the holier-than-thou attitude of which they are accused in the Gospels. However, that theory is no longer tenable, for it is now known that the Pharisees never called themselves by that name, which was a pejorative nickname given them by their opponents, the Sadducees, so that nothing can safely be inferred from it about the nature of Pharisaism, any more than the teachings of the Society of Friends can be inferred from the name 'Quakers' by which they are commonly known.

In saying that I am referring to an exhaustive study by the American Jewish historian Ellis Rivkin in which he proved with mathematical precision that the only passages in early Rabbinic literature in which the word undoubtedly refers to the Pharisees, rather than to 'dissenters' or 'heretics' in general, which the word can also mean, are cases in which the Sadducees are the speakers ('Defining the Pharisees: The Tannaitic Sources' in *Hebrew Union College Annual*, Vols. XL–XLI, 1969–70).

What, then, did the Pharisees call themselves? The answer is *chachamim*, which means 'sages', and that does bring us almost to the heart of the matter, for the Pharisees were essentially lay scholars, that is, people who, without necessarily being of priestly descent, were nevertheless expert expounders of the Scriptures and the Oral Tradition.

As such, they had an antecedent in the so-called *chasidim* or 'pious ones', that is to say, lay people who practised an intensive regimen of Scripture study and prayer, from whom the Maccabees drew much of their support (I Macc. 2:42).

What, then, were the conditions that gave rise, first, to the *chasidim* and then to the *chachamim*? The key fact is that the period after the Babylonian Exile, first under the Persians and then under the Greeks, was a period in which Judea was ruled by High Priests, who exercised both religious and political authority, and in which the Temple dominated the national life. But there was only the one Temple, in Jerusalem, where sacrifices were offered twice daily by a hereditary priesthood, for the book of Deuteronomy strictly forbade religious worship anywhere else.

This situation led to a growing sense of exclusion on the part of those (the great majority) who did not have the good fortune to be born into priestly families, especially if they were also prosperous and educated, as happened increasingly with the coming of Greek rule. For if they lived far from Jerusalem, they had no opportunities for regular worship, and even if they lived in Jerusalem and could go to the Temple, their role in it was passive. They attended, not as participants but as spectators, watching the priests perform the sacrificial rites.

The consequent resentment apparently came to a head during or immediately after the Maccabean War, and led to a democratising movement, which is essentially what Pharisaism was. In other words, the principal aim of the Pharisees was to make Judaism, which had been so largely a Temple religion, into a people's religion: to bring it into the daily lives of ordinary folk. Far from keeping aloof from the common people, the Pharisees addressed themselves to the common people, represented their interests, and were popular with them, as Josephus testifies.

Nevertheless, they did not have an easy time of it. For they were opposed, not only by the Sadducees, who, as the priestly party, possessed much wealth and influence, but also, some of the time, by the Hasmonean rulers. Alexander Jannai (101–78), for instance, persecuted them, though his widow and successor Salome Alexandra favoured them, and their history remained a chequered one until the destruction of the Temple in 70 CE. Then, of course, the priestly Sadducees lost their *raison d'être*, and from that time Pharisaism dominated virtually all Judaism, both in Palestine and in the Diaspora.

Synagogue

How, then, did the Pharisees set about achieving their democratising purpose? First and foremost through the Synagogue. There is indeed some doubt whether synagogues existed at all before their time, except in Egypt, where the first mention of synagogues dates from the reign of Ptolemy III, who reigned in the second half of the third century BCE. But if they existed in Palestine as early as that, we may be sure that the High Priest would have done his utmost to prevent them from gaining too much influence. The Pharisees, however, if they did not invent the Synagogue, used it for their purpose and made it a major institution of Jewish life, rivalling the Temple itself.

The very name 'synagogue', which is Greek for 'assembly', suggests a democratic institution. In it the Pharisees evolved a new form of worship, unprecedented in the whole history of religion, which involved no sacrifices and required no priesthood. Instead, it consisted of communal prayer and the public reading and expounding of Scripture; it was conducted by anybody, regardless of pedigree, who possessed the necessary knowledge; and it was participatory.

Soon synagogues sprang up in their hundreds wherever Jews lived, both in Palestine and in the Diaspora, and so spread the influence of Pharisaism far and wide. Admittedly, the number of Pharisees, in the sense of 'card-holding' members of the Pharisaic *chavurah* or brotherhood, was relatively small and centred in Jerusalem. According to Josephus there were only 800 in the time of Jesus. But they travelled extensively, as Paul did on his missionary journeys, and exerted great influence. It is therefore likely that Jesus would have become acquainted with Pharisaism, for instance, in the Capernaum synagogue.

Liturgy

The Synagogue, in turn, required an extensive liturgy, for in the Temple, apart from the chanting of Psalms, the use of words played only a subsidiary part. Here again the Pharisees were the pioneers. It was they who singled out the *Shema'* – that is, the passage beginning 'Hear, O Israel, the Eternal One is our God' from the sixth chapter of Deuteronomy, supplemented by two other Scriptural passages – as a declaration of loyalty to the Jewish faith, to be recited twice daily. It was they who composed the series of benedictions known as the *Tefillah* which became the core of the three daily services. Indeed, all the basic elements of the Jewish liturgy go back to the Pharisees.

Education

The Pharisees also understood that, in order to achieve their purpose, what they must do was not to level down but to level up; not to downgrade the priests but to upgrade the lay folk; in short, to implement the Scriptural ideal of 'a kingdom of priests and a holy nation' (Exod. 19:6). For this purpose education was all-important. The public reading of Scripture in the synagogue, and the exposition of it which became the sermon, served that purpose. But in addition, the Pharisees established schools in which children, admittedly only of the male sex, were taught to read and write, and to understand the sacred texts. Two Pharisaic teachers especially are mentioned in that connection. One was Simeon ben Shetach, brother of Queen Salome Alexandra, in the first century BCE; the other was Joshua ben Gamla, who was also a High Priest, in the first century CE.

If Jesus, as a child, attended a school in Nazareth, he would have benefited from a Pharisaic institution which, in addition to the synagogues he visited, would have introduced him to Pharisaic ideas.

Domestic Observance

The Pharisees brought Judaism out of the Temple into the synagogues and schools and therefore within reach of ordinary people. But they also brought it into their homes, by devising a whole regimen of domestic rituals. The most colourful of them is the domestic celebration of the Passover festival known as the *Seder*.

An even more illuminating example is the kindling of the Sabbath lights. According to the book of Exodus (35:3) it was forbidden to burn a fire on the Sabbath. The Sadducees took that literally and would therefore sit in darkness on Friday night. But the Pharisees pointed to a verse in Isaiah which says, 'You shall call the Sabbath a delight' (58:13), which they took to mean that the Sabbath is supposed to be a joyful day. Therefore they took the Exodus verse only as a prohibition against *kindling* a fire on the Sabbath and, to the consternation of the Sadducees, declared it to be a positive duty of the Jewish housewife to kindle lights before the onset of the holy day, so that Jewish homes would look bright and festive on the Sabbath Eve (Mishnah *Shab.* 2:6f). It was typical of their liberal, creative approach to Jewish observance.

Halachah

Central to the whole Pharisaic scheme was the doctrine of the

Twofold Torah: that, in addition to the Written Torah of the Bible, especially the Pentateuch, God had, at Mount Sinai, revealed a supplementary body of teachings which was to be handed down by word of mouth and augmented from generation to generation. Of this Oral Torah, elucidating and amplifying the Written Torah, the Pharisees claimed to be accredited exponents. They made this claim by asserting that it had been transmitted all along by a lay rather than a priestly chain of tradition: from Moses to Joshua, then to the Elders, then to the Prophets, then to the Men of the Great Assembly – who were the immediate predecessors of the Pharisees. By this opening statement of the *Ethics of the Fathers*, the Pharisees established their credentials.

The Oral Torah, in turn, had two aspects: *Halachah* and *Aggadah*. *Halachah* means 'law' and is the Pharisees' answer to the question of the Deuteronomist, 'And now, O Israel, what does the Eternal One your God require of you?' (10:12). It is an attempt, monumental in its comprehensiveness and mind-boggling in its detailedness, to construct out of the data of Scripture, supplemented by the Oral Tradition, a code of conduct governing every aspect of life, private and public, ritual and ethical, social and economic.

If we ask, more specifically, what was the approach of the Pharisees to civil and criminal law, I think we must say that its outstanding characteristic was humaneness. It was, for instance, the Pharisees who interpreted the biblical law of 'an eye for an eye' to mean that monetary compensation, commensurate with the injury, is to be paid to the injured party (*BK* 8:1). And it was the Pharisees who, out of regard for the sanctity of human life, weighted the rules of evidence in capital cases so heavily in favour of the defendant as to make conviction virtually impossible (*San.* 4–5). A Pharisaic teacher is quoted in the Mishnah as saying that a court that hands down one death penalty in seven years is considered cruel; another said 'one in seventy years'; and two more declared: 'If we had been in the Sanhedrin, no one would ever have been put to death' (*Mak.* 1:10).

Moreover, when the Pharisees considered the question, what is the essence of the Torah, they always tended to define it in ethical terms. When, for instance, Hillel the Elder, who was the greatest of the Pharisees, was challenged to sum up the Torah in a nutshell, his answer was: 'What is hateful to yourself, do not do to others. That is the gist of the Torah, the rest is a commentary on it. Go and learn' (Shab. 31a). Similarly, Rabbi Akiva taught that 'Love your neighbour as yourself' (Lev. 19:18) was the dominant principle of the Torah (Sifra 89b).

Aggadah

The other aspect of the Oral Torah, called *Aggadah*, which means narrative, covers everything non-legal, including Bible commentary, legends of all kinds, and general religious and ethical teachings. In this area, too, the Pharisees were extremely creative. As we already know from Josephus, they espoused the doctrine of resurrection, of the world-to-come, of reward and punishment, and of free will, even while affirming the paradox that, nevertheless, the ultimate control of human destiny is with God. They also adopted the belief in a messiah who would ultimately bring redemption to the Jewish people and to all humanity, but discouraged speculation about the time of his coming. Innumerable passages could be quoted from early Rabbinic Literature on these and other themes, including the justice and mercy of God, the good and evil inclinations in human nature, the power of repentance to obtain divine forgiveness, the special responsibility of the Jewish people, and the supreme ideal of peace.

From such an abundance it is hardly possible to make a meaningful selection, but perhaps something of the flavour of Pharisaism may be gauged from these aphorisms by its greatest exponent, Hillel. 'Be of the disciples of Aaron, loving peace and pursuing peace, loving your fellow human beings, and drawing them near to the Torah...If I am not for myself, who will be for me? But if I am only for myself, what am I? And if not now, when?...Do not separate yourself from the community...Do not judge others until you have been in their position...Where none behave like human beings, behave like a human being' (*Avot* 1:12, 1:14, 2:4, 2:5).

Preaching and Practising

Of course the Pharisees did not always practise what they preached, and there were no doubt hypocrites among them, as there are in all religious communities. At their best the Pharisees were people of extraordinary gentleness as well as spirituality. Of

Hillel, for instance, it is said that, no matter how hard one might try, it was impossible to rouse him to anger (*Shab.* 30b–31a). And of Hillel's disciples it is said that they were gentle and humble, and that they always cited the opinions of their opponents as well as their own, and even before their own (*'Eruvin* 13b). It is therefore hard to imagine Hillel using against his opponents the kind of vituperative language which the Evangelists put into the mouth of Jesus against the Pharisees. And when it comes to readiness to die for one's beliefs, nobody in the history of martyrdom has shown greater courage than, among many other Pharisees, Rabbi Akiva, who, as he was tortured to death by the Romans, recited the *Shema'*, happy in the knowledge that he was able to fulfil the commandment, 'You shall love the Eternal One your God . . . with all your soul' (*Ber.* 61b).

Jesus and the Pharisees

In spite of all the denunciations of the Pharisees attributed to Jesus in the Gospels, he probably had more in common with them than with any other Jewish sect. He held similar beliefs, for instance about life after death, and about the infinity of God's mercy. He used the same kind of language, not least in his prayers. The 'Lord's Prayer', for instance, is a string of characteristically Pharisaic phrases. He employed the same kinds of metaphors in his parables: father and son, king and subject, farmer and tenant. Often he taught in slightly enigmatic aphorisms just as Hillel did. And one could draw many more parallels. Above all, as we have seen, he advised his disciples to 'do what the Pharisees teach', which can only mean that in his view what they taught was, in the main, right.

It is therefore hard to believe that Jesus was as vehemently against the Pharisees as the Gospel writers make him out to have been. Furthermore, it is actually possible to prove that there occurred an intensification in the perception of their mutual hostility between the lifetime of Jesus and that of the Evangelists, and here is the best example.

According to the earliest Gospel, Mark, one of the Scribes, presumably a Pharisee, asks Jesus which is the greatest commandment, and Jesus replies with two: first, 'Hear, O Israel, the Eternal One is God, the Eternal God is One; and you shall love the Eternal One your God with all your heart, with all your soul, with all your mind, and with all your strength' (Deut. 6:4f); secondly, 'You shall love your neighbour as yourself' (Lev. 19:18). The Scribe is delighted with the answer; Jesus in turn says to him: 'You are not far from the kingdom of God' (12:28-34); and they part in perfect harmony.

But notice what happens in the subsequent transmission of the story. In Matthew the questioner, who is called a lawyer, again meaning a Pharisee, is out to 'test' Jesus, and there is no mutual commendation; the atmosphere has become distinctly chilly (22:34–40). In Luke the lawyer is again intent on 'testing' Jesus; he throws the question back at the lawyer, who duly quotes the same two commandments from Deuteronomy and Leviticus, and Jesus says to him: 'You have answered right; do this, and you will live.' But then Luke continues: 'But he, desiring to justify himself, said to Jesus, "And who is my neighbour?"' Whereupon Jesus tells the story of the Good Samaritan, with the implication that the Pharisee needed to be taught a lesson about good neighbourliness (10:25–37). As for John, he omits the story altogether, as if the merest hint of a suggestion that there were good Pharisees would be too great a concession.

So we can see that from generation to generation, as the conflict between the Church and the Synagogue grew sharper, so the perception of the relationship between Jesus and the Pharisees became sharper too. And if we extrapolate that tendency backwards in time, we come to the conclusion that the actual relationship must have been more harmonious than even the earliest strata of the Gospel process indicate.

CONCLUSION

We have looked at three sources of information about the Pharisees: the Gospels, which are mainly anti-Pharisaic and tell us very little; Josephus, who is neutral and tells us more but still not very much; and Rabbinic Literature, which is pro-Pharisaic and voluminous but rather late, so that much depends on the reliability of the oral traditions it enshrines. From these data, we must each make up our minds as best we can what the truth about the Pharisees is most likely to be.

The Suffering Servant

2 November 1993

The 'Servant Poems' to be found in the latter part of the book of the prophet Isaiah (42:1–4, 49:1–6, 50:4–9, 52:13–53:12) have always intrigued Jewish as well as Christian commentators, and given rise to a vast literature of interpretation to which it is hardly possible for a non-specialist to make an original contribution. What may nevertheless be useful, and will here be attempted, is a common-sense approach to the salient issues.

THE SCHOLARLY LITERATURE

Let me begin with one or two general remarks about the literature of Bible scholarship. It seems to me that much of it is vitiated by a lack of attention to methodology. Again and again, assertions are made with a degree of confidence that is not even remotely warranted by the weight of the evidence, and the crucial question of probability is not even considered. In addition, theological preconceptions often get in the way of objective judgment.

As an example let me refer to Christopher R. North's *The Suffering Servant in Deutero-Isaiah: An Historical and Critical Study*, published by Oxford University Press in 1948. For the most part it is an objective account of the exegetical history of the Servant Poems. Then, in his concluding chapter, the author makes all sorts of assertions that do not in the least follow from what has gone before but spring from his Christian faith and would be disputed by non-Christians. Thus, after examining a great variety of interpretations, including Jewish ones, in about 200 pages, he suddenly announces on page 216: 'It is agreed on all hands that the portrait of the Servant did ultimately find its actualization in Christ'! And he ends the book by invoking, like a *deus ex machina*, 'the principle of the unity of Scripture' (p. 218), which enables him to conclude: 'I find it hard to believe that the Prophet in his moments of deepest insight intended one thing and the Holy Spirit another. It seems more natural to conclude that both intended the same. Original and Fulfilment join hands across the centuries' (p. 219).

I find that kind of sleight-of-hand superimposition of pietistic dogma on literary-historical research a dereliction of academic responsibility and a reversion to medieval scholasticism. Furthermore, the particular dogma which North invokes, namely the 'principle of the unity of Scripture', seems to me manifest nonsense. For if one thing is certain about the literature of the Old and New Testaments, it is the great diversity of ideas to be found in it, as is to be expected of a collection of writings spanning more than a thousand years. If you may not investigate the meaning of a passage without presupposing that it must harmonise theologically with another, altogether different passage, then even the pretence of scholarly objectivity is abandoned.

By contrast, let me mention a book which I find free from any such fundamental flaw as well as generally persuasive. It is Sheldon H. Blank's *Prophetic Faith in Isaiah*, published by Adam and Charles Black in 1958; and I shall be quoting from it a number of times.

THE POET AND DEUTERO-ISAIAH

With these preliminaries, let me turn to the poems themselves and ask, first, whether they are all of a piece (a) with one another and (b) with the Deutero-Isaianic material in which they are embedded. That, it seems to me, is a good example of the sort of question which cannot be answered with certainty but only with one degree or another of probability.

That there are striking similarities between the four poems, is readily apparent, and it is therefore likely that they were written by the same author. But they are not so different from the surrounding chapters that it must have been a different author. Admittedly, they look like insertions. But then the last twenty-seven chapters of Isaiah are in any case a miscellany of prophecies, arranged according to an editorial plan that is no longer discernible. Therefore there is no means of knowing whether the Servant Poems were part of the original text or inserted subsequently, or, in the latter case, whether they were taken from another Deutero-Isaianic composition or from a different source altogether.

What is relevant here is, first, that the concept of the Servant features both in the poems and elsewhere in Deutero-Isaiah, and secondly, that a similar spirit pervades them. For the two hallmarks of Deutero-Isaiah are universalism and triumphalism. The God of Israel is the cosmic God and therefore, in spite of Israel's defeat, undefeated and undefeatable. Therefore the Exile, and the suffering it entailed, must be part of God's plan. It must be disciplinary, and it must be temporary. Soon the suffering will be over. Then the Israelites will return to their homeland, where a resplendent future lies ahead for them. And not only for them. For their restoration will finally, triumphantly demonstrate the universal sovereignty of Israel's God, and the nations will see it, and be redeemed. 'The glory of the Eternal One shall be revealed, and all flesh shall see it together' (40:5).

These *motifs*, which permeate Deutero-Isaiah's prophecy as a whole, are also present in the Servant Poems and, as Sheldon Blank points out, not least in the last of them. In particular, he makes much of the tenses that are used. An inspection of them, he says, reveals 'that all the verbs which in this fourth song describe the grim experience of the servant are verbs in the past tense, and conversely, that all the verbs in the future tense speak only of success and glory for the servant' (p. 90). Blank sums up: 'And so, throughout the composition, its author portrays the misery as past and looks to a future that is unmixed joy' (p. 92).

This important insight evidently strengthens the case for regarding the Servant Poems as Deutero-Isaianic. Nevertheless, the question of authorship remains, as I have said, unanswerable. Nor is it what chiefly concerns us. Much more interesting is the question of the identity and significance of the Servant.

THE IDENTITY OF THE SERVANT

Is the Servant an individual or a people, namely Israel? There is much in the text to support both contentions, and precisely because that is so, there is even more to be said for a third view: that he is an individual *personifying* the people, and that the poems are to be understood as a parable in that sense. But for the moment let us stay with the theory of the Servant as an individual. If it is correct, there are four possibilities: past, present, future, and imaginary.

The suggestion that the poems depict a hero of the past has been made many times throughout the ages. Christopher North lists no fewer than 15 such identifications: Isaiah, Uzziah, Hezekiah, Josiah, Jeremiah, Ezekiel, Job, Moses, Jehoiachin, Cyrus, Sheshbazzar, Zerubbabel, Meshullam, Nehemiah and Eleazar (*The Suffering Servant*, p. 192).

The idea that the Servant might have been a *contemporary* of the author, in which case the most obvious candidate is Deutero-Isaiah himself, was first put forward by Mowinckel in 1921. As North remarks, 'The suggestion was at once hailed by a number of famous scholars, all of them German, and including the redoubtable Ernst Sellin, who had already three times, and each time finally, settled the problem by proposing in turn Zerubbabel, Jehoiachin, and Moses.' It is even clearer from the second poem, in which the Servant says that God has made his mouth like a sharp sword (49:2), in conjunction with the third, which tells us that God has given him a well-taught tongue (50:4), and opened his ear to hear God's word (50:5). And it is echoed in the fourth poem, which describes the Servant as a righteous man who shall make many righteous (53:11), and ends with the statement that he 'made intercession for transgressors'. For that is one of the functions of a prophet. To quote Blank again: 'A prophet toils for his people. He spends his soul in intercessory prayer. He intervenes with God in a time of distress and defends his people before their divine judge and accuser' (*Prophetic Faith in Isaiah*, p. 95).

The second point is that the Servant *suffers*. He suffers because he does what prophets do: he speaks the truth, he speaks it in God's name, fearlessly, and he therefore incurs the wrath of those for whom the truth is inexpedient because their vested interest is in power, not in righteousness. He is therefore mocked, tormented, and perhaps killed, exactly as happened to Jeremiah.

Admittedly, that is not the only cause of his suffering. There is another, unrelated to the enmity of fellow human beings. The hero of the poems is also afflicted with leprosy, or some other disfiguring disease. How that motif relates to the main theme, is not at all clear, and one suspects that it is an intrusion, due to the conflation of two traditions, that of the persecuted prophet, like Jeremiah, and that of the patient leper, like Job, who really have only one thing in common: that both suffer innocently. But however that may be, the presence of the leprosy motif is undeniable. It is clearly stated in 52:14, which tells us that 'he was so disfigured that he looked no longer human', and in 53:3, where the old translation, 'a man of sorrows and acquainted with grief', is quite indefensible since the Hebrew unambiguously states that he was 'a man racked with pain and familiar with sickness'.

Here let me interject that the leper motif, combined with the mistaken identification of the Servant as the Messiah, gave rise in rabbinic times to the legend of Joshua ben Levi who, on the advice of the Prophet Elijah, went to the gates of Rome to find the Messiah sitting there among a group of lepers dressing and undressing their wounds but ready at any moment to respond to a signal from God that the time has come to redeem the world (San. 98a).

The third point is that the Servant's suffering *confers benefit* on those who, by persecuting him, have caused it. It makes them aware of their own guilt, which, they now realise, they have projected on to him. As they say, 'He was wounded on account of our sins, and crushed because of our iniquities' (53:5). And the realisation effects in them a moral regeneration: 'The chastisements he suffered were for our welfare, and there was healing for us in his bruises' (ibid.). If we think of the assassins of Jeremiah as contemplating with horror the enormity of what they have done, and becoming reformed characters as a result, we get the general idea of what seems to be meant here. Do such things happen in reality? Sometimes, undoubtedly, but, alas, only in relatively rare instances.

THE POEMS AS A PARABLE

If that is a correct analysis of the Servant depicted in the poems, we are still left with the question, what is the purpose of the depiction? And here there can surely be only one answer: the purpose is *parabolic*. Admittedly, the text does not say so; but then that is not usually the way of the Bible. Think, for example, of the song of the vineyard in the fifth chapter of Isaiah, which is not introduced as a parable either. As Rabbi Israel Mattuck pointed out in his excellent little book *The Thought of the Prophets* (George Allen and Unwin, London, 1953), 'The Prophets did not always mark the change from their statements to the parables illustrating them. The book of Jonah is an outstanding example, a parable told as history' (p. 132).

Whom, then, does the Servant parabolically represent? The answer can only be the Jewish people. Here, it seems to me, there is, for once, no room for any doubt at all. Just as Jonah (who, like the Servant, is a prophet) personifies the Jewish people, and just as 'the vineyard of the God of hosts' of Isaiah 5 is explicitly stated to be 'the house of Israel' (v. 7), so the Suffering Servant is a personification of Suffering Israel.

The whole prophecy of Deutero-Isaiah is, after all, addressed to, and concerns, the Jewish people: their suffering in exile, now mercifully drawing to a close, and their imminent, triumphant restoration, inaugurating a brave new world. That is what the surrounding chapters are all about, and therefore, unless all common sense is abandoned, any poems inserted into those chapters, even if derived from an extraneous source, can only be so understood in their context.

That would be so even if the poems themselves contained no clue as to the parabolic role which the Servant plays. But they contain the clearest possible clue, and not once but several times. The clue is quite simply the phrase '*Eved Adonai*, 'the servant of the Eternal One', which Deutero-Isaiah regularly employs in reference to the Jewish people. For instance, in 41:8 God apostrophises the people as 'Israel, My servant, Jacob whom I have chosen'. The reference is equally clear in 42:19, 'Who is blind, but My servant?'; in 43:10, 'You are My witnesses, says the Eternal One, and My servant whom I have chosen'; in 44:1, 'But now hear, O Jacob My servant, and Israel, whom I have chosen'; in 44:21, 'Remember these things, O Jacob, and Israel, for you are My servant'; and in 45:4, 'For the sake of Jacob My servant, and Israel My chosen one...'

If the individual of our poems were referred to only once as '*Eved Adonai*, even without any further identification, that would remove any last vestige of doubt one might have. But there are no less than six such references: one in the first of the poems (42:1), three in the second (49:3, 5, 6), and two in the fourth (52:13, 53:11); and one of them actually *spells out* the symbolism: 'You are My servant, Israel, in whom I will be glorified' (49:3).

In the face of such overwhelming evidence, to deny the parabolic function of the hero of the poems seems to me sheer perverseness, and to invite the comment: Who is blind but the interpreter of My servant?

DEATH AND RESURRECTION

Nevertheless, it may be thought that one problem remains. For there are two or three hints in the poems that the Servant dies and yet lives on. He is said to be 'like a sheep led to the slaughter' (53:7), 'cut off from the land of the living' (53:8); there is mention of his grave (53:9); and yet, we are told, 'he will enjoy long life' (53:10). Does not this motif of death and resurrection show that we are dealing, after all, with an individual rather than a people?

The answer is: on the contrary, it is precisely the death-and-resurrection motif which would furnish proof positive, if such were still needed, that the Servant personifies Israel. For the belief in individual resurrection was not yet entertained by the recognised teachers of Judaism in Deutero-Isaiah's time – or for about five centuries thereafter. That such a belief existed is not in question, which is why Ezekiel was able to make use of it in his prophecy about the valley of dry bones (37:1–14). But it was regarded as belonging to pagan mythology, and discountenanced. That is precisely why Ezekiel uses it only as a metaphor for the hoped-for national resurrection of the Jewish people. We therefore have the strongest possible indication that if the author of the Servant Poems, writing not long after Ezekiel, uses the same resurrection motif, he must be using it in the same metaphorical sense.

Let me clinch the point by quoting Sheldon Blank: 'The fourth song admirably supplements the others and strengthens the conclusion that the servant is Israel personified. It is not repeatedly stated and in so many words but it is the inevitable conclusion to be drawn from ... the fact that the servant dies and will live again ... It is just because the servant is not a person but a personification that the Second Isaiah can picture him living again after death . . . If he did not borrow the expectation directly from Ezekiel he found it among the hopes of his day, cherished by the sons and grandsons of Ezekiel's congregation . . . Because it was far too soon for a prophet to be speaking of bodily resurrection and because, on the other hand, resurrection as a symbol of national rebirth was already familiar in his day, the conclusion is justified that the Second Isaiah meant just this when he spoke of the one who had died and would live and that this servant can only be the people of Israel personified' (*Prophetic Faith in Isaiah*, pp. 98–100).

VICARIOUS SUFFERING AND ATONEMENT

But what about the significance of the Servant's, and therefore Israel's, suffering? The author stresses that it is undeserved. What happens to the Servant, happens even 'though he had done no violence and uttered no deceit' (53:9). That is not indeed the usual assessment of 'the state of the nation' one associates with the Prophets, who more commonly denounce the people for their sins. But the Babylonian Exile is different. At least after it had been going on for some time, the Prophets evidently became convinced that it was a time for encouragement, not castigation. The very beginning of Deutero-Isaiah announces the theme: 'Comfort now, comfort now My people, says your God. Speak tenderly to Jerusalem, and cry to her that she has served her term, that her penalty is paid, that she has received from God's hand double for all her sins' (40:1f.).

There was evidently a feeling that 'enough is enough', even from a divine point of view, so that any further suffering endured by Israel is, strictly speaking, unjust. Nevertheless it is still God's doing. To us that may seem scandalous. We might be inclined to say: if it is unjust, then it cannot be the doing of a just God; then it must be due to human beings acting *against* God's will. But that kind of radical acceptance of the implications of human free-will was not, apparently, an available option in the author's time. So, just as Deutero-Isaiah had said that it was 'from God's hand' that Jerusalem had received double for all her sins, so the author of our poems repeatedly states that it is God who has 'afflicted' the Servant (53:4), 'visited on him the guilt' of others (53:6), and 'chosen to crush him' (53:10).

On the one hand, therefore, the suffering is innocent, on the other it is divinely ordained. Therefore it must be in some paradoxical way beneficial or therapeutic, not only for Israel but for humanity. Sheldon Blank points out that the key verse (53:5) uses the word *musar*, which has precisely that connotation of 'redemptive punishment', especially in Jeremiah (*Prophetic Faith in Isaiah*, p. 96f.). 'Musar', he says, 'is divine discipline, suffering which might lead to someone's improvement, a bitter experience from which the wise might learn' (ibid., p. 96).

But how exactly the paradox is to be resolved, remains obscure. Clearly there is evil in the world. However, it is no longer Israel's but that of her oppressors. Therefore Israel's suffering is certainly vicarious, but how is it beneficial? The only rational explanation I can think of is the one I have already suggested: that the contemplation of Israel's suffering, and of the courage and patience with which it is borne, pricks the conscience of those who have caused it, namely the Babylonians, and elicits their repentance. As I said before, that sort of thing does sometimes happen, though not very often. It may very well have been a hope entertained – over-optimistically – by an exilic prophet.

But did the author of our poems also have in mind the non-rational, mythological concept of vicarious atonement, that the suffering of the sufferer actually removes the guilt or annuls the sin of the oppressor? Sheldon Blank thinks not. 'The idea of suffering for others', he writes, 'is unquestionably present here in the fourth song; but these are its forms: the toil of intercessory activity on others' behalf and the pain of affliction endured from which others would learn. The idea is present but it little resembles the "vicarious atonement" which is sometimes thought to be the theme of this song' (ibid., p. 97). Yehezkel Kaufmann, in his monumental *History of the Religion of Israel*, puts it more strongly: 'In the Hebrew Scriptures the idea of vicarious sacrifice, insofar as it is present, is limited strictly to the cultic sphere, and has no place in the doctrine of retribution' (Vol. IV, 'The Babylonian Exile and Deutero-Isaiah', UAHC, 1970, p. 145).

I think that both of these statements go too far. Admittedly, it is precisely where the poems seem to allude to vicarious atonement that the text is most obscure – linguistically as well as conceptually – and very probably corrupt. Therefore one can't be sure, and it would certainly be rash to build any elaborate theory on so shaky a basis. Nevertheless, the text as it has been transmitted does contain one or two words and phrases drawn from the language of the sacrificial cult which may very well refer to some kind of a notion of vicarious atonement, especially the 'lamb led to the slaughter' (53:7) and the word *asham*, for 'guilt-offering' (53:10). I am therefore inclined to agree with Samuel Sandmel, who does think that the concept of vicarious atonement is present in the last of the four poems but adds that it 'appears only here in Jewish literature and tradition' (*The Hebrew Scriptures*, Alfred A. Knopf, New York, 1963, p. 190), and that 'the theological idea contained in the poem found no acceptance in subsequent Judaism' (p. 193).

THE QUESTION OF 'FULFILMENT'

As I said before, the Servant is not the Messiah, for that apocalyptic concept did not exist in the author's time, nor are there any traces of it in the text of the poems. Similarly, the poems are not a prediction of a future historical personage in any other sense, for to entertain such a notion would be profoundly to misunderstand what sort of people the Prophets were and what sort of a literature Prophetic literature is. Prediction in that sense is a feature, not of classical Hebrew Prophecy but of Apocalypse, which is a web of escapist fantasies spun by charlatan imitators of classical Hebrew Prophecy.

Nevertheless it is perfectly legitimate to ask who, in the course of subsequent history, might be said as a matter of fact to have embodied the ideal of the Servant Poems. And indeed it is not difficult to think of examples in the history of martyrology, from Socrates and Jeremiah to Meir of Rothenburg, Thomas More and Martin Luther King. But of course it is for Jesus of Nazareth that the claim has most commonly been made; and therefore I should perhaps say a few words about that.

There is no doubt that the Evangelists *interpret* various episodes of Jesus' ministry in the light of the Servant Poems, using the *pesher* type of interpretation which has become so familiar to us from the Dead Sea Scrolls (e.g., Matt. 8:17 and 12:18–21). And sometimes they portray Jesus as deliberately *acting out* the role of the Suffering Servant (e.g., Luke 22:37). An interesting question which this raises is whether Jesus is so portrayed because the Servant had already been identified with the Messiah (as I would guess) or independently of such an identification.

However that may be, if we ask how well the historical Jesus fits the picture of the Suffering Servant, then we must note one or two minor discrepancies, for instance that Jesus was not a leper and did not enjoy 'long life', and one major one. The major one is that Deutero-Isaiah's Servant is a prophet who suffers and dies *because of the religious truth which he proclaims*. But though the belief is both grounded in the New Testament and widely held that the Passion and Crucifixion of Jesus are so to be explained, a number of scholarly studies of that aspect of the Gospel story have shown it to be highly questionable. (See, e.g. Paul Winter's *On the Trial of Jesus*, Walter de Guyter, Berlin, 1961, and Ellis Rivkin's *What Crucified Jesus?*, SCM Press, London, 1984.)

It is indeed likely enough that the religious teachings of Jesus aroused hostility among the Pharisees. But that hostility was greatly exaggerated by the Evangelists. I say that partly on *a priori* grounds, because there is so little in the authentic teachings of Jesus that differs significantly from what we know of Pharisaic teachings, and partly on the empirical ground that the growing hostility is actually traceable from Gospel to Gospel, e.g. in the story of the 'greatest commandment'. (See my 1982 St Paul's Lecture, 'The Greatest Commandment', published by the London Diocesan Council for Christian–Jewish Understanding.)

I am therefore convinced that the life of Jesus ended in tragedy, not because his religious teachings were rejected by his own people, but because, rightly or wrongly, he was widely regarded as the leader of a messianic movement, and because from the point of view of the Romans and those Jews who, like the High Priest, collaborated with them, such a movement was potentially insurrectionist. Jesus, in other words, was a victim, not of Jewish religious opposition but of Roman political oppression, as the titulus on the cross graphically confirms.

That is, I am sure, a disappointing conclusion from a Christian point of view, but I think it has been sufficiently demonstrated, and in the interest of historical truth as well as the prevention of anti-Semitism, should no longer be resisted.

CONCLUSION

Let me sum up. The Servant Poems depict a persecuted prophet who suffers innocently but whose suffering paradoxically rehabilitates his persecutors. But the depiction is a parable in which the prophet personifies the Jewish people, whose national suffering and quasi-death in Babylonian exile will soon end and give way to a glorious new age of national resurrection, when the God of Israel will be vindicated and Israel's suffering will be seen in retrospect to have been a means to the redemption of humanity.

That, I think, is the essence of the matter. But other themes are touched and other issues raised. There is the honest recognition, reminiscent of Job, that much human suffering is undeserved. There is the simultaneous assumption, which I would reject, that it is nevertheless God-willed. There is a struggle to make sense of that paradox, but no clear solution is offered, least of all in relation to the leprosy motif, the role of which is totally obscure. There is a hint of a suggestion that human suffering may sometimes be expiatory, like the guilt-offering of a sacrificial animal; but nothing is said to make the logic of the sacrificial cult any less illogical than it plainly is. Only one ray of light is thrown on the problem of undeserved suffering: that those who champion truth and justice must expect opposition, and that the fortitude with which they bear their consequent suffering may help, by inducing remorse, to win over the forces of evil. But that ray of light is very precious, and justifies all the ink that has been spilt in interpreting the Servant Poems.

Good and Evil in the Classical Sources of Judaism

17 March 1999

Two facts about the human condition stand out. The first is that like all animals, we are doomed to die; the second that, unlike other animals, or at least to an incomparably higher degree, we are capable of both good and evil – virtually unlimited good and evil. Of these two basic facts, it is the moral ambivalence that concerns us. Whether or not there is a hereafter, our life on earth is of limited duration. But while it lasts, we can and do perform both good and evil. The question is why.

BODY AND SOUL

One way of accounting for the duality of human beings in the moral sense is to point to their duality in a more fundamental, constitutional sense. They are, it is said, a compound of two kinds of stuff: matter and spirit. In so far as they are made of matter, they are prone to sin; in so far as they are made of spirit, they tend to act nobly.

This dualistic view is not, however, characteristic of the Hebrew Bible. Of course, the contrast between the high and low status of human beings is frequently noted and emphasised, not least in the eighth Psalm: 'When I look at Your heavens, the work of Your fingers, the moon and the stars which You have established – what are human beings that You are mindful of them, mortals that You care for them? Yet You have made them little less than divine, and crowned them with glory and honour!'

But the contrast is not generally stated in terms of a matter–spirit dualism in which matter is bad and spirit is good. To quote Otto Baab, 'Matter is not intrinsically evil or corrupt' (*The Theology of the Old Testament*, New York and Nashville, 1949, p. 108f.). And again: 'man's physical nature is not the reason for his sin...His proneness to yield to the lusts of the flesh results from his eagerness to escape the problem created by the conflict between his spiritual freedom and the limitations of his physical nature. His sin consists in *choosing* sensuality, not in the possession of a body which makes sensuality possible' (ibid., p. 248). On the contrary, the chief locus of sin is not *basar*, the flesh, but *lev*, the heart which, though in its literal sense a bodily organ, stands as a metaphor for the mind and the will.

There are indeed traces of matter–spirit dualism, showing Greek influence, especially in the later books of the Bible (e.g., 'The dust returns to the earth as it was, but the spirit returns to God who gave it,' Eccles. 12:7). But they become a great deal more pronounced in the Apocrypha, Philo and the New Testament, and they did leave their mark on Rabbinic Judaism.

Of special interest here is the Rabbinic interpretation of the phrase in the Second Creation Story that God 'formed Adam out of the dust of the ground' (Gen. 2:7), where the Hebrew word *va-yitzer* for 'formed' has a double *yod*, which is interpreted as pointing to the duality of human nature. According to one interpretation, which sees in the verb an allusion to the noun *yetzer* for 'inclination', God compounded Adam of two inclinations, good and evil (Gen.R. 14:4). According to another, which relates the verb to the noun *y'tzirah* for 'creation', the process involved two stages which brought into being respectively the earthly and heavenly aspects of human beings. This led the Rabbis to say of them: 'Like animals, they eat and drink, procreate, secrete and die; like angels, they stand erect, speak, think, and see visions' (Gen.R. 14:3).

That the matter–spirit duality of human nature is certainly found in Rabbinic literature can also be seen from the fact that the Rabbis could conceive of an *'olam ha-ba*, a world-to-come in which 'there is no eating or drinking or procreation or trading or jealousy, but the righteous sit with crowns on their heads, feasting on the radiance of the *sh'chinah*, the Divine Presence' (*Ber.* 17a) – in other words, a purely spiritual form of existence. Yet one senses a hesitancy to concede that the two components are ultimately separable, and therefore a reluctance to let go of the belief in a resurrection in which body and soul are finally reunited.

Above all, there is no straightforward identification of the two aspects with good and evil respectively. As George Foot Moore points out, it is not the case 'that the evil impulse resides in the body while the good impulse proceeds from the soul. That the physical organism, as material, is evil *per se*, sense the origin of error, the appetites and passions the source of moral evil – these ideas, which through prevalent philosophies had gained wide currency in the Hellenistic world, have no counterpart in Palestinian Judaism' (*Judaism in the First Centuries of the Christian Era*, Cambridge, MA, [1927], 1954, Vol. I, p. 485).

The general Rabbinic view sees the two components of human nature as different but inseparable, and both alike involved in good and evil. Typical is a well-known passage in which body and soul together appear before God to be judged, and each accuses the other, whereupon a parable, found also in other traditions, is told about two orchard keepers, one lame and one blind. During the royal owner's absence the lame man stands on the shoulders of the blind man, and picks the fruit. When the king returns to find the fruit gone, each has a ready excuse: the lame man that he can't walk and the blind man that he can't see. Then the king orders the lame man to climb on the blind man's back, and judges them together. So, too, is the moral, God judges body and soul together (*Mechilta* on Exod. 15:1; Lev.R. 4:5).

THE DIVINE IMAGE

As we continue our search for the causes of the moral ambivalence of human nature, we should remind ourselves that it is both sides of it, not only the evil but also the good, that call for an explanation. Why do we generally desire, and often though by no means always choose, what is good? About that, at least, Judaism has been clear and consistent all through the ages: the good in us is a consequence of our having been created in the image of God. God, says the first chapter of Genesis, created Adam in the divine image (1:27). In the divine likeness, reiterates the fifth chapter (5:1). And the greatest of the Rabbis, Akiva, remarked: 'How privileged we are to have been created in the divine image; how much more privileged still to have been made aware that we were created in God's image' (Avot 3:14).

This doctrine is central to the Jewish understanding of human nature. It has never been abandoned, and it has been regarded as a necessary and sufficient explanation of the Good Inclination, which is the voice within us that prompts us – often, alas, unheeded – to choose and do what is right. It does, however, raise a question, which we cannot ignore: what then of the story of the Garden of Eden? Does it not mean that the high status of human beings, and with it their Good Inclination, has long since been forfeited?

There is also a prior question: How seriously should the Garden-of-Eden story be taken? Some modern Bible scholars have regarded it, partly on account of its pessimism about human nature, as atypical of other Pentateuchal material and derived from a separate source which Otto Eissfeldt called L for 'Lay Source', Julian Morgenstern 'K' for 'Kenite' and Robert H. Pfeiffer 'S' for 'South' or 'Seir', meaning Edomite (Pfeiffer, *Introduction to the Old Testament*, London, [1941] 1948, pp. 161–65).

But whatever one makes of these views, the story is clearly mythological, and mythology is not dogma. On the contrary, myth is allusive. It lends itself to interpretation on a variety of levels. One obvious interpretation of the Garden-of-Eden myth is that it illustrates the dawning of the consciousness of choice, and therefore an advance rather than a retrogression. At any rate, there is not the slightest hint in the story that the wrong choice made by Adam and Eve deprived subsequent generations of the ability to choose rightly.

Nevertheless, something of that kind has been inferred from the story, chiefly in Christianity, but to some extent also in Judaism. Both in Apocryphal and Rabbinic literature we do occasionally encounter the view that on account of Adam and Eve's sin, death came into the world, and some kind of blemish is transmitted from generation to generation. Thus we read in Ben Sira: 'From a woman sin had its beginning, and because of her we all die' (25:24). And in the Fourth Book of Ezra: 'For a grain of evil seed was sown in Adam's heart from the beginning, and how much ungodliness it has produced until now, and will produce until the time of threshing comes!' (4:30). According to the Rabbis, when Adam sinned, the *Sh'chinah* distanced itself from the world (Gen.R. 19:7), and because of that first sin, all human beings are doomed to die (*BB* 17a; *Shab.* 55b).

But the typical Rabbinic view stresses rather the opposite. George Foot Moore sums up a passage in Midrash *Tanchuma*: 'Death came in with Adam, but every man has deserved it for himself; his descendants die in consequence of his sin, but not for the guilt of it' (*Judaism in the First Centuries of the Christian Era*, I, p. 476). More generally, he concludes: 'there is no notion that the original constitution of Adam underwent any change in consequence of the fall, so that he transmitted to his descendants a vitiated nature in which the appetites and passions necessarily prevail over reason and virtue, while the good is enfeebled or wholly impotent' (I, p. 479).

With reference to the assertion in the Ten Commandments that God visits the iniquity of parents on subsequent generations (Exod. 20:5), that principle was already challenged by the prophet Ezekiel (18:20), and the Rabbis took the sting out of it by explaining: only if the children are wicked in their turn (*Mechilta* to Exod. 20:5; cf. *San.* 27b on Exod. 34:7). Perhaps most characteristic of the Rabbinic attitude is a prayer which found its way from the Talmud (*Ber.* 60b) into the daily liturgy (*The Authorised Daily Prayer Book of the United Hebrew Congregations of the Commonwealth* ['Singer's'], 1990 edn., p. 15) and begins: 'My God, the soul which You have given me is pure. For You have formed it within me, and breathed it into me, and You preserve it within me...'

THE EVIL INCLINATION

We have seen that the Good Inclination is a necessary consequence of the Divine Image which Judaism regards as a continuing fact, uncancelled by the Garden-of-Eden myth. But if that is so, then all the more does its opposite, the Evil Inclination, call for an explanation.

In simplest terms, the answer of Rabbinic Judaism is that, just as God created the Good Inclination, so God created the Evil Inclination, in order that human beings may have the possibility, and the responsibility, of choice. Of course that raises the question how a good God can create an evil inclination; and the answer to that, at least in large part, is that the Evil Inclination, in spite of its name, is not intrinsically evil.

We have already seen that the double *yod* in the word *va-yitzer* in Genesis 2:7 gave rise to the interpretation that God created Adam with two kinds of *yetzer* or inclination. But that, of course, is not the origin of the term. The noun *yetzer* does indeed come from the verb *yatzar*, 'to form', and therefore means something like 'a fundamental aspect of the human make-up' or 'a basic human disposition'.

But the noun occurs already in the Bible, for instance at the beginning of the Flood story: 'God saw that the wickedness of humankind was great in the earth, and that every *yetzer* of the thoughts of their hearts was only evil continually' (Gen. 6:5). And again at the end of the Flood story: 'I will never again curse the ground because of humankind, for the *yetzer* of the human heart is evil from their youth' (Gen. 8:21). There are also other occurrences (e.g., Deut. 31:21), but these Genesis verses, whose negative context is to be noted, are the most relevant.

There are also one or two evidences of the concept in the intertestamental literature, for instance, when Ben Sira says that God 'created humankind in the beginning, and left them in the power of their own *yetzer*' (15:14). But it is in Rabbinic Judaism that the concept is fully developed, particularly as regards the Evil Inclination, *yetzer ha-ra'*. Indeed, when the word *yetzer* is used on its own, it usually refers to the Evil Inclination.

That the *yetzer ha-ra'* is not intrinsically evil is a clear implication of some of the most important Rabbinic teachings on the subject. For instance, the Creation Story reaches its climax with the creation of humankind, at which point the text says: 'and behold, it was very good' (Gen. 1:31). Here the pleonastic word 'and' is seen by the Rabbis as a hint that human beings were created with two inclinations, good and evil, the verdict 'very good' covering both. 'But,' continues the Midrash, 'can the Evil Inclination be called very good? That would be astonishing!' Then it explains: 'If it were not for the Evil Inclination no man would build a house, marry a wife, beget children, or engage in business'; and it concludes by quoting an Ecclesiastes verse (4:4) to the effect that all human effort is the result of rivalry between persons (Gen.R. 9:7).

What transpires from this illuminating passage is that the *yetzer ha-ra'* is an umbrella term for the self-regarding drives that motivate human beings: their desire for self-preservation, pleasure, power, property, prestige, popularity, and so forth. These drives are not evil. On the contrary, they are good in the sense that they are biologically beneficial. But they are extremely powerful and therefore, unless they are controlled by a lively conscience, they can easily lead us to disregard the rights and needs of others, and cause them harm. It is in *this* sense – because it so often prompts us to do wrong – that the *yetzer ha-ra'* is evil. But it need not do so; the psychic energy it represents can be directed to good ends.

That is the clear implication of a Rabbinic comment on the Deuteronomy verse, 'You shall love the Eternal One, your God, with all your heart' (6:5). Because the Hebrew word *l'vav'cha* for 'your heart' is spelt, slightly unusually, with a double *beit*, the lesson is drawn: with both your inclinations, the *yetzer tov* and the *yetzer ra'* (*Ber.* 9:5; *Sifrey* Deut. 32). That is to say, we should use even our self-regarding drives in the service of God.

Which of these drives is the most powerful? That question is not, so far as I know, directly discussed in the literature of the Rabbis, but the general impression one gets is that, like Freud, they would have been inclined to say: the desire for pleasure, or the libido. Often when the term *yetzer ha-ra'* is used without further qualification, it is clear from the context that the sex-drive is chiefly meant. At any rate, these drives, in their totality are, as we might say, what makes the world go round. As it is said in the Talmud, if the Evil Inclination were destroyed the world would go down (*Yoma* 69b). Nevertheless, to say it yet again, it is not evil in itself.

Another term sometimes used for it in Rabbinic literature is 'the leaven in the dough' (Gen.R. 34:10; *Ber.* 17a; *Mechilta* on Exod. 14:11). The leaven causes the dough to rise, and makes the bread palatable. But it can also cause fermentation, which serves as a metaphor for moral corruption. As Ephraim E. Urbach puts it, God 'put the leaven in the dough', 'but for the fermentation of the leaven man alone is responsible' (*The Sages*, Cambridge, MA, 1987, p. 482).

THE PERSONIFICATION OF THE EVIL INCLINATION

That the *yetzer ha-ra'*, in itself, is morally neutral, emerges very clearly from the key passages we have discussed. But it is not a view that is consistently maintained. For the Rabbis, we must remember, were not philosophers, and what they have to say about human nature is a product of experience and observation rather than the exposition of a clearly formulated intellectual system. And on the experiential level they did see the *yetzer ha-ra* as a nasty and insidious force which they did not hesitate, on occasion, to personify.

It begins, we are told, not indeed at conception, but at birth (Urbach, *The Sages*, p. 481). It grows stronger every day, and seeks to destroy us, and if God did not help us, we could not prevail over it (*Suk.* 52a–b). It entices us in this world and testifies against us in the world to come (*Suk.* 52b). At first it is like a spider's web, in the end it becomes like a cart-rope (*San.* 99b). At first it is a passer-by, then a guest, and in the end it occupies the house (*Suk.* 52b). It is called by seven epithets: evil, uncircumcised, unclean, enemy, stumbling-block, stone (as in Ezekiel's 'heart of stone') and the hidden one (ibid.; Solomon Schechter, *Aspects of Rabbinic Theology*, p. 243f.). Not surprisingly, therefore, the *yetzer ha-ra'* is sometimes seen as 'the tempter within' (Moore, *Judaism in the First Centuries of the Christian Era*, I, p. 482), 'a kind of malevolent second personality' (ibid.), humankind's 'implacable enemy' (ibid.); and even as a personification of Satan and the Angel of Death (*BB* 16a; Moore, p. 492).

The question, however, is how seriously these descriptions of the *yetzer ha-ra'* are to be taken. Are they merely graphic metaphors or do they imply belief in a truly evil force within and perhaps beyond human beings?

There is relatively little in Rabbinic literature to support the view that there is an inborn human impulse to do evil for evil's sake, to do wrong because it is wrong, to do what is forbidden because it is forbidden. There is more of that, as a matter of fact, in the Hebrew Bible. There we do encounter frequently the concept of sin as rebellion, as rejection of the Divine Will. The recurring description of the people of Israel as 'stiff-necked' (Exod. 32:10; 33:3, 5; 34:9) testifies to that. 'Evil,' says Otto Baab, 'appears, not so much as an extraneous force or supernatural power, as the inner pride of man, who defiantly sets himself against his Creator' (*The Theology of the Old Testament*, p. 230). But in the Hebrew Bible such rebelliousness is generally associated with idolatry, and that, in the view of the Rabbis, ceased to be a major problem shortly after the Babylonian Exile (*Yoma* 69b).

We do indeed hear in Rabbinic literature of the *epikoros*, who rejects all moral restraint (*San.* 10:1), the one who says that 'there is no judgment and no Judge' (Lev.R. 28:1), and the *kofer ba-ikkar*, who denies the very basis of religion (*Tos. Shevuot* 3:6). But by and large it is assumed that human beings mean well, that they are weak rather than wicked, though often so weak that they allow themselves to be lured by the *yetzer ha-ra* into very serious wrongdoing.

Here let me interject that Paul's confession in Romans 7, 'I do not do the good I want, but the evil I do not want is what I do' (v. 19) does not seem to me to contradict, but rather to confirm, that fundamentally positive view of human nature. For it clearly implies that we want good and not evil, though we continually fail to act accordingly; that we have a desire to do right but not a corresponding desire to do wrong.

To a large extent, at any rate, the Rabbinic analysis of sin is due to the *yetzer ha-ra'*, and of the *yetzer ha-ra'* as a set of drives that are in themselves ethically neutral though conducive to terrible consequences if uncontrolled, does seem to explain what needs to be explained, while the tendency to personify the *yetzer ha-ra* should be seen as the kind of metaphorical language which is the bread-and-butter of Rabbinic *Aggadah*.

Nevertheless, the occasional identification of the *yetzer ha-ra* with Satan requires some further comments. The whole concept of a superhuman cosmic power of evil independent of God, or even subservient to God, is manifestly incompatible with the purest monotheism. Hence Deutero-Isaiah's majestic proclamation, in God's name, against Zoroastrianism, 'I form light and create darkness, I make peace and create evil' (or, as the New Revised Standard Version translates the second clause, 'I make weal and create woe'); 'I the Eternal One do all these things' (45:7). In the words of Kaufmann Kohler, 'The Jewish conception of the unity of God necessitates the unity of the world, which leaves no place for a cosmic principle of evil' (*Jewish Theology*, Cincinnati, 1943, p. 189).

Therefore, too, the concept of a superhuman *person* embodying such an evil power did not gain ready admittance into Hebrew thought. Satan does indeed make one or two appearances in the Hebrew Bible, but only in its latest books, and even then only as a 'counsel for the prosecution'. In the words of Otto Baab: 'The occasional appearance of Satan or of minor demons has little significance in the religion of Israel...Throughout the literary records of Israel one finds no real belief that the power making for evil is outside of man; there is unanimity in asserting that this power resides in man himself' (*The Theology of the Old Testament*, p. 247).

It is true that in the Intertestamental and New-Testamental Literature, Satan assumes a malevolent personality and, along with a varied assortment of individually named demons and angels, plays a prominent role, which is generally taken with humourless seriousness. The same is true to some extent of the Rabbinic *Aggadah*, especially of Babylonian origin, and to a much greater extent of Jewish mystical texts. But with that last exception, Satan does not generally rise in Judaism above the level of folkloristic fantasy. As Kohler remarks, 'the belief in evil spirits and in Satan, the Evil One, remained rather a matter of popular credulity and never became a positive doctrine of the Synagogue' (ibid., p. 192).

Today, I should like to think, most Jews would go along, as I do, with Joseph Conrad's quip: 'The belief in a supernatural source of evil is not necessary; men alone are quite capable of every wickedness' (Nicolas Bentley and Evan Esar, *The Treasury of Humorous Quotations*, London, [1952] 1962, p. 61).

ORDINARY AND EXTRAORDINARY EVIL

The self-regarding drives, which constitute the *yetzer ha-ra'*, do seem to go a very long way towards accounting for the evil that men, and women, do. But do they go *all* the way? Is human evil basically nothing more than selfishness? At the end of the twentieth century, Conrad's phrase, that human beings alone are capable of every wickedness, conjures up horrendous images, of the murder of the little children of Dunblane, the killing fields of Cambodia, Bosnia and Rwanda, the Gulag Archipelago and, above all, the Holocaust. In the face of evils of such enormity, the Rabbinic account of the *yetzer ha-ra'* seems less than adequate.

Perhaps, therefore, we need to distinguish between two kinds of evil: ordinary and extraordinary. Sin, as such, is universal. We all do it. 'Surely there is no one on earth so righteous as to do good without ever sinning,' says Ecclesiastes (7:20; cf. I Kings 8:46, II Chron. 6:36; Prov. 20:9). The Rabbis do speak of three classes of human beings, good, bad and middling (*Ber.* 16b; RH 16b); but the implication always seems to be that most of us fall into the intermediate category. And they took a pretty realistic if not cynical view when they said: 'Most people are guilty of robbery, a minority of unchastity, and all of slander' (*BB* 165a).

Perhaps we may generalise and say that those sins which are committed out of selfishness, greed or lust can be satisfactorily explained in terms of the *yetzer ha-ra* as the Rabbis understood it; and they do seem to constitute the vast majority of 'ordinary' sins. But what about those that are committed out of hatred, anger or sheer cruelty and viciousness, and those that are to most of us altogether incomprehensible? It does seem that these call for some additional explanatory categories.

An obvious one is insanity. In that respect an important teaching of the Rabbis is that 'no person commits a transgression unless a spirit of *shetut* has entered into them' (*Sot.* 3a), where the word *shetut* is usually translated 'folly' but also means 'madness'.

There clearly is such a thing as criminal insanity, even though most forms of mental illness have no such implication. Are the kinds of evils which I have called 'extraordinary' to be explained as pathological? By calling sadism a perversion we do seem to imply that it is pathological. Is it, however, a mental or a moral condition? How does one explain the phenomenon of the psychopath, whose conscience is totally inoperative? And how are we to account for the frenzy that takes hold of crowds, and even whole populations, when they are brainwashed by an evil ideology like racism or mesmerised by a rabble-rousing demagogue like Hitler? What is the effect on human behaviour when a whole people is demonised? How large a part was played in the history that culminated in the Holocaust by Church teachings which held the Jewish people collectively responsible for the Crucifixion and portrayed them as rejected by God? Is there such a thing as mass psychopathology? If so, what are its causes and its *modus operandi*, and how much is to be attributed to the little understood forces of the occult, in which Hitler is said to have dabbled?

All these are questions to which there are no easy answers. They call for a concerted study to which theologians have no doubt important contributions to make, but which demand, at least equally, the scientific contributions of psychologists, sociologists and criminologists. What is not admissible, in my view, is to attribute all these phenomena to an evil force, personified or otherwise, outside humanity. That is merely a projection, and therefore an evasion of the real problem, as well as a huge oversimplification. It is the human psyche that needs to be understood.

COUNTERMEASURES

And therefore, too, the question, how to combat these extraordinary evils, cannot be easily answered. But let us, in conclusion, return to the ordinary, everyday evils which are a constant feature of human behaviour. Must they be accepted as inevitable or can they be overcome? The Jewish answer is clear. We have been given free will. That is the meaning of the Garden-of-Eden story, and it is implied in virtually all subsequent Jewish literature. Neither the commandments of the Pentateuch nor the exhortations of the Prophets make sense without it. 'I call heaven and earth to witness against you this day,' says God in Deuteronomy, 'that I have set before you life or death, blessing or curse: therefore keep the commandments, and to act faithfully is a matter of your choice' (30:19).

The Rabbis re-emphasised the point. 'Everything is foreseen,' they said, 'yet free will is given' (*Avot* 3:16). 'Everything is in the hand of God except the fear of God' (*Ber.* 33b). And again: 'Those who wish to pollute themselves with sin will find all the gates open to them, and those who desire to attain the highest purity will find all the forces of goodness ready to help them' (*Yoma* 38b). There is even, as that last saying implies, a cosmic bias in favour of goodness.

So it is *possible* for human beings to control the *yetzer ha-ra'* within them. But there is no suggestion that it is easy. On the contrary, 'Who is a hero?' asks Ben Zoma in Tractate *Avot*, and he answers: 'Those who subdue their Evil Inclination' (4:1). The problem, simply put, is how to cultivate and activate the Good Inclination so that it may exercise the necessary control. And the Rabbinic answer is: through study, prayer and observance.

Of major significance here is a parable which concludes by

making God say to the people of Israel: 'My children, I have created the *yetzer ha-ra'*, but I have also created the Torah as an antidote for it; if you occupy yourselves with the Torah you will not fall into its power' (Kid. 30b, interpreting Gen. 4:7; cf. *Sifrey* Deut. §45; *BB* 16a). To 'occupy oneself with the Torah' usually has a twofold meaning in Rabbinic Judaism. It means to study its teachings, for to do so is to be in touch with the Mind of God and is therefore a spiritual as well as an intellectual exercise. But it also means to practise the way of life which the Torah prescribes, which includes both an ethical code and a devotional discipline.

One Rabbi taught: 'Always stir up the Good Inclination against the Evil Inclination... If you succeed, well and good. If not, study Torah... If you succeed, well and good. If not, recite the *Shema'* (Deut. 6:4–9,11:13–21, Num. 15:37–41)... If you succeed, well and good. If not, remind yourself that one day you will die' (Resh Lakish, *Ber.* 5a, interpreting Psalm 4:5). Moore sums up: 'To stimulate the better self to contend against the worse; occupy one's self intensely with the word of God; confess one's faith in the one true God, and the duty of loving Him with all one's being, renewing thus the assumption of the yoke of the kingdom of Heaven; meditate on the hour of death (and the judgment of God) – these are the weapons with which victory may be won in this battle that man wages for the freedom of his soul' (*Judaism in the First Centuries of the Christian Era*, p. 491).

Some prayers of Rabbinic origin refer explicitly to the *yetzer ha-ra'*. One, from the Babylonian Talmud, begins: 'Eternal God, school us in Your teachings and make us loyal to Your commandments. May we never consent to evil, or surrender to temptation or self-contempt. Let not the Evil Inclination rule over us... but help us to cleave to the Good inclination...' (*Ber.* 60b). Another, from the Palestinian Talmud, reads: 'May it be Your will, Eternal One, our God and God of ancestors, to break and destroy the yoke of the Evil Inclination within our hearts. For You have created us to do Your will, and we know we ought to do it. Such is Your desire, and such is ours. What then hinders us? The leaven in the dough. You know that we ourselves have not the strength to overcome it. Therefore may it be Your will, Eternal One, our God and God of our ancestors, to destroy it and subdue it, so that we may do Your will wholeheartedly' (J. Ber. 4:2).

Of special relevance, of course, are the penitential prayers, which feature in the daily liturgy and pre-eminently during the Ten Days of Repentance, culminating in the Day of Atonement.

CONCLUSION

Our inquiry points to a hope and a task. The hope is for a time of redemption, which Judaism has traditionally associated with the coming of the Messiah, when good will finally triumph over evil or, as the Talmud graphically puts it, God will slay the *yetzer ha-ra'* in the presence of the righteous and the wicked *(Suk.* 52a). The task is to implement the will of God in all aspects of human life, and especially the commandment 'You shall love your neighbour as yourself' (Lev. 19:18). For if we do not love one another, says an ancient Midrash, we shall end by killing one another (*Sifrey* Deut. §187). But if we do learn to love one another, all things are possible, even the ultimate vindication of the risk God took in creating human beings on this planet.

Principles of Jewish Ethics

23 April 2002

DEFINITIONS

Ethics is concerned with questions of right and wrong, and of good and bad. But we must immediately qualify that because these terms are also used in non-ethical senses. For instance, a good car is simply an efficient car, and a bad car an inefficient one. There is no moral judgment implied because a car can't choose how it will perform. Therefore the use of ethical terms presupposes the possibility of choice.

Interestingly, we have for 'bad' the alternative 'evil' which nearly always does have an ethical sense. (I say 'nearly always' because we also have such expressions as 'an evil smell'.) Precisely for that reason we would not call an inefficient car an 'evil' car, for it can't help being made the way it is. What a pity that we don't have a similarly dual vocabulary for the other concepts I have mentioned. Therefore the word 'good' has to serve two quite different functions, to denote efficiency, as in 'a good car', and to denote an ethical quality, as in 'a good person' or 'a good deed'.

Similarly with regard to 'right' and 'wrong'. There is a right and a wrong way to treat a fellow human being, and that is a matter of ethics. But there is also a right and a wrong way to address an ambassador, or to eat spaghetti, but that is not a matter of ethics at all but only of etiquette. What then is it that makes the difference? That is not at all easy to say. It is partly that an ethical action is always one that is done by one human being to another, or at least to another sentient creature such as an animal. But that doesn't explain why the way we address an ambassador is not an ethical issue. Therefore we must add that in ethically right or wrong conduct there is also an element of a significant benefit being conferred or harm being done by one person to another.

ETHICAL EMPHASIS IN JUDAISM

If that clarifies sufficiently for our purpose what we mean by ethics, let us now ask how big a role it plays in Judaism. And before we attempt to answer that, let us ask a further question: compared with what? There are two possible rivals. One is belief and the other is ritual.

It is well known that in the history of Christianity there have been phases in which supreme emphasis was laid on correct belief, or orthodoxy, as against incorrect belief, otherwise known as heterodoxy or heresy. On the whole that has *not* been true of Judaism. It has indeed always insisted, as the most fundamental of all its demands, that only the One God shall be acknowledged and worshipped. But beyond that and a few other affirmations of great generality, it has hardly ever attempted to define in any detail what a Jew must believe. Its emphasis has been on what a Jew must do: on action rather than belief. But action can be of two kinds, ethical and ritual. So we are left with the question of the relative importance which Judaism gives to each of these.

Of course that depends on the kind of Judaism we are talking about. To the priestly writers of the Pentateuch, ritual was a matter of supreme importance, almost as if the world would come to an end if the correct sacrifices were not offered at the correct times in the correct manner. Yet the same writings also include moral injunctions such as 'You shall love your neighbour as yourself', sometimes in close juxtaposition with the most minute regulations of the sacrificial cult, as if they were of equal significance.

On the other hand, the greatest of the Prophets – Amos, Hosea, Isaiah, Micah, Jeremiah and Deutero-Isaiah – took a very different view. According to them the priestly emphasis on ritual was a misunderstanding, a hangover from a pagan past. The

God of monotheism, according to them, has no interest in sacrifices or any other rituals, but *only* in right conduct. 'I hate, I despise your feasts', says Amos in God's name, 'and I take no delight in your solemn assemblies...But let justice roll down like waters, and righteousness like an ever-flowing stream' (5:21–24). That is a recurring theme in all the Prophets I have named (for example, Hos. 6:6, Isa. 1:11–17, Micah 6:6–8, Jer. 7:21–23, Isa. 58:1–8).

But what about the rabbis? Which of the two trends did they follow? The short answer is: both. For they were essentially lawyers. Their chief enterprise, known as *Halakhah*, was the legal interpretation of the Pentateuch, and since that made no clear distinction between ethics and ritual, they didn't either. All the commandments of the Pentateuch were equally grist for their jurisprudential mill.

And yet the rabbis were also deeply influenced by the Prophets. This is seen in the humaneness that pervades the *Halakhah* when it deals with matters of ethical import, such as civil and criminal law. But it is seen even more clearly in the other area of rabbinic activity, known as *Aggadah*. For when the rabbis stood back from their preoccupation with halakhic matters and reflected on the relative importance of ritual and ethics *in general terms*, they nearly always came down on the ethical side. Hence the Golden Rule as taught by Hillel and again by Rabbi Akiva – and we shall come back to that. Hence Rabbi Simlai's reduction of the 613 commandments to 11, then six, then three, then one, all of ethical import (*Makkot* 23b–24a). Hence, to give only one more example, the remarkable fact that the *viddui gadol* or 'Great Confession' recited on *Yom Kippur* lists *only* offences of a moral nature (cf. Routledge *Machzor*, Day of Atonement I, pp. 26–28). It doesn't, for example, include: 'For the sin we have committed against you by eating leaven during *Pesach*.'

We may sum up by saying that, halakhically, Rabbinic Judaism follows the Pentateuch in giving equal weight to ritual and ethics; aggadically, it follows the Prophets in giving greater weight to ethics. As for Progressive Judaism, it began by shifting the emphasis decidedly towards the Prophets, even to the extent of treating ritual with disdain. But in more recent times there has been a reversal of that trend, and whether that has now gone too far or not yet far enough is a matter of opinion.

THREE FUNDAMENTAL PRINCIPLES

The fundamental principles of Jewish ethics are, I suggest, three, and the first is the *Imitation of God*. This is grounded in the repeated injunction of the Torah that we are to walk in God's ways (for example, Deut. 10:12, 11:22, 13:5, 28:9) and more specifically in the exhortation, 'You shall be holy, for I the Eternal One your God am holy' (Lev. 19:2). It is exemplified by the teaching of Deuteronomy that, as God loves the stranger, so we should love the stranger (10:18f.), and further elaborated by the rabbis. Thus, on the phrase, 'to walk in God's ways' (Deut. 11:22), they commented: 'As God is called merciful, so you should be merciful; as God is called gracious, so you should be gracious; as God is called righteous, so you should be righteous; as God is called faithful, so you should be faithful' (*Sifrey* Deut. 49). Similarly, they taught that to walk after God's ways (Deut. 13:5) means to act in accordance with God's attributes: 'As God clothes the naked, visits the sick, comforts the mourners, and buries the dead, so should you' (*Sotah* 14a).

All this implies, of course, that we know what the divine attributes are. But even if we take the view that this is not a matter of revelation but that we merely ascribe to God all those qualities which we admire most in human beings, even then to try to live in accordance with those qualities, although the argument is then circular, is still a noble ambition.

Incidentally, this principle was included by Maimonides in his *Sefer ha-Mitzvot* (*Book of the Commandments*), listing the 613 commandments of the Torah – in spite of his well-known insistence that it is impossible for human beings to say anything positive about the nature of God; but he expresses himself carefully. Thus he concludes his account of the eighth of the 248 positive commandments by saying that it means 'to imitate (*l'hit dammot*) the good deeds and lofty attributes by which God is described *in a figurative way*, even though God is exalted above all such descriptions'.

The second and third fundamental principles of Jewish ethics are interlinked. They begin with the teaching that all humanity is descended from a common ancestor, *created in God's image*. Whatever the biblical author may have meant by 'image' (*tzelem* or *d'mut*, Gen. 1:26f., 5:1), it is clear that the concept confers on human beings the highest possible dignity, with the implication, which is what matters for our purpose, that every one of them is entitled to be treated with a kind of reverential respect. But to this must be added the *Golden Rule* to which I have already referred. As taught by Hillel, this means that what is hateful to ourselves we should not do to others (*Shab.* 31a). But the classical expression of it is the positive one in the nineteenth chapter of Leviticus, *V'ahavta l're-'acha kamocha*, 'You shall love your neighbour as yourself' (v. 18). It was this which Rabbi Akiva singled out as *k'lal gadol ba-torah*, the greatest principle of the Torah (*Sifra* 89b, Gen. R. 24:7).

Why do we need *both*, the Divine Image and the Golden Rule? Because the Golden Rule by itself could be taken to mean that we should care for others *only* as much as we care for ourselves – which, when our self-respect is low, might mean very little. But as Ben Azzai and Rabbi Tanchuma pointed out, when you think of the Divine Image in every human being, you are reminded that only the highest respect for others (as well as for yourself) is acceptable. Thus the principle of the Divine Image teaches us the *quality* of the way we should treat others; the Golden Rule teaches us the *equality* with which we should apply that principle to all our fellow men and women.

And why do we need both Hillel's negative formulation of the Golden Rule and the positive formulation of the Torah? Because each has a different set of consequences. Because we should not do to others what is hateful to ourselves, therefore all these are forbidden: murder (Ex. 20:13), manslaughter (Deut. 22:8), kidnapping (Ex. 20:15 as interpreted in the *Mechilta*), assault (Ex. 21:18), robbery (Lev. 19:13), theft (Lev. 19:11), lying (Lev. 19:11, Ex. 23:7), promise-breaking (Num. 30:3), slander (Lev. 19:16), insulting others (Lev. 25:17, *BM* 58b), coveting what they have (Ex. 20:14), judging them hastily (*Avot* 2:4) or uncharitably (*Avot* 1:6), cursing others (Lev. 1914), hating them (Lev. 19:17) and looking the other way when they are in danger (Lev. 19:16).

Because we should positively love – that is, care for – others, therefore we should respect their dignity (*Avot* 2:10) as well as their property (*Avot* 2:12), speak truthfully to them (Zech. 8:16), greet them cheerfully (*Avot* 1:15), spread peace among them (*Avot* 1:12), and perform acts of kindness (*g'milut chasadim*) towards them (*Pe'ah* 1:1, *Avot* 1:2).

FIVE SUPREME VALUES

In addition to these fundamental principles, it would be useful at this stage to identify the supreme values which suffuse all areas of Jewish ethics. They are, I suggest, five in number.

The first is the *sanctity of life* – at least of human life. (To what extent similar considerations apply to animal life is another subject, also important, but which we can't deal with in the time available.) It would not be quite correct to speak of the 'infinite' value of human life, as some writers do, for that would preclude the taking of it in contexts such as capital punishment and warfare which have in the past been considered legitimate. But that human life is considered *extremely precious* and in all normal circumstances inviolable, is clear. This may be inferred from the horror with which the Bible regards murder because it is the destruction of a being created in God's image (Gen. 9:6) and from its many life-affirming injunctions such as *u-vacharta ba-chayyim*, 'therefore choose life' (Deut. 30:19). But perhaps the most eloquent expression of the all-but-infinite value of human life is in the statement of the Mishnah that 'one who saves a single life is considered as if they had saved the whole world, and one who destroys a single life as if they had destroyed the whole world' (*Sanh.* 4:5).

The preciousness of human life also plays a major role in the *Halakhah*, where *pikkuach nefesh*, the saving of life, overrides practically all other considerations (*Pes.* 25a), even to the extent that the mere possibility of a human life being saved is sufficient, and questions of probability are set aside (*Ket.* 15b).

So far as capital punishment is concerned, it should be noted that, while the Bible demands it for the most serious offences, the Rabbis were clearly uncomfortable with it and tried to make conviction in capital cases virtually impossible (*Sanh.* 4–5, *Mak.* 1:10). It should also be added that nowadays many Jews would reject capital punishment altogether, in theory as well as in practice. As for warfare, many Jews nowadays tend towards pacifism, at least to the extent of believing that it can be justified only as a very last resort, when all attempts at a political solution of the conflict have failed, and then strictly in self-defence.

The next three major values of Jewish ethics are juxtaposed in the famous aphorism of Rabban Simeon ben Gamaliel, that the world, that is, civilisation, rests on three foundations: truth, justice and peace (*Avot* 1:18).

'Truth is God's seal', said the Rabbis (*chotamo shel ha-kadosh baruch hu emet, Shab.* 55a). Therefore, by the principle of the imitation of God, *truth* should inform all our thoughts, words and deeds. 'We should always revere God', says an ancient Jewish prayer, 'privately as well as publicly, acknowledge the truth and speak the truth in our hearts' (cf. Psalm 15:2). 'Keep far from anything that is false', warns the Torah (Exod. 23:7). 'Guard your tongue from evil, and your lips from speaking deceit', enjoins the Psalmist (34:14).

That *justice* is a major value in Judaism must be obvious to everybody. It can be seen in the repetition for emphasis when the Torah commands, *tzedek tzedek tirdof,* 'justice, justice shall you follow' (Deut. 16:20). It is a recurring theme in the Prophets, as when Amos thunders, 'Let justice roll down like waters, and righteousness like an ever-flowing stream' (5:24). It is enshrined in innumerable provisions of Jewish law. And the Rabbis added a significant point when they taught that 'the sword enters the world because of justice delayed and justice denied' (*Avot* 5:8).

As for *peace*, its praises resound like a refrain all through Jewish literature, beginning with Isaiah's celebrated prophecy of the day when they 'will beat their swords into ploughshares, and their spears into pruning-hooks, nation will not lift up sword against nation, and never again train for war' (2:4) and Micah's idyllic postscript, 'But everyone shall sit under their vine and under their fig-tree, and none shall make them afraid' (4:4). The Priestly Benediction, as the Rabbis liked to point out, concludes with the word 'peace' (Num. 3:26; Num. R. 11:7) as the greatest of all blessings. What the book of Proverbs says about wisdom was applied by the Rabbis to the Torah: that 'its ways are ways of pleasantness, and all its paths are peace' (Prov. 3:17, *Git.* 59b). The same repetition for emphasis which we have noted about justice is found in Psalm 34 when it says, 'Seek peace, and pursue it' (v. 14), and in Hillel's evocation of that verse in his famous motto, 'Be of the disciples of Aaron, loving peace, and pursuing peace, loving your fellow human beings, and drawing them towards Torah' (*Avot* 1:12).

The fifth supreme value of Jewish ethics is compassion, in Hebrew *rachamim*. It is a quality frequently attributed to God. Indeed, the famous passage in the book of Exodus known as

'The Thirteen Attributes of God' (34:6), which is solemnly recited on the High Holydays, was so interpreted by the Rabbis as to make all thirteen more or less synonymous with compassion (Num. R. 21:16, *Pes. K.* 57a). So, too, one of the commonest appellations of God in Rabbinic literature is *ha-rachaman*, 'The Merciful One'. And by the same 'imitation' logic we have already noted more than once, compassion is constantly enjoined on human beings. 'As God is merciful, so you should be merciful' (*Sifrey* Deut. 49). One talmudic passage speaks of compassion as one of three distinguishing characteristics of the Jewish people, the other two being modesty and kindness (*Yev.* 79a). We may wish to comment *hal'vai*, would it were always true, but the implied aspiration is itself significant.

LIKE AND UNLIKE

So far we have considered only the fundamental principles and general values which should govern the mutual behaviour of any two individuals simply because of their common humanity. But many ethical problems arise from the fact that human beings are not alike. On the contrary, they are infinitely various. As the Mishnah teaches, 'God stamped every human being with the seal of Adam, yet not one of them is like another' (*Sanh.* 4:5). Unfortunately, we tend to react negatively to conspicuous differences, whether in appearance or manner or speech or opinion: to view them with suspicion, or to see them as a threat, or as betokening inferiority, and therefore as rendering inapplicable, or less cogent, the general principles we have discussed. Consequently Judaism warns against that temptation.

Individual differences, it teaches, are not to be deplored but celebrated as tokens of God's creative wisdom. On the phrase *elohey ha-ruchot l'chol basar*, 'God of the spirits of all flesh' (Num. 27:16), the Midrash, noting the plural, comments: 'When you see a great multitude of people, say: I praise You, Eternal God, Sovereign of the universe, to whom the innermost secrets of every one of them is known. For as their faces are not alike, so their minds are not alike, but every one of them has a mind of their own' (Num. R. 21:2). Similarly, the Mishnah teaches that just because human beings are infinitely various, therefore every one must say: *Bishvili nivra ha-'olam*, 'the world was created for my sake' (*Sanh.* 4:5). And among the blessings for various occasions the traditional liturgy includes one to be recited 'on seeing strangely formed persons, such as giants or dwarfs', which praises God *m'shanneh ha-b'riyyot*, for having created human beings in various forms.

Therefore the general principles and values we have considered most certainly do apply to the way we conduct ourselves towards those who are different from ourselves, and indeed are all the more to be emphasised just because they are liable to be thought inapplicable.

STRONG AND WEAK

Not only do human beings differ from each other in innumerable ways, but some are stronger and some are weaker – physically or mentally or economically or politically. And therefore the chief test of any ethical code is how it instructs the stronger to behave towards the weaker, what concern it evinces towards the most vulnerable members of society.

Among the most vulnerable in most societies have been *women*. Here two things must be said. The first is that prior to modern times Judaism compared well with most societies in its attitude to women. According to the first Creation Story, though not the second, men and women were created simultaneously – 'male and female God created them' (Gen. 1:27). The Matriarchs and other women, like Miriam, Deborah and Hannah, play a prominent role in the biblical narrative. A number of laws were enacted for the protection of women, especially widows. The last chapter of the book of Proverbs paints a dignified picture of *eshet chayil*, the 'virtuous wife'. And all these trends were continued and developed in post-biblical times.

On the other hand the role which women were encouraged or even allowed to play outside the home, in society, was severely limited. They were exempted from religious duties which had to be performed at specified times (*Kid.* 1:7), theoretically for their own benefit but in practice often to the point of forbidding them to do these things. They were debarred from playing an equal role with men in synagogue worship. And in spite of all improvements in their status, such as the medieval prohibition of polygamy, they continued to suffer from several disadvantages in the laws of marriage and divorce.

So it came about that by the time of the Enlightenment, Gentile society had begun to overtake Judaism in its treatment of women and was moving towards giving them complete equality with men. And since traditional Judaism could not modernise itself sufficiently quickly, it was left to the Progressive movement to institute corresponding changes within Judaism.

Next to women, the most vulnerable members of any society are those who are 'in it but not of it', in other words, resident aliens or *strangers*. Accordingly, they are frequently commended in the Bible as particularly requiring sympathy and generosity on the part of the indigenous majority. 'The strangers who live with you,' says the nineteenth chapter of Leviticus, 'shall be to you like the natives among you, and you shall love them as yourselves, for you were strangers in the land of Egypt' (19:34). There are numerous such passages in the Torah and corresponding exhortations in the Prophets, and they raise serious questions about the treatment of asylum seekers in contemporary societies.

Another vulnerable group are of course the *poor* and, as one would expect, they are constantly singled out for special concern and compassion on the part of their fellow citizens. Again and again the rich are enjoined to give to the poor and reprimanded if they do so stingily or grudgingly (Deut. 15:7–11). In Rabbinic Judaism there is enormous stress on charity, called *tz'dakah*, a word which in biblical times had meant 'justice' or 'righteousness' and retained something of that connotation in that giving to the poor was considered not so much an act of generosity as a duty incumbent on everybody. Its purpose was to rectify an unfair situation, and it was therefore to be performed without condescension and anonymously, so that the recipient would not be embarrassed. There are also attempts to construct, at least in theory, a social order in which excessive impoverishment is periodically remedied. The twenty-fifth chapter of Leviticus, with its sabbatical year and jubilee, is the best example of that.

Other vulnerable categories are orphans, often commended in the sources of Judaism as calling for compassionate concern, as well as the bodily disabled and the mentally sick, and those whose sexual orientation is unconventional. How a society treats all these vulnerable groups is as good a test as any of how civilised it is.

SPECIALISED RELATIONSHIPS

The general principles and values of Jewish ethics require special applications in special contexts, when we are dealing with the mutual obligations of two or more persons, not simply because of their common humanity, but because they stand in a special relationship to one another. Examples are the relations between husbands and wives, parents and children, teachers and pupils, employers and employees, merchants and customers, doctors and patients, media and public, judges and litigants, governments and citizens, nation and nation, humanity and environment. Each of these is a subject for a whole evening, or even several, so that I cannot go into them now, but I am glad to know that several will be dealt with in future sessions of this series.

THE SOURCES OF JEWISH ETHICS

Let me conclude by raising a question which logically should have come at the beginning. What are the sources of Jewish ethical teachings? Where are they to be found? To a large extent, the answer will have emerged from what has been said already, and especially from the sorts of quotations that have been adduced. But it may be useful to clarify and amplify a little.

Clearly, one of the major sources is the Prophetic literature with its many moral exhortations. For instance, Isaiah: 'Cease to do evil, learn to do good; seek justice, rescue the oppressed, defend the orphan, plead for the widow' (1:16f.). Or Deutero-Isaiah: 'Is not this the fast I look for: to release the shackles of injustice, to undo the fetters of bondage, to let the oppressed go free, and to break every cruel chain? Is it not to share your bred with the hungry, and to bring the homeless poor into your house? When you see the naked, to cover them, and never to hide yourself from your own flesh?' (58:6f.). Or Zechariah: 'These are the things that you shall do: speak the truth to one another, render in your gates judgements that are true and make for peace' (8:16).

Another major source are the commandments of the Torah in so far as they are of a general ethical nature. Because they occur in the Pentateuch and are expressed in the imperative, the Rabbis treated them as legislation rather than only exhortation, and subjected them to legal interpretation. But in themselves they are not necessarily very different from the Prophetic exhortations. Examples are some of the Ten Commandments, for instance: 'Honour your father and your mother … You shall not murder. You shall not commit adultery. You shall not steal. You shall not bear false witness against your neighbour' (Ex. 20:12f.). Or, from the Holiness Code: 'You shall not curse the deaf, or put a stumbling block before the blind' (Lev. 19:14).

Some fine ethical teachings are to be found in the Apocrypha and Pseudepigrapha, for instance in the Testaments of the Twelve Patriarchs: 'And now, my children, I beg you: love one another. Drive hatred out of your hearts. Love one another in deed, word and thought' (Testament of Gad 6:1).

Most important for the subsequent development of Judaism is of course the vast Rabbinic literature. But here we must distinguish between its two *genres*, *Halakhah* and *Aggadah*. Many of the ethical values of the Bible, whether expressed in legislative or hortatory form, were embodied by the Rabbis in the minute rules and regulations of the *Halakhah*. For instance, the mutual obligations of husbands and wives, and of parents and children, are spelt out in minute jurisprudential detail. But side by side with these, the aggadic literature includes many ethical teachings that are, once again, in the form of exhortation rather than legislation. Best known perhaps are those to be found in the Ethics of the Fathers, such as 'Let your neighbour's honour be as dear to you as your own' and 'Let your neighbour's property be as dear to you as your own' (Avot 2:10, 12).

But we should note that *Halakhah* and *Aggadah* are not always in perfect synchronisation with one another. For the *Halakhah*, being subject to a strict methodology, can only advance slowly, whereas the *Aggadah*, being untrammelled by procedural rules, can respond more readily to changing attitudes. An example of that is the Golden Rule which has already been quoted two or three times. Halakhically, 'you shall love your neighbour as yourself' was understood to refer to fellow Jews only (see, for example, *Sifra* to Lev. 19:18 and Maimonides, *Sefer ha-Mitzvot*, Positive Commandment 206). Even the injunction to love the stranger, which occurs in the same chapter of Leviticus (19:34), was not applied to non-Jews, since the Hebrew word *ger* was understood to mean 'proselyte'. Of course the decent treatment of unconverted non-Jews is also enjoined, but in other contexts

(for example, *Git.* 61a). But the *Aggadah* has always understood
'your neighbour' to refer to any human being, as is clear, for
instance, from Hillel's famous teaching, 'Be of the disciples of
Aaron, loving peace and pursuing peace, *ohev et ha-b'riyyot*,
loving your fellow human beings, and drawing them near to the
Torah' (*Avot* 1:12). Needless to say, most Jews nowadays
understand the Golden Rule in the universalistic sense of the
Aggadah, and a Progressive *Halakhah* would so interpret it for all
purposes.

To these sources we must add a number of medieval and later
works of a moralistic nature such as *The Duties of the Heart* by
Bachya ibn Pakuda (eleventh century), *The Book of the Pious* by
Judah he-Chasid (twelfth century) and *The Path of the Upright* by
Moses Chayyim Luzzatto (eighteenth century). There is also an
extensive literature of 'Hebrew Ethical Wills' an excellent
anthology of which, edited by Israel Abrahams, was published
by the Jewish Publication Society in 1926. In addition, the huge
literature of Chasidism contains many fine ethical teachings.

The modern period has been one of scholarly research rather
than creative development. But it is surprising, especially
considering the emphasis on ethics in Progressive Judaism, how
little attempt has been made to isolate the ethical teachings of
Judaism from the broader literature in which they are
embedded, and present them in a systematic way. Virtually the
first scholar to do so was the philosophy professor Moritz
Lazarus in his book *Die Ethik des Judentums*, published in 1901.
There is also an excellent little book entitled *Jewish Ethics* by my
teacher Rabbi Israel Mattuck, published in 1953. But as both of
these have long been out of print you may be interested to know
that my own attempt to summarise the topic, although only in
pamphlet form, is available. It was published four years ago
under the title *Principles of Jewish Ethics*.

Judaism and Animal Welfare: Overview and Some Questions

18 March 2000

INTRODUCTION

Writers about Judaism have often extolled its humaneness towards animals: from Josephus, who wrote of Moses, 'So thorough a lesson has he given us in gentleness and humanity that he does not overlook even the brute beasts, authorising their use only in accordance with the Law, and forbidding all other employment of them',[1] to Joseph Hertz, who saw in its consideration for animals a characteristic of the Hebrew Bible which has been 'strangely overlooked in most ethical systems, not excluding Christianity'.[2]

In these eulogies there is much truth, but also some exaggeration. Not everything in the Jewish garden is lovely, nor is everywhere else a wasteland. Hinduism, Buddhism, Taoism and Jainism all have teachings about animals which in some respects go beyond Judaism.[3] Our task is not to praise but to appraise: to give a soberly factual account of what Judaism has taught on our subject in the past, and then to ask in what respects it may now need to go further.

1. HUMAN BEINGS AND OTHER ANIMALS

Although our inquiry is a practical one, we must begin with a theoretical question: what, according to Judaism, is the status of animals in the divine scheme?

There is a sense in which human beings are part and parcel of the animal world, not essentially different from other species. That view is not generally found in Jewish tradition, except in Kohelet who says explicitly that we are nothing but animals, and adds: 'For the fate of humans and the fate of animals is the same: as one dies, so dies the other... they all have the same spirit, and the pre-eminence of humans over animals is nothing' (3:18f.).

Although that last phrase is familiar to observant Jews from the daily morning prayer in which it is quoted,[4] it is far from typical. On the contrary, Judaism normally teaches that 'the pre-eminence of humans over animals' is vast. Furthermore, that view is surely to be endorsed both from a biological and from a theological point of view. For in their ability to think and to feel, to remember and communicate, to build machines and manipulate their environment, to produce art, music and literature, to discern between right and wrong, to apprehend divinity, to create and transmit culture: in all these respects human beings are, if not unique, enormously superior to all other animals.

This note is struck already in the Creation Story, with its announcement that human beings were created in God's image, and commanded: 'Be fruitful and multiply, fill the earth and subdue it, and have dominion over the fish of the sea and the birds of the air and every living thing that moves upon the earth' (Gen. 1:28); and it is echoed in Psalm 8 with its triumphant exclamation: 'You have made human beings little less than divine, and crowned them with glory and honour. You have given them dominion over the works of Your hands; You have put all things under their feet, all sheep and oxen, and also the beasts of the field, the birds of the air, and the fish of the sea, and all who swim the pathways of the sea' (vv. 7–9).

Here let me interject that much hinges on the meaning of 'have dominion', which in the Creation Story comes from the verb *radah* and in Psalm 8 from the verb *mashal*. Both connote rulership but leave open the question whether the power it confers is absolute or conditional.

That it is conditional is suggested by the affirmation that *God cares* for animals. The Creation Story, for instance, declares that vegetation was created to provide food not only for humans but for animals as well (Gen. 1:29f.). In the Flood Story, God commands Noah to go to great lengths to save every animal species (Gen. 6:19; cf. 8:1). The book of Jonah memorably ends with God's rebuke to the reluctant prophet: 'And should not I have pity on Nineveh, that great city, in which there are more than a hundred and twenty thousand persons who do not know their right hand from their left, *and also much cattle*?' (4:11). Psalm 104 describes in loving detail how God provides food for all creatures (vv. 11–29; cf. Psalms 36:9, 145:16, 147:9; Job 38:41). And a Midrash sums up, 'Just as God has compassion on humans, so God has compassion on animals' (Deut. R. 6:1). The clear implication of all this is that what God cherishes *we* must cherish.

The condition on which God has given us 'dominion' over animals is that we exercise it *responsibly*. If we do so, all will be well; if not, disaster will ensue. That point is made in a Rabbinic comment based on the fact that the imperative *r'du* in the divine command to Adam and Eve (Gen. 1:28) could grammatically be taken either from the verb *radah*, 'to have dominion', or from the verb *yarad*, 'to go down', the comment being that if we are worthy, we shall have dominion over other animals; if not, we shall descend to their level (Gen. R. 8:12).

If we now ask whether this is a satisfactory philosophy of the relationship between humans and animals, we have to say two things. On the one hand, it contrasts favourably with the attitude to animals that prevailed in the Western world until the nineteenth century. Prior to that, according to the historian Cecil Roth, 'cruelty to animals was nowhere illegal – except under Jewish Law'.[5] In England, as he goes on to point out, a major shift in attitude occurred as recently as 1824, which saw the publication of a book entitled *Moral Enquiries on the Situation of Men and Brutes* by Lewis Gompertz, who was a Jew, and, partly as result of that, the establishment of the Society for the Prevention of Cruelty to Animals.[6]

On the other hand, the traditional Jewish view falls short of the most advanced thinking of our time, which, influenced by Darwinian and post-Darwinian biology, has stressed anew, in a manner reminiscent of Kohelet, how much all living things, humans included, have in common. As Dr John Launer wrote in a recent article in *Manna*, 'We are the comparatively recent descendants of tree shrews and the distant progeny of bacteria... A fuller understanding of our connectedness to other life forms... might lead us to reconsider our superiority. It might also prompt us to reassess our attitudes towards our multi-farious biological relations.'[7]

This kind of thinking also underlies the modern emphasis on 'animal rights'.[8] Whether there really are such rights is, I suggest, an academic question.[9] For from a common-sense point of view rights and duties are simply correlatives. If A has a duty to B, then B has a right to the benefit of the fulfilment of that duty. But the advantage of 'animal rights' language is that it challenges the anthropocentrism which has hitherto dominated Jewish, and Western, thought about animals. Judaism, for instance, has characteristically taught that all animals were created solely or primarily for the benefit of humanity.[10]

Here then is the first of my questions: as Progressive Jews, should we not be in the vanguard of those who acknowledge the inadequacy of the traditional anthropocentrism, and try to see the animal world from a cosmic rather than merely a human point of view? Should we not say that the myriads of species of animals serve many purposes which are fully known only to the Creator and among which their usefulness to humanity is at best only one?

2. THE CONSERVATION OF ANIMALS

The relevance of this becomes immediately apparent when we consider how many millions[11] of species of animals have already become extinct as a direct or indirect result of anthropocentrically motivated human activity. This calamity could of course not be foreseen in pre-modern times, and therefore we must not expect to find much guidance concerning it in the classical sources of Judaism; and yet one or two hints may be found already there.

Most obviously, the Flood Story is itself an object lesson in the conservation of species. Even more explicitly, there is a Midrash on it according to which a raven said to Noah: 'You must hate me, for you did not send a scout from the species of birds of which there are seven pairs in the ark, but from a species of which there is only one pair. Therefore, if I had been struck down by the power of the sun or of the cold, would not the world be missing a species?' (*San.* 108b).[12]

That human irresponsibility can lead to ecological disaster was strikingly perceived, even earlier, by the prophet Hosea when, after denouncing various social evils, he continued: 'Therefore the land mourns, and all who live in it languish;

together with the wild animals and the birds of the air, even the fish of the sea are perishing' (4:3).

Which brings me to my second question: to the commandments of Judaism, should we not add this twofold ecological one: negatively, to refrain from any activity, such as deforestation and environmental pollution, which may destroy essential animal habitats and, positively, to take all necessary steps to save endangered species from extinction?

3. THE TREATMENT OF ANIMALS

We have said that our 'dominion' over animals is granted to us on the condition that we exercise it responsibly. Another way of putting that may be taken from a comment on the Psalm verse, 'The heavens are the heavens of the Eternal One, but the earth God has given to humankind' (115:16). On this Abraham ibn Ezra remarks 'that humanity is like God's steward on earth in charge of all that it contains' (ad loc.).

This concept of stewardship is central to our subject, and, as we have already seen, what it primarily entails is conservation. But equally obviously, it has implications for the way we treat animals, especially domestic ones, since by domesticating them we assume responsibility for them. That this requires considerate behaviour on our part is a major theme of Jewish literature, expressed in exhortations, stories and regulations.

The fundamental principle is stated positively in the book of Proverbs when it says, 'A righteous man knows the soul [that is, considers the feelings] of his domestic animals' (12.10). The corresponding negative principle is *tza'ar ba'aley chayyim*, animal suffering. This is a rabbinic term, and there is an unresolved debate as to whether the prohibition of it is *d'oraita or d'rabbanan*, that is, whether it has Sinaitic or only post-Sinaitic authority (Tos. *BM* 32b).[13] But, as Rabbi J. David Bleich points out, the question 'is of no significance whatsoever insofar as the normative regulations prohibiting overt acts of cruelty vis-à-vis animals are concerned'.[14]

Relevant narratives include, once again, the story of the Flood, which the aggadists greatly elaborated, stressing how much trouble Noah and his family took, even to the point of denying themselves sleep, to ensure that the animals in the Ark were adequately fed (*Tanchuma, Noach* 9, 15a; *Midrash Tehillim* on Psalm 37:1). There is also the story of how Rebekah made a favourable impression on Abraham's servant by giving water not only to him but also to his camels (Gen. 24:46).

In the *Aggadah*, Moses, by his tender care for a straying lamb, proves his worthiness to become the shepherd of God's flock, the people of Israel (Exod. R. 2:2). And there is the story of how Judah the Prince, when a terrified calf, about to be slaughtered, sought refuge under his coat, said to it, 'Go, for this you were created', and was divinely punished for his heartlessness until he redeemed himself by saving a litter of newborn weasels whom his maidservant was about to sweep out of the house (*BM* 85a).

Turning from narrative to legislation, we must note a number of specific laws forbidding cruelty and enjoining kindness to animals as found in the Bible and supplemented in the Talmud.

It is forbidden to eat what the Rabbis called *ever min ha-chai*, a limb torn from a living animal (*Sifrey* Deut. 76). This prohibition is first found in the Noah story (Gen. 9:4) and restated in Deuteronomy (12:23) and was considered so fundamental that it was included among the seven laws incumbent on the descendants of Noah and therefore on all human beings (*Tosefta AZ* 8:4–6; *San.* 56b). Here I must interject, however, that the traditional hard-and-fast distinction between laws applicable only to Jews and laws applicable to human beings generally cannot be sustained from a Progressive point of view. For ethical precepts are by their very nature universal, which is indeed particularly obvious where the welfare of animals is concerned, since they suffer just as much whether ill-treated by Jews or by non-Jews.

Crossbreeding of cattle is forbidden (Lev. 19:19). An ox and a donkey may not be yoked together when ploughing (Deut. 22:10), for the obvious reason, spelt out by Ibn Ezra, that it would be cruel, since a donkey is not as strong as an ox, and 'God has mercy on all creatures' (ad loc.). An ox may not be muzzled when treading the corn (Deut. 25:4). A sacrificial animal must be allowed to live for at least seven days, and even after that it is forbidden to slaughter the mother and its young on the same day (Lev. 22:27f.). Similarly, a mother bird must not be taken from its nest together with its young (Deut. 22:6f.).

Domestic animals, like servants, must be allowed to rest on the sabbath (Exod. 20:10, 23:12, Deut. 5:14). Even the 'beasts of the field', that is, wild animals, may help themselves to what grows of itself in the sabbatical year, when the land lies fallow (Exod. 23:11). A domestic animal that has strayed from its owner's domain must be taken back to him, even if he is your enemy (Exod. 23:4). An animal that has collapsed under its burden must be helped up, even if its owner is your enemy (Exod. 23:5, Deut. 22:4).

The biblical legislation was amplified by the rabbis in various ways. They ruled, for instance, that it is forbidden to buy a domestic or a wild animal or a bird if one does not have the means to feed it. (*J. Yev.* 15:3; *J. Kid.* 4:8). From the verse, 'I will give grass in your fields for your cattle, and you shall eat and be satisfied' (Deut. 11:15) they inferred: 'It is forbidden to eat before giving food to one's animals' (*Ber.* 40a). The laws of sabbath rest were relaxed when necessary to rescue an animal that had fallen into a ditch (*Shab.* 126b).

Some of the medieval authorities went even further. Maimonides, for instance, ruled that the prohibition against muzzling an ox when treading the corn applies equally to other animals and other produce;[15] and commenting on the biblical prohibition against killing an animal and its young on the same day (Lev. 22:28), he explained that maternal love is just as strong in animals as it is in humans.[16] Judah he-Chasid taught that whoever causes suffering to an animal by overloading it or by hitting it will be held to account before the heavenly court,[17] and that if a strange dog enters your house you may chase it away, but only by gentle means.[18] And Abraham Gumbiner remarked that even with respect to somebody else's animal, it is a good deed to feed it.[19]

All this is splendid and has prompted modern expounders of Judaism to praise it unreservedly.[20] But to do so is to gloss over the less favourable evidence which, in loyalty to truth, needs also to be acknowledged. For one thing, the regulations we have noted, with only two exceptions, apply to *domestic* rather than wild animals. Furthermore, there is a strong tendency in Jewish tradition to regard these laws as enacted, not so much for the physical good of animals as for the moral good of human beings, so that they may not acquire cruel habits and so come to behave cruelly to one another (anthropocentrism again!).[21] There is even some disagreement whether the law about helping a collapsed animal applies when its owner is a non-Jew.[22]

The story of the *Akedah* was no doubt intended to evoke horror at the thought of Abraham sacrificing his son, but there is no hint of a suggestion that there is any cause to feel sorry for the ram that is slaughtered in his place.[23] Likewise, the Samson story betrays no squeamishness when it relates how he tore a young lion asunder with his bare hands (Jud. 14:6).

The ritual of the scapegoat (Lev. 16:7–10), as understood in the Mishnah, involved pushing the unfortunate animal backwards over a precipice so that, by the time it was half-way down it was broken to pieces (Yoma 6:6). Similarly, the expiation of an unexplained murder required a ritual which involved the breaking of the neck of a heifer by the elders of he nearest town (Deut. 21:1–9; *Sotah* 9:1–9). Again, an ox that had gored a human being was to be stoned to death (Exod. 21:28; *San.* 7:4). Although these practices ceased with the destruction of the Temple or were subsequently discontinued, Rabbinic Literature nowhere expresses any qualms about them on grounds of cruelty.

The truth is that in this matter ancient Judaism was indeed far ahead of its time, but to credit it with a modern fastidiousness about animal welfare is anachronistic, and to that extent Judaism has still some catching up to do.

For instance, the traditional *Halakhah* has not yet addressed some problems which have become acute only in recent times as a result either of new developments in farming technology or of enhanced sensitivity about animal suffering. Perhaps the most serious of these is factory farming, including the obscene practice of confining hens in battery cages so small that they can never flap their wings.

Here then is a third question: should not any animal food produced under such conditions be forbidden on grounds of cruelty to animals?

4. KILLING ANIMALS FOR NUTRITIONAL PURPOSES

This brings us to a crucial question: for what purposes may human beings kill animals? In the past, six such purposes have been considered legitimate: nutritional, sacrificial, recreational, ecological, commercial and experimental. Let us examine each in turn.

On the question whether it is permissible to kill animals for food, the traditional answer can be stated briefly. Because the

Creation Story speaks of 'every herb yielding seed' as permitted to Adam and Eve (Gen. 1:29), it was assumed that our earliest ancestors were vegetarians. But because in the Flood Story God says to Noah and his sons: 'Every living thing that moves shall be food for you' (Gen. 9:3), therefore the tradition teaches that from that time onwards the consumption of meat was permitted (*San.* 59b) – albeit on the condition we have already noted that the prohibition against tearing a limb from a living animal, was observed. Subsequently, the tradition continues, to the Jewish people only, an elaborate code was revealed as to which animals might be eaten and how they were to be killed.

To the obvious question, how the killing of animals could be reconciled with the rule against causing them suffering, the answer was given, either that it is an exception to the rule or that the rule is sufficiently satisfied if the killing is done in the most humane way possible.[24]

Either way, meat eating has been considered perfectly legitimate in Jewish tradition all through the ages. There is even something of a bias in its favour, for the Torah says explicitly that the craving for meat may be satisfied (Deut. 12:20f.), and meat featured in the joyful celebration of the festivals. In the words of Maimonides, 'there is no rejoicing without meat'.[25]

There is indeed a question whether meat eating should not be confined to the learned, who understand the legislation involved, and forbidden to the ignorant, who do not (*Pes.* 49b). Nevertheless, vegetarianism has never been common among Jews, and when individuals opted for it they were regarded as practising a kind of supererogatory piety which was not even commanded to all and sundry.[26]

From an Orthodox point of view that is the end of the matter, since it does not admit the possibility of any valid ethical principles unstated in the Torah. Thus Rabbi J. David Bleich begins his exhaustive essay on 'Vegetarianism and Judaism' by saying: 'In Jewish teaching, not only are normative laws regarded as binding solely upon the authority of divine revelation, but ethical principles as well are regarded as endowed with validity and commended as goals of human aspiration only if they, too, are divinely revealed'.[27] In other words, there have been no genuine ethical advances since Sinai. Since Progressive Judaism emphatically rejects that view, the traditional position is not necessarily to be accepted as final.

Consequently the question – my fourth – arises whether the time has not come to go one step further and, instead of looking on vegetarianism as a pardonable eccentricity, declare it to be positively commendable, even though not obligatory.

If, however, meat eating is to continue to be regarded as legitimate, then two further questions arise. First, whether the biblical and traditional distinctions between permitted and forbidden species are to be upheld. From a non-fundamentalist point of view, the laws in question can hardly be said to be divinely revealed. Neither can they all be justified on hygienic grounds, though that may be true of *some* of them. In short, they cannot, in their entirety, be rationally justified, and therefore Progressive Judaism has never officially endorsed them.

Nevertheless I think it would accord with the prevailing mood among Progressive Jews today to recognise that every society has such food taboos, going back to ancient times; that, since they are essentially non-rational, there is little point in arguing about them; and that, if we wish to identify ourselves with *k'lal yisrael*, the Jewish people as a whole, we may as well go along with those which Jewish tradition has upheld.

Therefore my next question (number five) is whether something to that effect should now be taught in the name of Progressive Judaism.

The other question, on which Progressive Judaism has likewise never committed itself, is whether *shechitah*, the traditional Jewish method of slaughter, is to be regarded as obligatory. Here, again, we can hardly go along with the fundamentalist view of it as divinely ordained. Therefore it must be judged by its humaneness. Of course defenders of traditional Judaism maintain that it *is* the most humane method, and they may well be right. However, whether that is the case is a scientific, not a theological, question. And because scientific opinion is divided, therefore it must remain, to that extent, open.

All I think we can do in the name of Progressive Judaism – and my sixth question is whether I am right in so thinking – is to make this conditional three-part statement. If shechitah is more humane than other ways of slaughtering animals, then we should not only insist on it for ourselves but urge it upon non-Jews as well. And even if it is only as humane as any other method, we should still adhere to it for the sake of k'lal yisrael. But if and when there is a clear consensus in the scientific world that it is less humane than some other method, such as prior stunning, then we should opt for that other method, for the universal-ethical principle of tza'ar ba'aley chayyim *has a much stronger claim on us than the technicalities of any ancient ritual code.*

5. KILLING ANIMALS FOR SACRIFICIAL PURPOSES

A second purpose which has in the past been regarded as a legitimate reason for killing animals is the religious ritual of sacrifice. Fortunately, this is not, in Judaism, operative law, since the Jewish sacrificial cult ceased with the destruction of the Temple nearly 2,000 years ago. Even so, it is messianic law, in the sense that the hope for its ultimate restoration is a principle of Orthodox Judaism and a major theme of its liturgy. As the late Chief Rabbi Lord Jakobovits pointed out, 'The truth is that sacrifices are absolutely central to the very structure of our daily prayers'.[28]

This theme links up with the preceding one because the institution of sacrifice derives from the belief that the gods were sufficiently like humans to require food. Admittedly, the Hebrew Bible occasionally repudiates that belief (for example, Psalm 50:12f.), and Rabbi Bernard J. Bamberger was no doubt right when he wrote, 'Very likely the authors of Leviticus regarded sacrifice as simply an act of homage to God and not as a means of satisfying His hunger.'[29] Nevertheless, traces of the primitive notion survive in the term 'the food of God', which occurs six times in the Torah (Lev. 21:6, 8, 17, 21, 22, 22:25), and in the related expression *re'ach nicho'ach*, referring to the 'sweet odour' of the burnt offerings, intended to give God pleasure, which occurs no less than 39 times.

Furthermore, some of the sacrificial animals, after being symbolically offered to God, were actually consumed by the worshippers who brought them or the priests who slaughtered them. But that does not apply to the burnt offering, which, as its name implies, was wholly destroyed and therefore served no utilitarian purpose at all.

From a non-fundamentalist point of view, there can be no religiously valid ritual that requires the killing of animals; consequently such an act would be tantamount to wanton destruction, which Jewish tradition forbids on the basis of the biblical prohibition against destroying fruit trees when besieging a city (Deut. 20:19).

Therefore my seventh question is: should not Progressive Judaism declare that, if ever it should become possible to rebuild the Temple and restore the ancient sacrificial cult, to do so would be not only theologically absurd but also morally wrong?

6. KILLING ANIMALS FOR RECREATIONAL PURPOSES

It could be said that the secular equivalent of killing animals as a religious ritual is to kill them by way of sport and entertainment. This, however, is something Judaism has generally frowned upon. The gladiatorial contests, in which animals as well as humans were 'butchered to make a Roman holiday',[30] held little attraction for Jews, and those who refrained from attending them are commended in the Talmud (*AZ* 18b) with the Psalm verse, 'Happy is the one who has not walked in the counsel of the wicked' (1:1).

On the particular subject of hunting there is a responsum by the famous eighteenth-century rabbi of Prague, Ezekiel Laudau, who disallows it, not exactly on the ground of the suffering it inflicts on the hunted animals, but because it is an uncalled-for and cruel activity which, furthermore, endangers the life of the hunter in contravention of the principle, 'Take good care of yourselves' (Deut. 4:15), which forbids such unnecessary risk-taking.[31]

To me it seems very clear that killing animals as a sport, rather than for food or for some other valid purpose, must be ethically wrong for the double reason that it involves unnecessary destruction and that it inflicts unnecessary suffering. That applies not only to bear-baiting, dog-fighting and cock-fighting, which are today illegal in most countries, and to bull-fighting, which is still legal in some, but also to deer-hunting, fox-hunting and game-shooting, and indeed to fishing as well, as long as these activities cannot be shown to be necessary for a valid purpose beyond the sporting pleasure they provide.

With this proviso, should not Progressive Judaism call on its adherents both to abstain from such activities and to urge legislation prohibiting them as and when the state of public opinion makes such legislation possible? That is my eighth question.

7. KILLING ANIMALS FOR ECOLOGICAL PURPOSES

It is sometimes alleged by defenders of fox-hunting and similar sports that they are a necessary or the most efficient means of animal population control. Such claims should not be dismissed out of hand: there may be an element of truth in some of them.

In any case, it can hardly be doubted that human beings have a right to protect themselves, their livestock and their crops against destructive animals. This applies to microbes, parasites, insects, birds of prey, rodents, foxes, wolves and other predators, and no restrictions are specified in Jewish law as to the methods that may be used to destroy them. Nevertheless it follows from the spirit of Jewish law that it should always be done in the most humane way possible.

Just as it is permissible to protect human beings from animals, so it is permissible to protect animals from one another. In other words, culling, too, is legitimate, with the same proviso, that it is done as humanely as possible. Indeed, the more human activity disturbs the self-regulation of nature, the greater is our obligation to do what we can to restore the ecological balance.

8. KILLING ANIMALS FOR COMMERCIAL PURPOSES

In addition to the purposes already mentioned, it has almost universally been thought legitimate to kill animals as a source of raw materials for the manufacture of commercial products such as fur, leather, ivory, and cosmetics. Rabbinic law, too, has generally taken this view, on the ground that animals exist for the sake of human beings, who may therefore use them in any way that is beneficial to them, although to kill them for no purpose at all would be to transgress the law which forbids all wanton destruction, just as to cause them pain without reason would be cruelty.

Today, however, that assumption is being challenged by various animal welfare organisations, and to my mind they are right. To kill animals for food, or to maintain an ecological balance, is one thing. To kill them for the manufacture of luxury goods and for commercial profit, is quite another. For animals, although they rank below human beings, nevertheless rank above mineral and vegetables. They are sentient beings, and therefore 'important entities' (*Zevachim* 72b, 73a). They do not exist solely for our benefit. They serve all sorts of purposes which we may or may not fully understand. Their life may not be as precious as human life, but it is still precious. Therefore to kill them for what are essentially frivolous purposes cannot be ethically right.

Of course, if the luxury goods to which I have referred are merely by-products of the killing of animals for legitimate purposes such as food production and ecological control, there can be no objection. But in many cases that is not so. Mink coats, crocodile handbags and ivory ornaments, for example, result from killings that have no morally legitimate purpose and that, as with the clubbing to death of young seals, involve great cruelty.

Surely a Progressive Halakhah *should make it clear that to engage in such activities, and to derive benefit from them, is unacceptable. That is my ninth question.*

9. KILLING ANIMALS FOR EXPERIMENTAL PURPOSES

Apart from food and control, the only justification for killing animals is to provide for human beings, not merely a benefit, but a *life-saving*, or potentially life-saving, benefit. Hence there is general agreement that it is legitimate to carry out medical experiments on animals, even though they usually involve suffering and death, as long as there is good reason to believe that they will lead to significant advances in the treatment of human – and incidentally also animal – diseases. But of course the scope for abuse in this area is enormous, and therefore the need for stringent legislative control is both evident and urgent.

Among the restrictions that should be imposed are the following.

1. All such experiments should be strictly controlled, as to their number, method and purpose, by a statutory supervisory body that has no commercial interest in them.
2. They should be carried out only by accredited researchers who have the necessary competence and responsibility.
3. They should be carried out in the most humane way, including the use of anaesthetics whenever possible.

4. They should be kept to a minimum, which means that they should be prohibited altogether whenever the desired result can be obtained by other means, and there should be no more repetition of the same experiment by different institutions than is scientifically necessary.

5. There should be the greatest vigilance to ensure that ethical considerations, such as humaneness, are not sacrificed to commercial gain.[32]

NOTES

1. Against Apion, II, 29.
2. *The Pentateuch and Haftorahs*, p. 854b. He quotes I Corinthians 9:9, as if Christianity had never taught anything else about animal welfare. See also the writings of Andrew Linzey of Mansfield College, Oxford, for Christian views on animal welfare.
3. 'The mode of living which is founded upon a total harmlessness toward all creatures ... is the highest morality' (Hinduism). 'Pure and earnest *bhikshus* [mendicant monks] will never wear ... shoes made of leather, for it involves the taking of life' (Buddhism). 'How commendable is abstinence that dispenses with the butcher! While walking be mindful of worms and ants' (Taoism). 'One should not injure, subjugate, enslave, torture, or kill any animal' (Jainism). These quotations are from *World Scripture: A Comparative Anthology of Sacred Texts*, ed. Andrew Wilson, New York, 1991, p. 208f.
4. The one beginning *ribbon kol ha-'olamim* (Singer's, 1990 edn., p. 19).
5. *The Jewish Contribution to Civilisation*, p. 299.
6. Now under royal patronage.
7. *Manna*, Winter 2000, p. 32c.
8. There is even a Universal Declaration of Animal Rights, proclaimed in Paris in 1978 and submitted to UNESCO in 1990.
9. See the discussion of this question in J. David Bleich, *Contemporary Halakhic Problems*, Vol. III, 1989, p. 203f.
10. So, for example, R. Eleazar, *Ber.* 6b, and R. Simeon b. Eleazar, *Kid.* 82; Bleich, p. 220.
11. According to *Chronicle of the Twentieth Century*, p.1294, we are destroying six species every hour.
12. Quoted in *Siddur Lev Chadash* (ULPS), p. 167.
13. See Bleich, op. cit., p. 200ff.
14. Ibid., p. 200.
15. *Sefer ha-Mitzvot*, Prohibition 219.
16. *Moreh Nevuchim* III, 48.
17. *Sefer Chasidim* 666.
18. Ibid., 700.
19. *Shulchan Aruch, Orach Chayyim* 324, note 7, referring to Exod. 22:30.
20. For a particularly eloquent example, see Morris Joseph, *Judaism as Creed and Life*, 1925 edn., pp. 471–7.
21. See, for example, Gen. R. 44:1, and *Sefer ha-Chinnuch* 596.
22. *Shulchan Aruch, Choshen Mishpat* 272:9.

23. On the contrary, it may well be one of the purposes of the story to commend animal sacrifice in the Jerusalem Temple as a legitimate form of worship; see Shalom Spiegel, *The Last Trial*, p. 73.
24. Bleich, p. 213f.
25. *Mishneh Torah, Hilchot Yom Tov* 6:18.
26. For a full exploration of the traditional sources, see Bleich, op. cit., Ch. XX, pp. 237–50.
27. Ibid., p. 237.
28. *The Authorised Daily Prayer Book of the United Hebrew Congregations of the Commonwealth*, 1990, p. 897.
29. *The Torah: A Modern Commentary*, UAHC, 1881, p. 751b.
30. John Byron, *Child Harold's Pilgrimage*, canto 4, stanza 14.
31. *Noda biyhudah, YD*, No. 10; for an abridged translation, see Solomon B. Freehof, *A Treasury of Responsa*, JPS, 1963, No. 41.
32. Further on the subject of medical experiments on animals, see Rabbi Walter Jacob, 'Jewish Involvement in Genetic Engineering', March 1989, in *Questions and Reform Jewish Answers: New American Reform Responsa*, New York, 1992; and Rabbi J. David Bleich, *Contemporary Halakhic Problems*, Vol. III, New York, 1989, Ch. IX, 'Animal Experimentation'.

Some Glimpses of the History of the Jewish Liturgy

28 December 1994

Of the many thousands of books that make up the literature of Judaism, none can make a better claim to be considered normative than the prayerbook. It is itself an anthology of Jewish literature; it spans almost every age and country of Jewish history; it is the most widely owned and frequently used of all Jewish books – more so than the Bible itself; and it has done more than any other book both to express, and in turn to influence, the collective Jewish psyche. Nevertheless, its history remains little known except to specialists. This chapter will, it is hoped, afford a few glimpses into that fascinating aspect of the history of Judaism for the general reader.

ORIGINS OF THE JEWISH LITURGY

The word 'liturgy' literally means 'worship'. It can therefore refer to the worship of the Temple, for which the Hebrew is *avodah*. But that was largely sacrificial, with the use of words playing only a subsidiary role. The sources do indeed tell us that the Levites chanted Psalms and that the *Kohanim* recited the Ten Commandments, the Shema and five short prayers, including the Priestly Benediction (see *Tamid* 5:1). But some of that information may apply only to the Second Temple period, or even to the latter part of it, and therefore may already reflect the influence of the Synagogue.

At any rate, it was in the Synagogue that Jewish worship took on the form with which we are familiar, consisting entirely of prayer and the reading of sacred texts; and it is in this sense, for which the Hebrew is *t'fillah*, that the term 'Jewish liturgy' is generally used. In this sense, therefore, the Jewish liturgy is as old as the Synagogue. But how old is that?

Nearly all the text-books tell us that it goes back to the Babylonian Exile or at least the early Second Temple period. But on what grounds? Chiefly because it is argued that, since the exiles had no Temple, they must have held synagogue-type gatherings in order to keep up their morale and maintain their identity. But 'must have' is not historical evidence.

We do indeed read in the book of Ezekiel about gatherings of elders that took place occasionally in the prophet's home (8:1, 14:1, 20:1), but there is no indication that they involved either prayer or the study of Scripture.

Then, in the Mishnah and Talmud, we hear about an institution called the 'Great Assembly', which is said to have consisted of 120 elders including several prophets, and to have laid the foundations of the Jewish liturgy (*Avot* 1:1; *Ber.* 33a; *Meg.* 17b). We also hear about the so-called *ma'amadot* or contingents of lay people who served in the Temple by rotation, a week at a time, and studied the Creation Story (*Ta'an.* 4:2–3). But how early in the Second Temple period these institutions came into existence, and how much reliance is to be placed on the traditions concerning them, recorded centuries later, is not clear.

That is the sum-total of the case, and, as the American Jewish historian Ellis Rivkin has pointed out, it has to be set against two weighty counter-arguments. The first is an argument from silence. If synagogues existed already in the Babylonian Exile or soon after, why are they never mentioned in the Bible, much of which was written in the post-exilic period, or even in the apocryphal book of Ben Sira, which gives a vivid account of Judean society round about 200 BCE? The only possible answer is that they did not exist or, if they did, played no significant role in Jewish life.

The second counter-argument is an argument from improbability. Everything we know about the dictatorial powers exercised by the High Priests, in matters spiritual as well as political, under the Persians and Greeks, makes it unlikely in the extreme that they would have tolerated the emergence of a new institution, rivalling the Temple, namely the Synagogue, or a new class of lay teachers of Torah, rivalling the priests, namely the *soferim* 'Scribes', as the conventional view also alleges.

What is clear, however, is that the coming of Greek rule brought into being a newly prosperous and educated middle class of merchants and artisans who would have resented their exclusion from any active participation, let alone leadership, in religious worship, legislation or education.

Here we need to remind ourselves that prior to the emergence of the Synagogue, Jewish worship was strictly confined to the Temple, so that only those who lived in or near Jerusalem could attend it regularly. Even then they attended as spectators rather than participants. They sat in the Court of the Israelites or the Court of the Women, as the case might be, and watched from a distance while the *Kohanim*, whose office was strictly hereditary and confined to a few families, performed the sacrificial rituals. Similarly, the master-copy of the Torah was kept under lock and key in the Temple, and only the *Kohanim* were considered competent to expound it.

This state of affairs was a far cry from the democratic ideal enunciated in the Torah when it speaks of the Jewish people as 'a kingdom of priests and a holy nation' (Exod. 19:6), and it is not difficult to imagine the resentment which it would have aroused among those members of the new middle class who, not being born of priestly stock, were thus religiously unempowered.

It was the Maccabean War of 167–164 BCE which brought this resentment to a head and gave it an unprecedented opportunity to express itself. About this time we hear of *Chasidim*, 'Pious Ones', who devoted their lives to prayer and study, and who were the first to answer Mattathias's call for volunteers to take up arms in defence of the Torah. And soon after we hear of *Chachamim*, 'Wise Ones' or 'Lay Scholars', which is what the Pharisees called themselves.

To cut a long story short: I believe with Ellis Rivkin that 'it all happened' in the second century BCE. It was then that the Pharisees emerged and created the Synagogue or, if it already existed, used it for their democratising purpose, to evolve a new form of worship, independent of Temple, sacrifice and priesthood, in which all could participate as equals. And this in turn necessitated the creation of an appropriate liturgy. Here, too, I believe, the Pharisees were the pioneers. At any rate, all attempts to trace the basic prayers of the Jewish liturgy back to their origins fizzle out in the period immediately preceding that of the *Tannaim*, which was the period of the Pharisees, and cannot be pushed any further back than that.

As for the *Sof'rim*, they are a puzzle for two reasons. First, because Ben Sira, who prides himself on being a *Sofer*, in his lengthy eulogy of the great figures of Jewish history, beginning 'Let us now praise famous men,' fails to mention Ezra, the supposed founder of the Soferic profession. And secondly, because his own book is in no sense a commentary on the Torah. Perhaps, therefore, as Ellis Rivkin suggests, the *Sof'rim* were simply writers of Wisdom Literature, like Ben Sira himself. Or perhaps the title was used in different senses at different times.

Similarly, it may be that the *Keneset ha-G'dolah* and the Ma'amadot were Pharisaic institutions, or concessions to the democratising pressures which preceded and occasioned the emergence of Pharisaism.

Before leaving this topic, let me emphasise the immensity of the change involved in the transition from Temple to Synagogue: a change uncannily anticipated by the eighth-century prophet Hosea when he said: 'Take with you words, and return to the Eternal One; say to God, Forgive all iniquity, and accept that which is good; so we will bring instead of bullocks the offering of our lips' (14:3).

Whatever one may think of sacrificial worship, prayer is immeasurably more versatile. For there were only a few types of sacrifice, each with its distinctive symbolic significance; but language is capable of expressing an infinitude of meanings. Therefore the emergence of the Synagogue enabled Judaism, as never before, to express its whole theology liturgically.

It should also be noted that, since the new kind of worship did not involve sacrifice, therefore it enabled Judaism to survive the destruction of the Temple. But therefore, too, synagogues could be established wherever Jews lived, both in Eretz Yisrael and in the Diaspora, and this made it possible for Judaism to become a more universal religion than would otherwise have been the case.

THE *TEFILLAH*

We now turn our attention to a few specific prayers, chosen largely for the light they throw on the question of what the Jewish liturgy reveals about the attitude of Judaism to the non-Jewish world.

We begin with the principal prayer of the Jewish liturgy, variously known as *t'fillah*, meaning 'prayer', *'amidah*, meaning 'standing', or the *sh'moneh 'esreh*, meaning 'Eighteen'. Since, however, it has long consisted of nineteen benedictions, the obvious question to ask about it is how the Eighteen became Nineteen.

An answer commonly given is that the odd one out is No. 12, known as *birkat ha-minim*, the 'Benediction [or, more accurately, Malediction] against Heretics'. About the origin of that prayer we do indeed have an uncharacteristically precise piece of information in the Talmud, which tells us that it was composed by one Samuel the Little on the order of Rabban Gamliel of Yavneh (*Ber.* 28a). That would have been shortly after the Roman War – say, about 90 CE – when Jewish feelings against enemies within and without were running high.

Unfortunately, we do not know how the prayer was worded. That is indeed a problem besetting all study of the early Jewish liturgy. For the Rabbinic literature rarely gives the full text of a prayer. Mostly it only cites a snippet or two, leaving us to guess what the full text might have been in those days. For the liturgy was considered part of the oral law, transmitted orally for about a thousand years before the first prayerbook, known as *Seder Rav Amram*, was compiled in Babylonia about 860 CE. Even then the texts varied considerably for another two or three centuries, and to a lesser extent after that. At any rate, any attempt to reconstruct the textual history of any particular prayer prior to *Seder Rav Amram* is largely a matter of guesswork.

But in the case of *Birkat ha-Minim*, because of its history of censorship, we do not even know what the key word originally was, and therefore against whom it was directed: whether it was against the Sadducees, Gnostics, Romans, Judeo-Christians, Christians generally, Apostates, or Informers. And therefore no inference can be safely drawn from this prayer as to how Jews saw their relationship with the non-Jewish world.

In any case, it is extremely doubtful whether this malediction is the odd one out numerically. For if the *Tefillah* consisted of nineteen benedictions already about 90 CE, it seems most unlikely that the Mishnah, over a century later, would still have referred to it as the Eighteen Benedictions.

Besides, there is a telltale passage in *Midrash B'midbar Rabbah* which points to quite another benediction as the odd one out. It refers to the Hosea verse I have already mentioned, which it understands anachronistically as a plea for God's acceptance of Israel's prayer in the narrower sense of *Tefillah*, and points out that the word *tov* for 'good' in the phrase, 'accept that which is good', has a numerical value of seventeen. But surely, it asks, there are nineteen benedictions! Yes, it answers, but from these you must deduct, first, *Birkat ha-Minim* and, secondly, the one about *tzemach David*, the offspring of David, 'which was composed after it' (18:21).

There could not be a clearer statement of the sequence of events, and I am not aware of any good reason to doubt that it is correct. First, the *Birkat ha-Minim* was composed at Yavneh about 90 CE, which increased the number of benedictions from seventeen to eighteen, so that the Mishnah correctly refers to the prayer as *Shemoneh 'Esreh*. Then, in the third century, in Babylonia, another benediction was composed, specifically about the restoration of the Davidic dynasty, perhaps because the Exilarchs claimed Davidic descent; that became No. 15 in the sequence and increased the total number from eighteen to nineteen.

If any further proof is wanted, it may be found in the fact that in the liturgy of *Eretz Yisrael* down to about the ninth century, as preserved in the Cairo Genizah, No. 15 is missing. In other words, the Jews of *Eretz Yisrael* continued to have only eighteen benedictions, as in the Mishnah, during all those centuries.

Before we leave this topic, let us broaden it and ask what the *Tefillah* as a whole reveals about the Jewish attitude to non-Jews. As we have seen, there is a *possible* hostile reference in *Birkat ha-Minim*. Against that, there is a friendly reference, but only to those who convert to Judaism, in the following benediction, known as the 'Benediction of the Righteous', which commends 'true' or 'righteous proselytes'.

Other than that, the *Tefillah* does not mention non-Jews. Nor is that at all surprising, for it stems from a time when our ancestors saw themselves as the sole monotheists and everybody else as idolaters, so that Jewish prayer was conceived as essentially a matter between the Jewish people and the God whom they alone recognised.

But what we must add to that is the eschatological dimension, the way the Jews perceived the 'end of days'. They hoped, of course, that ultimately all human beings would come to recognise the true God. That hope is not explicitly expressed in the *Tefillah*, though it is elsewhere, as we shall see presently. But even then it is combined with a particularistic view of Jewish destiny. More generally, the traditional Jewish liturgy as a whole is permeated by what one might call a back-to-square-one view of history. As it was in the beginning, so it will be in the end, only better. The people will return to their land; the Davidic monarchy will be restored; the Temple will be rebuilt; the sacrificial cult will be re-instituted; the hereditary priesthood will be re-activated; and all the laws that have been in abeyance for the last two thousand years will come into force again.

The *Tefillah* is therefore a highly particularistic prayer, which pays little attention to the non-Jewish world and sees the historic role of the Jewish people as one of separateness from it rather than identification with it. For instance, it speaks of 'the Redeemer of Israel', 'the One who heals the sick of His people Israel', 'who gathers the dispersed of His people Israel', 'who will rebuild Jerusalem', 'who will restore the Divine Presence to Zion', which is a reference to the rebuilding of the Temple, and 'who will bless His people Israel with peace'.

There are many Jews who would go along with that perception of the role of the Jewish people in human history; and some would add that the events of the twentieth century, including the Holocaust and the establishment of the State of Israel, have given it renewed force. But there are other Jews, with whom my sympathies lie, who tend to take a different view. They would stress that the destiny of the Jewish people is bound up with the destiny of humanity; that healing, redemption and peace are indivisible; and that it is therefore necessary to rephrase some of the language of the Tefillah in a more universalistic spirit.

THE *'ALEYNU*

The question of particularism versus universalism is highlighted by the *'Aleynu*, by general consent one of the finest prayers of the entire Jewish liturgy. But is it one prayer? I must confess that I used to think so, until I read Joseph Heinemann's book, *Prayer in the Period of the Tanna'im and the Amora'im* (Jerusalem, 1966). What his form-critical approach shows becomes blindingly obvious as soon as it is pointed out: that we are actually dealing with two quite different prayers.

The first half, beginning '*aleynu*, refers to God in the third person, and never uses the Tetragrammaton but always circumlocutions such as 'the Sovereign of the universe', and 'the Holy One who is ever to be praised'. These, according to Heinemann, are sure signs of a prayer that originated, not in a context of worship but in a context of study. But whereas other such prayers, like the Kaddish, emanate from the rabbinic colleges, where they served the purpose of concluding a lecture on a note of prayer, and especially a hopeful prayer looking forward to the messianic age, the first half of the '*Aleynu* has some further features which point to an even earlier origin.

For instance, one of the circumlocutions by which it refers to God is 'the Supreme King of Kings', which alludes to one of the titles of the Persian emperors and suggests that the prayer might have been composed at a time when the memory of the Persian empire was not yet remote. More importantly, it includes the phrase, *va-anachnu kor'im u-mishtachavim*, referring to kneeling and prostration, which were features of Temple worship, discontinued in the Synagogue.

These considerations led Heinemann to conjecture that the prayer might go back to the *Ma'amadot* who, as I mentioned earlier, used to meet in the Temple and study the Creation Story from the first chapter of Genesis. That would explain the emphasis on God as the Creator, 'who stretched out the heavens and established the earth'. It would also account for phrases such as 'God's glorious throne is in the heavens above, and the abode of God's power in the loftiest heights'; for, as Heinemann points out, precisely in the days of the Temple was there a danger that people might naively suppose that God dwelt in the earthly sanctuary, and precisely then was it therefore necessary to stress God's transcendence. And only in the time of the Temple, he adds, was it possible to understand 'the kingdom of Heaven', 'as a present reality and not only an eschatological hope'.

In one sense, therefore, the '*Aleynu* (and I am still speaking only of the first half) is highly universalistic. But in another sense it is extremely particularistic. It is universalistic about God but particularistic about the Jewish people. It emphasises that God 'has not made us like the nations of the world, nor placed us like other families of the earth, has not made our portion like theirs, nor our destiny like that of their multitude'.

The contrast between the Jewish people, who worship the true

God, and the rest of humanity, who worship idols, could hardly be more sharply drawn. But it was even sharper in the original text, which included a phrase, still preserved in the Sefardi liturgy, which has been omitted from most Ashkenazi prayerbooks, for reasons of censorship, since the beginning of the 18th century. The phrase, taken from two Isaiah verses (30:7 and 45:20), reads: 'For they prostrate themselves before vanity and emptiness, and pray to a God who cannot save.'

God is the transcendent Creator of the cosmos, but the chasm here on earth between the Jewish people, who worship Him, and the rest of humanity, who do not, is vast. That is one way of combining universalism and particularism.

But there is another, which is exemplified by the second half of the *'Aleynu*, beginning 'Therefore we hope in You, Eternal One, our God ...' As already that opening phrase shows, this prayer is cast in an altogether different liturgical style. It addresses God in the second person, and uses the Tetragrammaton. The style, according to Heinemann, is typical of prayers composed for use in synagogue worship. Furthermore, we know for which service it was composed, namely *Musaf* (i.e., the Additional Service) of *Rosh Hashanah*. For that was its original position in the liturgy. Only with *Machzor Vitry*, a prayerbook compiled in France by a disciple of Rashi around 1100, did it also become a daily prayer.

Now there are various indications in the Talmud that the liturgy for *Rosh Hashanah Musaf*, which includes the blowing of the Shofar, was composed by the 'House' or 'School' of Rav, i.e., Abba Aricha, founder of the Babylonian academy of Sura in the first half of the third century (*J. RH* 1:3; *AZ* 1:2). It is therefore to him that the *'Aleynu* is usually attributed, and Joseph Heinemann accepts the attribution, but only as regards the second half. The first half is, as we have seen, much older and, according to Heinemann, was simply used by Rav as a readily available hymnological preface to his own composition.

Here I must interject that some doubt has been cast on Heinemann's theory by the discovery of a manuscript belonging to the *He'chalot* mystical literature which Gershom Sholem dates from the third century, where both parts of the *'Aleynu* are attributed to Rabbi Akiva, but the first half is couched in the first person singular, so that it begins 'It is my duty to praise . . .' (*Jewish Gnosticism, Merkabah Mysticism, and the Talmud Tradition*, New York, 1969, 24:105). If that is historically correct, the credit for the combination of the two prayers may belong to Akiva rather than Rav, but the two halves nevertheless remain distinct, and the first half may still go back beyond Akiva to the Ma'amadot, as Heinemann conjectured.

But to return to the second half: the way it deals with the issue of universalism versus particularism is not to deny what the first half asserts about the enormous gulf that separates the Jewish people from all other peoples, but to affirm that ultimately that gulf will be bridged, when the one true God will be acknowledged and worshipped by all humanity, and to express the fervent hope that that time will come soon. Thus it speaks of 'all who dwell on earth' – not only Jews but human beings generally, and says: 'May they realise and know that to You every knee must bend, and every tongue swear loyalty...Let them all accept the yoke of Your kingdom, and may You reign over them speedily and for ever...'

So the *'Aleynu* prayer, in its second half, resolves the universalism–particularism paradox in the eschatological future. *Then* all will be united in the worship of the true God. 'On that day the Eternal God shall be One, and God's name One,' it quotes from Zechariah (14:9).

It is an inspiring thought, but it raises the question whether the bridging of the gulf needs to be postponed until the messianic age. As I mentioned earlier, the ancient parts of the Jewish liturgy stem from a time when the non-Jewish world in its entirety was perceived as idolatrous. But since then Christianity and Islam have arisen, and some of the greatest Jewish authorities, already in the Middle Ages, have taught that their adherents are to be regarded as fellow monotheists. And in recent times we have begun to learn to respect the religions of the Far East also. We live in a whole new age of inter-faith dialogue and understanding. In these circumstances, is the gulf between us and the rest of humanity really as vast as the first half of the Aleynu depicts it? Can we use unmodified a liturgy which implies that nothing has changed in that respect in the last two thousand years?

THE *MA'OZ TZUR*

We now turn to an entirely different genre of Jewish liturgy, known as Piyyut, a Hebrew word of Greek origin, referring to Hebrew religious poetry of a kind which was written in great abundance in the post-talmudic period and throughout the Middle Ages, in Palestine, Italy, Germany, Spain and other countries. Much of it found its way into the Jewish liturgy, though different communities made different selections from it, and much of it is of a high quality, both theologically and stylistically. One outstanding example is the *Adon 'olam*. Here we turn our attention to a medieval composition of less exalted quality which is nevertheless very popular among Ashkenazi (though not Sefardi) Jews because of its association with the festival of Chanukkah, and because of its relevance to our special topic of the relationship between Israel and humanity.

Its popularity is partly due to the catchy tune to which it has been sung since at least 1744 (*Encyclopaedia Judaica*, Vol. 11, p. 910) – a tune which is said to date from the first half of the fifteenth century and to bear a close resemblance to German soldiers' songs and Bohemian church songs.

But the text, which concerns us, is somewhat older. It was written by a Hebrew poet called Mordecai, possibly Mordecai ben Isaac, who lived in Germany in the 13th century. It consists of five stanzas, which acrostically spell out the name of the author, Mordecai, and a sixth stanza, which only appears in some prayerbooks, whose first three words acrostically spell out the word 'Be strong'. The middle stanzas celebrate in the manner of a victory song the Jewish people's deliverance, first from Egyptian slavery, then from Babylonian exile, then from Haman's plot to destroy the Jews of Persia, and finally from the Greeks who defiled the Temple in the episode commemorated at Chanukkah.

These stanzas are therefore reminiscent of the tradition, first found in the *Yerushalmi* (*Pes.* 10:1), which explains the Four Cups of the Seder as symbolising the four world empires which must be overthrown before the Messianic Age can dawn.

The first and last stanzas are a fervent plea for redemption, including the hope for the restoration of the Temple. They are not only particularistic but express deep anger against the oppressive non-Jewish world by which the author saw the Jews surrounded. No doubt the anger was inspired by the Crusades, which would make it entirely understandable. But what is understandable is not necessarily edifying. Here, for instance, is a translation of the last, not so well-known stanza, taken from the latest (1990) edition of Singer's prayerbook (previous editions didn't have it):

O bare Your holy arm, And hasten the time of salvation. Wreak vengeance upon the wicked nation, On behalf of Your faithful servants. For deliverance has too long been delayed. And the evil days are endless. O thrust the enemy into the shadow of death. And set up for us the seven Shepherds. (p. 710)

The 'seven Shepherds' are an allusion to a Micah verse (5:4) and are identified in the Talmud as Adam, Seth and Methuselah on one side, Abraham, Jacob and Moses on the other, with David in the middle (*Suk.* 52b).

But it is the first and best-known stanza which I suggest we look at more closely. It begins: 'Refuge, Rock of my salvation, to You our praise is due.' It continues: 'Let our house of prayer be restored, and there we will bring You our thank-offerings.' The term 'house of prayer' is taken from Deutero-Isaiah's prophecy, 'My house shall be called a house of prayer for all peoples' (56:7), which, in spite of the word 'prayer', is an allusion to the Temple. Finally, the stanza concludes: 'When You, God, prepare a slaughter of the barking foe,' 'Then we will complete, with songs of praise, the re-dedication of the altar'.

It is the penultimate clause, about the slaughter of the barking foe, which calls for closer scrutiny. It expresses the same spirit of anger and revenge which we have noted in the sixth stanza, and is reminiscent of the Psalm verse, 'Pour out Your wrath upon the nations that do not acknowledge You...' (79:6), traditionally recited when the door is opened during the *Seder*. But it raises a moral question: Is it right to pray for the destruction of the wicked?

Not according to Ezekiel's famous prophecy, 'As I live, says the Eternal God, I do not desire the death of the wicked, but that they turn from their ways and live...' (33:1). Nor according to the well known story in the Talmud about Rabbi Meir who, after a series of attacks by highwaymen, prayed that they should die. But his wife Beruria rebuked him, pointing out that the last verse of Psalm 104 should be read to mean 'Let sin cease', not 'Let sinners cease' (*Ber.* 10a).

Any Jew who is sensitive to that tradition is therefore bound to feel uneasy about asking God to 'prepare a slaughter of the barking foe'. Such squeamish persons were David Woolf Marks and Morris Joseph, Ministers of the West London Synagogue when it issued in 1898 the Fifth Edition of its prayerbook, *Forms of Prayer*. There the clause we are discussing is amended to read, 'When thou shalt have put an end to carnage and to the war-hound's fury'. The amendment reverses the meaning, for instead of being asked to *prepare* a slaughter, God is now asked to *end* all slaughter.

The same amendment appears in the 1931 revision of that prayerbook, but without a translation. Instead, the facing page gives an English hymn, beginning 'Rock of ages', which was written in America by Rabbi Marcus Jastrow (1829–1903), author of the famous talmudic dictionary, and Rabbi Gustav Gottheil (1827–1903) on the model of a German hymn by Rabbi Leopold Stein (1810–82).

Another squeamish individual was Chief Rabbi Joseph H. Hertz (1872–1946). He is best known for his ungrammatically entitled *Pentateuch and Haftorahs*, which is largely a misguided polemic against Bible criticism. But he also edited, in 1946, *The Authorised Daily Prayer Book of the United Hebrew Congregations of the British Empire*, and in the Revised Edition of 1947 almost the same amendment appears as in the prayerbook of the West London Synagogue. It reads: 'When thou shalt cause all slaughter to cease, and the blaspheming foe.'

This amendment passed into the 1954 edition of 'Singer's' (the standard prayerbook of the United Synagogue) but remained in use only for a few years, for the Revised Edition of 1962 reverted to the traditional text. So, too, the latest, 1990 edition, which has moved even further to the Right, although there the meaning of the Hebrew is nicely disguised in the translation, which reads, 'When You will have utterly *silenced* the loud-mouthed foe.'

More surprisingly, the editors of the new *Siddur* of the Reform Synagogues of Great Britain, published in 1977, thought it wise, after the movement had lived with the amended version for 79 years, to revert to the traditional one, while discrepantly translating it according to the now abandoned revised version. Similarly, the Central Conference of American Rabbis, which had never before included the Hebrew *Ma'oz Tzur* in its liturgy, but made do with 'Rock of Ages', opted in its new *Siddur*, *Gates of Prayer*, published in 1975, for the traditional text.

Never mind Ezekiel, never mind Beruria, never mind David Woolf Marks and Morris Joseph, never mind Joseph H. Hertz, never mind moral fastidiousness: if an obscure Hebrew poet of thirteenth-century Germany felt impelled to beseech God to prepare a slaughter of the barking foe, then that is what we must sing, and teach our children to sing, from generation to generation. Such is the prevailing mentality of our community.

CONCLUSION

If we search the Jewish liturgy for some expression of a generous or at any rate positive sentiment towards the non-Jewish world, not relating to the perfect future but to the imperfect present, the obvious place to look is the Prayer for the Government.

As already pointed out, the Jewish prayerbook is an unequalled expression of the collective Jewish psyche. What it reveals, among other things, is a deep devotion to the One God, a passionate belief in the unique role of the Jewish people in the Divine Scheme, and a fervent hope for the coming of the Messianic Age, when not only Israel but all humanity will be redeemed. What it does *not* show, except in very rare instances, is any concern for the well-being of the rest of humanity in the pre-messianic present. To that extent the collective psyche of the Jewish people which the traditional liturgy reveals is one of self-preoccupation. In that there is, to repeat, nothing at all surprising. It is the price we have paid for centuries of isolation and persecution.

But now, some of us believe, the time has come, if it is not long overdue, to express in our liturgy sympathetic concern, not only for our own people, but also for the other 99.9% of the human family, who are likewise God's children, created in the Divine Image. The various reforming movements in Judaism have been trying to do that – not always consistently or sensibly – for nearly two hundred years; and Chief Rabbi Joseph H. Hertz has shown that it is possible to do it, to some extent at least, within Orthodox Judaism.

In the ancient Temple in Jerusalem, during the Festival of *Sukkot*, seventy sacrifices were offered for the seventy nations of the world; so the Mishnah informs us (*Suk.* 5:6; 55b). Something of that spirit, it seems to me, needs now to be expressed in the liturgy of the Synagogue. Surely we should pray for the peace of all the dwellers on earth, not only because Jeremiah was right, that only in their peace shall we find our peace, but also because their peace is itself devoutly to be wished.

The Four Children of the Passover Haggadah

9 January 1991

ORIGIN OF THE *SEDER*

The centrepiece of the domestic celebration of the Passover festival, known in Ashkenazi tradition as the *Seder* ('Order'), is the annual retelling of the story of the Exodus. The idea derives from the Scriptural verse, 'You shall tell (*v'higgadta*) your child on that day: It is because of what the Eternal One did for me when I came out of Egypt' (Exod. 13:8). That verse is also the source of the term Haggadah ('Narration'), found already in the Talmud (*Pes.* 116b), which is used by Sefardim to designate the celebration and by Ashkenazim to refer to the prayerbook containing its liturgy.

Some time between the redaction of the Pentateuch around 400 BCE and that of the Mishnah around 200 CE, the narration became formalised and standardised. No doubt that was a gradual process, but it is likely that the Pharisees, who emerged in the 2nd century BCE, played a major part in it. For it accords well with their general aim of bringing religious ritual out of the Temple into the home (as well as the synagogue) and with what we know of their liturgical creativity.

The same inference may be drawn from the fact that the earliest account of the *Seder*, in the tenth chapter of Mishnah *P'sachim*, cites Pharisaic and Tannaitic authorities of the periods immediately before and after the Destruction of the Temple, including the schools of Hillel and Shammai, Rabban Gamliel the Elder, Eliezer ben Tzadok, Tarfon, Akiva and Ishmael.

FOCUS ON CHILDREN

One of the striking features of the *Seder* is the special attention it pays to children. That is evident already in the Mishnah account, which insists that the child must ask: *mah nishtannah ha-lailah ha-zeh mi-kol ha-leylot* (*Pes.* 10:4). Grammatically, that is an exclamation: 'How different this night is from all other nights!' But the Mishnah makes it quite clear that it is meant as a question, or at least as an introduction to a series of questions that call for answers.

Evidently, the *Seder* was deliberately carried out in such a way as to arouse the curiosity of any children present, which shows a keen insight into the psychology of education. Further evidence of this is provided by the *Tosefta*, where we read in the name of Rabbi Eliezer: *chot'fin matzah la-tinokot*, which Saul Lieberman takes to mean that the grown-ups play a game of snatching pieces of Matzah from each other, so as to intrigue the children and keep them awake (*Pischa* 10:9). Another version of that tradition is found in the Babylonian Talmud (*Pes.* 109b) and variously interpreted to mean that the Matzot are eaten in haste, or that the dish containing them is held up, or that they are taken away from the children while they are still hungry. The same source also tells us that Rabbi Judah and Rabbi Akiva used to distribute parched corn and nuts to the children, so as to keep them alert and induce them to ask questions (*Pes.* 108b–109a).

BOYS AND GIRLS

The most interesting illustration of emphasis on the instruction of children in the context of the *Seder* is the Midrash of the Four Children, which is *not* in the Mishnah and therefore must have been incorporated into the *Seder* somewhat later. But since it is more commonly known as the Midrash of the Four *Sons*, the question needs to be raised whether the word *banim*, in that context, should or should not be understood in a gender-exclusive sense.

It is of course well known that Rabbinic Judaism *ultimately* took a negative view about the position of women and girls in relation to religious education: a view that found expression in

Rabbi Eliezer's unfortunate remark that 'whoever teaches his daughter Torah is as if he had taught her frivolity' (*Sot.* 3:4).

But it should not be assumed that it was so from the beginning. Contrary indications include the fact that women were explicitly included in the ceremony of *Hakhel* ('Assemble the people, men, women and children...', Deut. 31:12) and in the great gathering at the water gate, when Ezra 'brought the Torah before the congregation, both men and women' and read it aloud 'in the presence of the men and the women' (Neh. 8:2f.).

Even more striking is the Rabbis' emphasis on the inclusion of women in God's Revelation to the assembled people at Sinai. On the phrase, 'Thus shall you say to the house of Jacob and tell the children of Israel' (Exod. 19:30), they commented: 'the house of Jacob' refers to the women, 'the children of Israel' to the men (*Mechilta* ad loc.).

Given such a background, it should not be taken for granted that the author of our Midrash – while he would no doubt have had boys chiefly in mind – deliberately intended to exclude girls. Accordingly, there is a good case for abandoning the time-honoured translation of its title as 'The Midrash of the Four Sons' and understanding it, rather, as 'The Midrash of the Four Children'.

SOURCES OF THE MIDRASH

As already mentioned, the Midrash does not feature in the Mishnah's account of the *Seder*. But it is found in two sources of almost equal antiquity. One is the *Mechilta* of Rabbi Ishmael (*Bo*, Chapter 18; ed. Lauterbach, Schiff Library of Jewish Classics, 1949, Vol. I, p. 166f.; ed. Horovitz-Rabin, Jerusalem, 1960, p. 73f.). The other is the Palestinian Talmud, popularly known as the *Yerushalmi* (*Pes.* 10:4).

There are, as we shall see, some significant differences between the two versions, and neither is quite identical with the Haggadah text of the first Jewish prayerbook, *Seder Rav Amram* (II, 82; ed. Daniel Goldschmidt, p. 114), which, however, follows the *Mechilta* version more closely than the *Yerushalmi* one.

The idea underlying the Midrash is succinctly expressed in another ancient source, the *Mechilta* of Simeon ben Yochai. Commenting on the verse, 'When your child asks you in time to come, what is this? you shall say to him: by strength of hand the Eternal One brought us out of Egypt' (Exod. 13:14), it remarks: 'From the question children ask, and the way they talk, you can tell something of their state of mind' (ed. J.N. Epstein and E.Z. Melamed, Jerusalem 1955, p. 44).

There are two other such question-and-answer passages in the Torah, making three with the one just quoted and four if one adds, although it does not postulate a question, Exodus 13:8, mentioned above. The Midrash of the Four Children is an interpretation of those four passages.

In the *Mechilta* the Midrash is given anonymously. It occurs in a discussion of Exodus 13:14 which goes on to quote Deuteronomy 6:20, then continues: 'Thus you have to say: There are four types of child: one who is wise, one who is stupid, one who is wicked, and one who does not know how to ask.'

In the *Yerushalmi* the Midrash occurs as a comment on the Mishnah account of the *Seder*, specifically the questions to be asked by the child, after which the Mishnah states: 'And according to the child's state of mind, his (or her) father (or mother) teaches him (or her)' (10:4). The comment of the *Yerushalmi* on that phrase begins 'Rabbi Chiyya taught: The Torah alludes to four types of child: a wise child, a wicked child, a stupid child, and a child who does not know how to ask.'

RABBI CHIYYA

Thus the *Yerushalmi*, unlike the *Mechilta*, identifies the author of the Midrash; and though the identification cannot be taken as certain, there is no particular reason to doubt it. Yet in the numerous commentaries on the Haggadah, its significance is, to my knowledge, never discussed.

Rabbi Chiyya, also known as Chiyya Rabba, 'Chiyya the Great', is unique among the Rabbis in that he is regarded as belonging both to the last generation of *Tannaim* and the first generation of *Amoraim*. That he was considered a *Tanna* is confirmed by the word *t'nei* with which the *Yerushalmi* passage begins, introducing as it always does a *Baraita*, i.e., a Tannaitic teaching not included in the Mishnah. Thus 'The Midrash of the Four Children' could also be called 'The *Baraita* of the Four Children'.

Rabbi Chiyya was born in Babylonia but migrated to Palestine and studied under Judah ha-Nasi, editor of the Mishnah, who held him in highest esteem. There is some doubt whether he died before or after Judah, but in either case the chronology of his life would explain why his Midrash did not find its way into the Mishnah: it had not yet been conceived, or too recently conceived, when the Mishnah was compiled.

But there is a further interest in the attribution of the Midrash to Rabbi Chiyya: he was a great educationalist. The Babylonian Talmud, for instance, relates that he used to grow flax in order to make nets with which to hunt deer; then he would give the meat to orphans, and make scrolls out of the skins. After that he would go to a town where there was a shortage of teachers, write out the five books of the Torah on separate scrolls for each of a group of five children, and teach the six orders of the Mishnah to six more children. Then he would tell the children to teach each other in rotation until his return. Thus, it is said, he preserved the Torah from being forgotten in Israel (*Ket.* 103b; *BM* 85b).

A man so dedicated to education might well have reflected on the way children differ from each other, how from the questions they ask you can tell much about their ability and motivation, and how you must take these factors into account if you wish to teach them effectively.

The Talmud further informs us that Rabbi Chiyya had four children: twin sons called Judah and Hezekiah (*Suk.* 20a) and twin daughters called Pazi and Tavi (*Yev.* 65b–66a). This circumstance may well have given him a personal interest in observing similarities and dissimilarities between children.

Let us now review the four Scripture passages which Rabbi Chiyya's Midrash interprets, and the four types of child with which they have been identified.

PASSAGE 1: EXODUS 12:26–27

The first passage (taking them in the order in which they occur in the Bible) comes from Exodus 12, which refers to the annual commemoration of the Exodus and reads: 'When your children say to you, "What is this service to you?", you shall answer: "It is the sacrifice of the passover of the Eternal One, who passed over the houses of the children of Israel in Egypt…".'

Here all the sources agree that the question typifies the 'wicked' child. For instance, the *Mechilta* of Rabbi Simeon ben Yochai comments: 'This refers to a wicked child who excludes himself (or herself) from the community'. Evidently, it is the word *lachem* that is stressed in this interpretation: 'What is this service to *you*?'

This point is spelt out in the *Mechilta* of Rabbi Ishmael version of the *Baraita* of the Four Children: 'What does the wicked one say? "What is this service to you?" – to you but not to him.' Exactly that is the version of *Seder Rav Amram* and hence of the traditional Haggadah.

The *Yerushalmi* version of the *Baraita*, however, takes a different line. It paraphrases the question: 'What is this trouble you impose on us every year?' This interpretation emphasises the word *'avodah* which is taken not in the sense of 'service' but of 'work' or 'slavery'. (See Menachem Kasher, *Haggadah Shlemah*, Jerusalem, 1967, p. 23, note 118.)

According to one commentator, this interpretation is further reinforced by the fact that the questioner fails to mention the name of God, showing that he (or she) thinks of *'avodah* as an empty routine rather than an act of worship (ibid., note 122).

Still another interpretation fastens on the word *yom'ru* 'when your children *say* to you' – not 'when they *ask* you' – and infers that they do not ask in order to know the inner meaning and truth of the ritual, but only to deny and refute (ibid., note 116).

PASSAGE 2: EXODUS 13:8

The second passage comes from Exodus 13 and is part of Moses' exhortation to the Israelites to remember the Exodus and observe the Passover by the eating of unleavened bread. It is also the 'odd one out' of the four passages, in that it mentions no question but simply commands: 'You shall tell your child on that day: it is because of what the Eternal One did for me when I came out of Egypt.' As we have previously noted, that verse is the source of the term Haggadah.

Because there is no mention in it of any question, it is the proof-text for the child 'who does not know how to ask'. About that, too, the sources are agreed. Both the *Mechilta* and the *Yerushalmi* versions of our Baraita say that, in the case of a child who does not know how to ask, 'you must take the initiative'. The *Mechilta*, followed by *Seder Rav Amram* and the traditional Haggadah, goes on to quote the proof-text: 'Because it says, "You shall tell your child on that day".'

PASSAGE 3: EXODUS 13:14

The third passage also comes from Exodus 13. Its context is the redemption of the firstborn, a ritual instituted in grateful remembrance of the Exodus, when the firstborn of the Israelites were spared. It reads: 'When in time to come your child asks you "What is this?", you shall say to him (or her): "By strength of hand the Eternal One brought us out of Egypt, from the house of bondage".'

Because of the inarticulate nature of the question, the obvious inference is that the questioner in this instance is 'simple'. That is indeed the view taken in all the sources, but with an interesting difference in terminology. In the *Yerushalmi* the term used is *tippesh*, 'stupid'. The *Mechilta* reading is also *tippesh* according to the best manuscripts, including the Oxford MS dated 1291 and the Munich MS dated 1435, but printed editions usually follow *Seder Rav Amram* and the *Haggadot* in substituting the word *tam* which means 'simple' in the sense of 'unsophisticated' rather than 'stupid'.

No doubt the substitution was made because the word *tippesh* seemed too harsh. But the word *tam* has its own and opposite difficulty, since it comes from a root meaning 'to be perfect', so that it has almost too positive a connotation for the intended purpose. There are, however, one or two biblical passages in which the abstract noun *tom* seems to mean 'innocence' (II Sam. 15:11; I Kings 22:34). (It is an interesting fact that in English, too, 'innocence' has the double meaning of blamelessness and *naïveté*.)

PASSAGE 4: DEUTERONOMY 6:20–25

The fourth passage comes from Deuteronomy 6 and has a more general context than the preceding ones. Moses exhorts the people to observe God's commandments, then adds: 'When your child asks you in time to come, saying, "What are the testimonies and the statutes and the ordinances which the Eternal One our God has commanded you?" then you shall answer your child: "We were slaves to Pharaoh in Egypt, and the Eternal One our God led us out from there with a mighty hand and an outstretched arm . . . ".'

By universal consent this passage refers to the 'wise' child, since the question is a sophisticated one, calling for an elaborate response. The only difficulty is that it uses the second person plural, 'which the Eternal One our God has commanded *you*', from which it might appear that, as in the case of the wicked child, so here too the questioner excludes himself (or herself) from the community. To overcome the difficulty, several suggestions have been made. First, that the questioner does at least say 'our God' (Kasher, *Haggadah Shelemah*, p. 21, note 99). Secondly, that by 'you' he only means 'you who came out of Egypt and received the Torah at Sinai', a category in which he (or she) cannot truthfully include himself (or herself), although he (or she) does accept the obligation to obey the commandments (ibid., note 100). Thirdly, that the problematic word should be read, or understood in the sense of, *itt'chem*, '*with* you' (ibid., notes 101 and 103).

There is, however, a strong possibility that the Deuteronomy text did not originally have 'you', at all, but 'us'. For that, contrary to the Masoretic text, is the implied reading of the Septuagint and the actual reading of both the Mechilta and the Yerushalmi versions of our *Baraita*. Only in *Seder Rav Amram* is the reading brought into conformity with the Masoretic text, thus creating for the commentators a problem which may be a non-problem.

HOW TO TEACH THE WISE CHILD

Having established the Scriptural derivations of the four types of child, we now turn to the various ways in which they are to be instructed. Here the two ancient versions of the *Baraita* differ considerably. What they nevertheless have in common is the striking fact that they do not generally take the 'answers' from the same passages as the 'questions'. Evidently Rabbi Chiyya felt free to pick in each case the answer that seemed to fit it best as a matter of educational psychology.

In the case of the wise child, the *Yerushalmi* version is surprising. It says: 'You, in return, should say to him: "By strength of hand the Eternal One brought us out of Egypt, from the house of bondage".' Thus the answer to the wise child, derived from passage 4, is taken from passage 3, which is the source of the 'simple' child. Surely it is far too simplistic an answer to give the wise one, and it is therefore hard to believe that the *Yerushalmi* text can be correct.

The *Mechilta* has an entirely different answer, not derived from *any* of the Scripture passages. It reads: 'You, in return, should take the initiative by expounding to him (or her) the laws of Passover, including the rule that "we do not conclude the Passover meal with *afikoman*".'

As usual, it is the *Mechilta* version that is followed in Seder Rav Amram and the *Haggadot*, except that they adopt the Yerushalmi's opening phrase, 'You, in return, should *say* to him,' in preference to the *Mechilta*'s 'You, in return, should *take the initiative*,' which obviously belongs to the child 'who does not know how to ask' and is quite inappropriate here.

The rule about the *afikoman* is quoted from the Mishnah (Pes. 10:8), where it occurs almost at the end of the whole tractate; therefore the implication may be that the 'wise' child is to have all the laws of Passover expounded to him (or her), down to the very last. However, the law of the *afikoman* is *not quite* the last, and therefore another explanation would be preferable.

The fact is that the meaning of the word *afikoman* is quite uncertain. Already in the Talmud there is a disagreement about it between Rabbi Chiyya's nephew Rav and Rav's great friend and rival Samuel (*Pes.* 119b). Evidently, therefore, the meaning of the word is not only obscure to us: it was so already within a generation after the compilation of the Mishnah. And it is this obscurity which may well explain the answer to be given to the 'wise' child: he (or she) is to be taught all the laws of Passover, down to the most obscure.

Among modern theories about the word *afikoman*, the most persuasive was put forward in 1925 by Robert Eisler (*Zeitschrift für die Neutestamentliche Wissenschaft*, No. 24, p. 161ff.) and reformulated by Professor David Daube in 1966 in a lecture given in the Crypt of St Paul's Cathedral, London, which was subsequently published as a pamphlet under the title *He that Cometh* by the London Diocesan Council for Christian–Jewish

Understanding. The essence of the theory is that *afikoman* derives from a Greek word meaning 'he who is coming' and is a cryptic reference to the Messiah. If that is correct, then the extra piece of *Matzah* which was not eaten at the end of the *Seder* – like the extra (fifth) cup of wine, later associated with Elijah, which was not drunk – symbolised the hope for the speedy coming of the Messiah. Such a symbolism would have been politically dangerous in Roman-occupied Palestine, and would therefore have been treated with a degree of secrecy. That might explain why the meaning of the word *afikoman* was so quickly forgotten, and it would give added point to the singling out of just this law of the Mishnah for the instruction of the 'wise' child: he (or she) alone was to be initiated into its esoteric meaning.

HOW TO TEACH THE WICKED CHILD

About the 'wicked' child, derived from passage 1, the sources are agreed that he (or she) is to be answered out of passage 2: 'It is because of what the Eternal One did for me when I came out of Egypt.' To which the Mechilta version adds: 'Me and not you; if you had been there you would not have been redeemed.' The *Yerushalmi* spells it out more fully: 'For me did God do it, for that man God did not do it; if he had been in Egypt he would never have been fit to be redeemed.' *Seder Rav Amram* follows the *Mechilta* version but transposes it from the second into the third person.

The reply to the 'wicked' child is introduced in the Yerushalmi with this phrase: 'Since he (or she) excludes himself (or herself) from the community, you, in return, should say to him (or her)...' Here the *Mechilta*, followed by *Seder Rav Amram*, is more elaborate: 'Since he (or she) excludes himself (or herself) from the community, and denies the essence of our faith, you should make him eat his words (literally 'blunt his teeth') by saying...'

HOW TO TEACH THE SIMPLE CHILD

According to the *Mechilta*, the 'stupid' or 'simple' child is to be taught in the words of the same passage, Number 3, from which he (or she) is derived: 'By strength of hand the Eternal One brought us out of Egypt, from the house of bondage.' But the Yerushalmi, having already used that verse in its answer to the 'wise' child, commits the absurdity of saying that the 'stupid' or 'simple' child, of all people, is to be taught the obscure Mishnah rule about the *afikoman*! Needless to say, *Seder Rav Amram* follows the *Mechilta*.

HOW TO TEACH THE CHILD WHO DOES NOT KNOW HOW TO ASK

With regard to the child 'who does not know how to ask', derived from passage 2, the sources agree that the parent must take the initiative; but while the Yerushalmi stops there, the *Mechilta* goes on to quote the opening words of the Scripture passage, 'You shall tell your child on that day,' and *Seder Rav Amram* completes the quotation: 'saying, it is because of what the Eternal One did for me when I came out of Egypt,' which spoils the symmetry since that verse has already been used in answer to the 'wicked' child. There can be little doubt, therefore, that *Seder Rav Amram*, and consequently the traditional *Haggadah*, are wrong, and that we should go back to the *Mechilta* or *Yerushalmi* version, both of which imply, or at least can be taken to mean, that the child 'who does not know how to ask' is not to be taught in the terms of any Scripture verse at all but in the parent's own words.

THE SEQUENCE OF THE TYPES

If we now look at the structure of the Midrash, there are two questions to be considered. The first is the *sequence* in which it deals with the four types of child, which is not the sequence of their Scriptural provenance, but as we have just gone through it: first the 'wise' child, derived from passage 4; then the 'wicked' one, derived from passage 1; then the 'simple' one, derived from passage 3; then the one 'who does not know how to ask', derived from passage 2.

Since the sequence is not Scriptural, it is presumably logical. If so, as good an explanation as any is the one suggested by the fourteenth-century scholar David Abudarham of Seville.

According to him the author 'wished to mention the four types of child in the order of their wisdom: first the 'wise' child; then the wicked one, for he too is wise and it is only out of rebelliousness that his heart has grown wicked; then the simple child, who is not really wise but has just enough wisdom to ask questions; and finally the one 'who is unable to ask', who has no wisdom at all' (J.D. Eisenstein, *Otzar perushim ve-tziyyurim 'al haggadah shel pesach*, Israel, 1970, p. 172a).

THE INTERRELATIONSHIP OF THE TYPES ACCORDING TO THE VILNA GAON

The other question concerns the interrelationship of the four types. About that very little has been written. An exception is Elijah ben Solomon, the Vilna Gaon. He sees the four types as two pairs of opposites. The 'wise' child, he says, is a *talmid chacham*, a Torah scholar, and his opposite is the one who does not even know how to ask a question. As for the other pair, the *tam* is one *ha-holech bit'mimut*, who behaves impeccably, and therefore his opposite is the wicked child. In support of the second pairing, the Vilna Gaon quotes a Scripture verse where the two words occur in juxtaposition: 'God destroys the innocent and the wicked' (Job 9:22).

That interpretation evidently depends on taking the word *tam* in a purely ethical sense, as meaning 'morally blameless' rather than 'mentally simple'. But that is extremely improbable, especially considering that in the ancient sources the alternative term *tippesh*, 'stupid', is much better attested. What we may nevertheless take from the Vilna Gaon is that the four types represent two sets of qualities – qualities of mind and qualities of character.

A NOVEL SUGGESTION

A possible key to another understanding of the interrelationship of the four types is the fact that in Jewish thought wisdom is not only a mental quality but also a moral quality; it is not only to be learned but also to be religious. Hence 'the fear of God is the beginning of wisdom' (Prov. 9:10). Similarly, the 'wicked' child, as Abudarham pointed out, is not necessarily ignorant; on the contrary, scoffers are often intellectually sophisticated. Then again, the 'simple' child is indeed unlearned or even unintelligent (if *tippesh* is the correct reading) but not therefore lacking in goodness (but quite possibly the contrary, especially if *tam* is the correct reading). As for the child 'who does not know how to ask', he (or she) is perhaps as yet too young to have given any clear indication how he (or she) will turn out in either respect.

It is then possible to see in our Midrash all the possible combinations of two qualities: an intellectual quality, say learning, and a moral quality, say goodness. Thus the 'wise' child is both learned and good; the 'wicked' child is learned but not good; the 'simple' child is good but not learned; and the one 'who is unable to ask' is as yet neither learned nor good. Expressed in symbolic logic, the pattern is A and B, A but not B, B but not A, and neither A nor B. Such an analysis of the four types makes them not only mutually exclusive but also collectively exhaustive.

It is not suggested that it can be proved that Rabbi Chiyya had such a pattern consciously in mind; but it is at least possible, and even if not, he still created a Midrash that lends itself to such an interpretation. Furthermore, it would not be a unique case of such a construction. On the contrary, one encounters it frequently in Rabbinic Literature.

In the fifth chapter of *Avot* there are several examples. It is said there, for instance, that there are four kinds of temperament: easy to provoke and easy to appease, hard to provoke and hard to appease, hard to provoke but easy to appease, easy to provoke but hard to appease (5:11); that there are four types of student: quick to learn and quick to forget, slow to learn and slow to forget, quick to learn but slow to forget, slow to learn but quick to forget (5:12); that some go to the house of study but don't practise what they learn there, some practise but don't go, some go but don't practise, and some neither go nor practise (5:14).

Another case in point is the Midrash about the 'Four Species' used in the celebration of *Sukkot*. The *Etrog*, it says, has both taste and smell, the date has taste but no smell, the myrtle has smell but no taste, and the willow has neither. Between them, they represent four types of Jew, for taste is a metaphor for knowledge of Torah and smell for good deeds (Lev.R. 30:12).

THE MORAL OF THE MIDRASH

These aphorisms are partly *jeux d'esprit*, but they also have a serious purpose, which is positively to *commend* an ideal type: the person who is hard to provoke but easy to appease, or who is quick to learn but slow to forget, or who both studies and practises, or who is both knowledgeable in Torah and a doer of good deeds. So, too, the purpose of the Midrash of the Four Children is to hold up the ideal of the 'wise' child, who is both learned and good, and in particular, who both desires to know the history of his or her people and to identify himself or herself with its communal life.

Universalising Tendencies in Anglo-Jewish Liturgy

15 July 2003

PARTICULARISM AND UNIVERSALISM IN JUDAISM AND TRADITIONAL JEWISH LITURGY

There has always been in Judaism a tension between particularism and universalism. But the relative emphasis has varied in the different phases of Jewish history and the different genres of Jewish literature. In the traditional Jewish liturgy, which concerns us, particularism predominates. To a very large extent Jewish worship is a 'private conversation' between the Jewish people and its God, the people addressing God in prayer, God addressing the people in the Scripture readings. Thus the non-Jewish world does not receive much attention in the traditional Jewish liturgy.

Of course there are expressions of the hope for the coming of a time when the nations will be united in the worship of the One God and live together in freedom, justice, friendship and peace. But that is an eschatological hope. If we look for expressions of concern for the well-being of non-Jewish humanity in the pre-messianic here-and-now, they are not easy to find. There is indeed a daily prayer invoking God's compassion on, among others, *gerey tzedek*, sincere proselytes, but they of course are Jews. There is, above all, the prayer for the government, which goes back to the Middle Ages. But even that has usually been expressed in terms of Jewish self-interest.

A typical one, which appeared in the first edition of the

Anglo-Jewish Orthodox prayer book, known after its translator as 'Singer's', dating from 1890 and hence referring to Queen Victoria, beseeches God to 'put compassion into her heart and into the hearts of all her counsellors and nobles, that they may deal kindly with us and with all Israel'. And it concludes: 'In her days and ours may Judah be saved, and Israel dwell securely, and may the Redeemer come unto Zion.' No concern is expressed for the welfare of Her Majesty's non-Jewish subjects, although, as we shall see, that omission has since been remedied.

THE IMPACT OF THE EMANCIPATION

The Emancipation changed the way in which most Jews perceived their relationship with the non-Jewish world. They were now inclined to identify themselves with humanity in a way they had not done before. And they could not very well leave that perception behind whenever they crossed the threshold of the synagogue. Therefore the proportion between particularism and universalism of the traditional Jewish liturgy, which had seemed right in the past, no longer seemed right. A need was felt for a little less particularism and a little more universalism.

UNIVERSALISING TENDENCY IN ORTHODOX JUDAISM: PRAYER FOR THE ROYAL FAMILY

This need was felt, here and there, even in Orthodox Judaism. An example is the Prayer for the Royal Family in Singer's prayer book. Within ten years of its first publication, the supplication that the Queen and her counsellors 'may deal kindly with us and with all Israel' had been enlarged to read '*that they may uphold the peace of the realm, advance the welfare of the nation,* and deal kindly and truly with all Israel'. And in 1935 Chief Rabbi Dr Joseph Hertz took the further step of universalising the conclusion of the prayer as well, so that it read: 'May the Heavenly Father *spread the tabernacle of peace over all the dwellers on earth*; and may the redeemer come unto Zion.'

But that is a rare exception. By and large, Orthodox Jews have not felt the urge – or else have not considered themselves entitled – to make changes in the traditional liturgy in order to universalise it, or for any other reason. It is therefore almost exclusively in Progressive Judaism that the universalising tendency has manifested itself.

THE PRAYER BOOKS OF REFORM AND LIBERAL JUDAISM IN BRITAIN

A large part of that story relates to Germany, the United States and some other countries. Our concern, however, is only with Britain and its two Progressive movements, popularly known as 'Reform' and 'Liberal' respectively.

The liturgy of the Reform movement, entitled *Forms of Prayer*, goes back to 1841 and the first rabbi of the West London Synagogue, David Woolf Marks. It was substantially revised in 1931 under the influence of Morris Joseph and Harold Reinhart, and replaced by a new generation of prayer books, edited by Lionel Blue and Jonathan Magonet, in 1977. I shall refer to these books as 'Reform' plus the date of publication.

The liturgy of Liberal Judaism goes back primarily to Rabbi Israel Mattuck's *Liberal Jewish Prayer Book* of 1926, revised in 1937. It was replaced in 1967 by *Service of the Heart*, and again in 1995 by *Siddur Lev Chadash*, both co-edited by myself and the late Rabbi Chaim Stern. I shall refer to these books as 'Liberal' plus date of publication.

Now let us examine how these liturgies have dealt with six test cases, all taken from the daily prayer known as '*Amidah* or *T'fillah* or *Sh'moneh Esreh*.

1. 'GOD WILL SEND A REDEEMER'

The first of the 19 (originally 18) benedictions which comprise it is called *Avot*, referring to the Patriarchs whose piety it invokes. It includes assuring the worshipper that 'God will send a redeemer to their children's children for His name's sake, in love'. This is clearly a reference to the Messiah. The concept is not necessarily particularistic, for it is possible to believe, as indeed Judaism has traditionally taught, that the Messiah will inaugurate a golden age for all humanity. Nevertheless the more immediate connotation of the word is that of an anointed king of the Davidic line who will reign over a restored Jewish commonwealth.

The Reformers found it problematic because it seemed to them to run counter to their desire to identify themselves permanently with the societies that had granted them citizenship. It also seemed to contradict their belief that, however desirable the restoration of Jewish sovereignty in their ancient homeland might be, nevertheless Judaism was *in principle* a universal religion, capable of being practised anywhere on God's earth. For this reason among others, they tended to play down, or even to reject, the concept of a personal Messiah and to emphasise, instead, the hope for a 'messianic age', understood in a universalistic sense. What then did they do with the *go'el*, 'redeemer', of the *Avot*?

The Liberal liturgy, following an American Reform tradition that goes back to 1856, has always changed *go'el* to *ge'ullah*, 'Redemption'. The Reform liturgy, on the other hand, has always retained the traditional *go'el*, but the translation of the word has undergone some interesting changes. The early editions had 'Redeemer' with a capital 'R', perhaps with the intention that it should be taken to refer to God, although that is syntactically impossible in this case, where God is said to be the one who *sends* the *go'el*. Perhaps that is why the 1931 edition changed the translation to 'redeemer' with a small 'r', thus making it refer to the Messiah, after all. Most curiously, the 1977 edition translates *go'el* as 'rescue', which has a twofold implication. On the one hand the editors chose an abstract noun, presumably because they were uncomfortable with the concept of a personal Messiah. On the other hand they opted for the sudden-divine-intervention form of the messianic hope rather than the gradual-amelioration form which Progressive Judaism has generally espoused.

2. 'HEALER OF THE SICK OF HIS PEOPLE ISRAEL'

The eighth benediction of the '*Amidah* traditionally concludes with the eulogy that God 'heals the sick of His people Israel'. This is an unfortunate particularism, since the healing processes of nature work impartially for all peoples, and nobody would wish it to be otherwise. It is also easy to universalise since the more general eulogy, that God 'heals the sick' *sans phrase*, is well attested in the ancient sources (*Sifrey* Deut. to Deut. 33:2, *J. Ber.*

2:4). Surprisingly, though, not all Progressive liturgies have adopted that remedy. In England, the Liberals have done so since 1967, the Reformers since 1977.

3. 'GATHER US TOGETHER FROM THE FOUR CORNERS OF THE EARTH'

The tenth benediction of the '*Amidah*, known as 'The Ingathering of the Exiles', traditionally includes the petition, 'Gather us together from the four corners of the earth' and concludes by eulogising God 'who gathers the dispersed of His people Israel'. This is another expression of what might be called the 'back-to-square-one' view of Jewish history, that as in ancient times the Jews were a sovereign people in their own land, so they will be again in the messianic future. But this is not how emancipated Jews saw themselves. On the contrary, they regarded themselves as permanent residents of the countries in which they lived. What then did they do with this prayer?

Reform 1841 kept the traditional Sephardi text, Reform 1931 omitted the benediction altogether, and Reform 1977 introduced a new version, in which the key phrase reads: 'and speedily may the voice of liberty (*pedut*) be heard in the cities of our lands'. Unfortunately, the word for 'voice' is missing in the Hebrew; the word for 'liberty' should, by analogy with Leviticus 25:10, be *deror* rather than *pedut*, and the reference to 'the cities of our lands' is peculiar. The concluding eulogy praises God 'who redeems His people Israel in mercy'.

Liberal 1967 as well as 1995 universalises the prayer, making it a petition on behalf of the oppressed in general rather than only the Jewish people. The key phrase reads 'and let the song of freedom be heard in the four corners of the earth', and the concluding eulogy praises God as 'Redeemer of the oppressed'.

4. 'SPEEDILY RE-ESTABLISH THE THRONE OF DAVID'

The fourteenth and fifteenth benedictions of the '*Amidah*, which were originally one, are known respectively as *boneh yerushalayim*, about the rebuilding of Jerusalem, and *birkat david*, the benediction about David. In the first of these, according to the Ashkenazi text, God is implored to return to Jerusalem, to rebuild it, and speedily to re-establish in it the throne of David. And in the second there is a further supplication that 'the sprout of David may flourish speedily', that is, that the restoration of David's kingdom, under his descendant the Messiah, may come about soon. The problems which this raises from a Progressive point of view have already been indicated. How have the liturgies of Progressive Judaism dealt with them?

Reform 1841 reproduced the traditional Sephardi text of both benedictions. Reform 1977 has a strange mixture of theological inconsistency and inept innovation. Benediction 14, for instance, begins in the traditional way, except that the Hebrew text implores God to 'return' whereas the English translation asks only that He should 'turn' to Jerusalem. It then beseeches God to rebuild 'the city of righteousness' and continues with a fine allusion to Isaiah 56:7, 'For My house shall be called a house of prayer for all peoples', except that Deutero-Isaiah's 'house' has been unaccountably changed to *machon*, 'institute', which in turn is mistranslated as 'centre', and that his 'peoples', in the plural, has sadly become 'people' in the singular. Benediction 15 has been completely re-written. It begins, 'Fulfil in our time the words of Your servant David', which is odd since David is not known as the author of any messianic prophecy. It then continues by referring to God's promise to rule the world in justice and compassion, and to bring to it light and salvation, and concludes with the traditional eulogy.

Liberal 1967 and again, slightly differently, Liberal 1995 modify both benedictions. The later version of Benediction 14, as translated, reads: 'Let Your presence dwell in Jerusalem, and Zion be filled with justice and righteousness. May peace be in her gates and quietness in the hearts of her inhabitants. Let Your teaching go forth from Zion, and Your word from Jerusalem.' In short, it is all about Jerusalem, but without suggesting that God has been absent from the city, and without any reference to the throne of David. It concludes in the traditional way with 'Builder of Jerusalem'. Benediction 15 retains the traditional text, but universalises it by the simple device of substituting 'the sprout of righteousness', a phrase taken from Jeremiah (33:15), for 'the sprout of David'.

5. THE RETURN OF THE *SHECHINAH*

The seventeenth benediction of the *'Amidah* concludes by praising God 'who will cause the Divine Presence to return to Zion'. The phrase is a poetic metaphor for the rebuilding of the Temple. There is, moreover, reason to believe that the traditional wording of the benediction dates from after the destruction of the Temple and replaced an earlier one which concluded 'whom alone we worship in reverence' (*J. Sotah* 7:6). This pre-Destruction version is, furthermore, found in the Cairo Genizah and is still traditionally used in the re-enactment of the ritual of the Priestly Benediction on festivals.

However, Progressive Judaism has always rejected the traditional hope for the restoration of the Temple with its sacrificial ritual, and looked on the synagogue as having permanently replaced it. In addition, the notion that God has been absent from Jerusalem and needs to return is inconsistent with a liberal theology. Therefore the obvious thing for Progressive liturgies to do would be to revert to the older, pre-Destruction version of this benediction and interpret it as a petition for God's acceptance of present-day, synagogue worship. And indeed most of them have done just that, but not all.

Reform 1841 had the traditional *ha-machazir sh'chinato l'-tziyyon*, but Reform 1931 significantly changed that to *ha-mashreh sh'chinato 'al tziyyon*, translated 'who causest thy holy spirit to rest upon Zion', thus eliminating any suggestion either that God has been absent or that His presence depends on the Temple. Reform 1977, however, reverts to the traditional text, which it translates 'who restores His presence to Zion'. Liberal 1967 and 1995, however, have 'whom alone we worship in reverence'.

6. THE BLESSING OF PEACE

The last benediction of the Amidah is known as *birkat kohanim*, because it is modelled on the Priestly Benediction, and sometimes as *birkat shalom* because, like the Priestly Benediction, it empha-sises the blessing of peace. Its concluding eulogy traditionally praises God 'who blesses His people Israel with peace'.

The problem this raises is obvious. Whether we understand *shalom* in the narrower sense of the absence of war or in the broader sense of welfare, surely it is neither possible nor desirable that it should be conferred on the Jewish people alone but withheld from the rest of humanity. Surely peace is indivisible. And did not the prophet Jeremiah make just that point when he wrote to the exiles in Babylonia, 'Seek the peace of the city where I have sent you into exile, and pray to God on its behalf, for in its peace you will find your peace' (29:7)? Surely the case for universalising this prayer is overwhelming. Furthermore, there is an easy way of doing it, since we have another version of the concluding eulogy which simply praises God as 'the Maker of peace': a version which is found already in an ancient source (Lev. R. 9:9) as well as the Cairo Genizah and which is in fact used in the Ashkenazi tradition during the Ten Days of Repentance. One would therefore expect all Progressive prayer books to opt for the universalistic conclusion, and indeed most of them have done so, but not all.

Reform Judaism has always thought it preferable to pray for the peace of Israel only, and that applies even to its current, 1977 prayer book. But Liberal Judaism has since 1923 praised God as 'the Maker of peace' *sans phrase.*

CONCLUSION

All Progressive prayer books show a tendency to shift the traditional balance from particularism towards universalism, but the extent to which they do so varies considerably. Those of the Liberal movement go a great deal further in that direction than those of the Reform movement. It is idle to speculate what the future will bring. But it seems safe to assume that however the Jewish people see their relationship with the rest of humanity – which will continue to be influenced by historical circumstances – that view will sooner or later reflect itself in their liturgy.

The Ethical Issues Surrounding the Middle East

12 December 2001

PRINCIPLES OF JEWISH ETHICS

Judaism is a strongly ethical religion. Central to it is the belief in a moral God who demands that human beings shall act morally towards one another.[1]

The basic principles of Jewish ethics are, first, the dignity of every human being, created in God's image,[2] and secondly, 'You shall love your neighbour as yourself'.[3] In short, we are required to treat our fellow men and women with respect, and to seek their welfare.

On this twin foundation Judaism has built a comprehensive code of conduct governing the relations between person and person, rich and poor, husband and wife, parents and children, teachers and pupils, employers and employees, merchants and customers, doctors and patients, rulers and ruled.[4]

Like any ethical code worthy of the name, it is universal in application. The Hebrew Bible repeatedly enjoins concern for 'the strangers who live among you', even to the extent of demanding that we love them, too, as ourselves.[5] And the Talmud teaches that acts of kindness such as maintaining the poor, visiting the sick and burying the dead should be performed towards Jews and non-Jews alike.[6]

INTERNATIONAL RELATIONS

Like other ethical codes, Judaism's is primarily concerned with relations between individuals rather than collectivities. But there is nevertheless an implication that the same principles should govern relations between social units, from families up to nations.

Unfortunately, human beings are notoriously slow to make that transition. The larger the group, the less inclined they are to feel that it has any moral responsibility towards other groups. That individuals should care for their neighbours is readily enough accepted, at least in theory. But a nation is commonly regarded as entitled to pursue its own self-interest, with little or no regard for other nations. The only code it is supposed to observe is the non-ethical one of *Realpolitik*.

All the more does it need to be emphasised that moral imperatives do apply between nations. The Hebrew prophets frequently castigate not only individuals but also peoples, and not only other peoples but also their own. Amos, for instance, castigates in turn the neighbouring kingdoms of Syria, Philistia, Phoenicia, Edom, Ammon and Moab before rounding all the more severely on the kingdoms of Judah and Israel.[7]

Similarly, the Prophets affirm that God cares for all peoples, with the implication that we should do likewise. 'Are you not like the Ethiopians to Me, O people of Israel?' says Amos in God's name.[8] And Isaiah makes God declare: 'Blessed be Egypt My people, and Assyria the work of My hands, and Israel My heritage.'[9]

Then again, the Prophets depict the ultimate future as a time of international harmony and peace,[10] with the implication that in order to get 'from here to there', the nations had better learn to behave morally towards one another.

Similarly, the Mishnah teaches that 'the world rests on three pillars: truth, justice and peace';[11] and a commentator explains that these virtues need to be practised between nations as well as between individuals.[12]

Thus it is clear that the same moral principles which apply to personal relations should also govern international relations. But it has to be admitted that the full implications of that principle have not been worked out in Judaism as thoroughly as those relating to personal ethics. To that extent its teachings need to be supplemented by the more recently created instruments of international law such as the various United Nations declarations and conventions, themselves largely influenced by Hebraic values.

There is one further difficulty with the transference of moral values from the personal to the international sphere. Although personal behaviour is largely left to the individual conscience, it is nevertheless backed up by state legislation. By contrast, international law is largely unenforceable, and will remain so until there is some kind of world government.

WHOSE LAND?

Let us now apply these principles to the Middle East conflict. Our point of departure is the obvious one that it concerns the conflicting claims of two peoples to the same strip of land on the eastern seaboard of the Mediterranean, geographically known as Palestine.

To whom then does it belong? There is an important sense in which its only rightful Owner is God.[13] But then the Divine Freeholder may conceivably lease it to a particular people. Just that is what the ancient Israelites believed. For the Hebrew Bible is replete with passages in which God is said to have promised the land to Abraham,[14] Isaac,[15] Jacob,[16] Moses[17] and Joshua,[18] to be inherited by the Jewish people in perpetuity – either unconditionally[19] or provided that they remain loyal to the Covenant.[20]

Unfortunately, there are fundamentalists who read the Bible as a divine book and therefore take these promises at face value,[21] which means that they place theological considerations above ethical considerations. Against this, liberally minded Jews would assert the common-sense view that the Bible, though divinely inspired, is a human book, and that nothing may ever override ethical considerations. On this view, God does not make long-term geopolitical dispositions in disregard of historical events such as conquests and migrations which may materially alter the ethical situation.

But this doesn't mean that the Jewish people's claim to Palestine is invalid. Admittedly, it is not as clear-cut as that of the Palestinians. Theirs is simple and straightforward. It rests on the fact that for many centuries, until the nineteenth and well into the twentieth, they constituted the large majority of the indigenous population.

The Jewish claim, by contrast, is complex. It rests on several facts none of which is decisive in isolation but which, cumulatively, make a very powerful case. Among these is the fact that in biblical times the Jews not only were the majority in the land but, as long as they remained unconquered by neighbouring empires, exercised sovereignty in it – the only indigenous people to have done so since then. Another is the fact that when eventually they left the land they did not, for the most part, do so voluntarily but because the Romans expelled them. A third fact is that even then some remained in the land and that thereafter they returned to it in smaller or larger numbers whenever conditions allowed.[22]

Not only did they never completely abandon the land, but they maintained an extraordinarily close emotional bond with it, and never ceased to pray that ultimately they would be able to return to it. Jewish literature from the Bible onwards abounds with expressions of a passionate love and longing for the land. And any dismissal of these as only pious sentiments is refuted by the colossal outpouring of energy which that ancient hope has elicited from the Jewish people in modern times. Here I am referring to the extraordinary dedication, self-sacrifice and resourcefulness with which the Zionist pioneers and the builders of the State of Israel have drained the swamps and made the deserts blossom and generally transformed the land into an oasis of agricultural and industrial prosperity.

To all that we must add that the experience of the Jewish people outside the land was often precarious and ultimately became catastrophic. In Muslim lands they rarely fared better than second-class citizenship. In Christendom they were generally treated as pariahs and periodically persecuted and expelled. And when, with the Emancipation, a new age of tolerance seemed at last to dawn, that hope was soon shattered by a resurgence of anti-Semitism more horrific than Dante's *Inferno*. The need of the Jewish people for a homeland which might serve as a dependable haven of refuge became desperately urgent.

Here I must interject that there are varieties of Zionism, which should not all be judged alike. There is a chauvinistic, militaristic, territorially maximalist kind, at present seemingly on the ascendant, which I find morally unacceptable. But what was and will again be mainstream Zionism seems to me a legitimate, honourable and even noble enterprise which deserves, as it has to a large extent received, the sympathy, support and admiration of humanity.

That view was taken by the British Government (although some historians would maintain that it acted out of a mistaken perception of national self-interest) when it issued the Balfour Declaration in 1917, and by the League of Nations when it mandated Britain to implement it.

THE PARTITION PRINCIPLE

I would maintain, then, that the Palestinian and Jewish claims to the land, although differently grounded, are equally valid and, in so far as such matters can be quantified, of approximately equal weight. If so, then justice demands that the two peoples must, in one way or another, *share* the land.

One way might have been a bi-national state, as advocated by some eminent Jews in the 1920s and 30s.[23] But it would not have provided a guaranteed haven of refuge, and was rejected by both peoples.

The only remaining solution, consistent with any kind of justice, was *partition*. Accordingly, that was proposed by various commissions of inquiry, and adopted by the United Nations General Assembly when, by a majority of 33 votes to 13, it passed the Partition Resolution of 29 November 1947.

Furthermore, the partition principle has been implicitly reaffirmed by the UN in Resolution 242 of 1967, Resolution 338 of 1973, the Preamble of the Camp David Accords of 1979, and the Oslo Accords of 1993. It may therefore be said to express the collective will of humanity. Indeed, it has been implicitly endorsed by successive Israeli governments as well as by Egypt and Jordan and, since 1988, the Palestinians.

In view of such remarkable unanimity, the essential basis for a just settlement of the conflict has long been crystal-clear. Yet the conflict continues, and its resolution seems as distant as ever.

For this lamentable fact both peoples, Jewish and Palestinian, as well as their sponsors, must bear a heavy responsibility; and as Amos criticised other peoples before criticising his own, so let me proceed in the same order.

THE ARAB-PALESTINIAN RECORD

The Arabs of Palestine, who had always been less than friendly to non-Muslim immigrants, resented the arrival of Zionist pioneers which began towards the end of the nineteenth century, accelerated after the Balfour Declaration, and became a flood with the rise of Hitlerism in Germany. Their resentment was understandable but regrettable. It was ungenerous. And when it inspired anti-Jewish riots in the 1920s and 30s, it became positively reprehensible, and set a pattern of violence which has bedevilled the conflict ever since.

When the UN voted for partition and the British withdrew, the violence degenerated into all-out war. That the Arab states should have rejected the Partition Plan is, again, understandable but regrettable. For if there is to be international law and order, then the collective will of humanity as expressed through the UN, created for that purpose, must be accepted even when it is not to the liking of a particular member state. The Arabs cannot simultaneously defend their rejection of the Partition Resolution and condemn the State of Israel for its defiance of other UN resolutions. And if their rejection was motivated by some dogma to the effect that a non-Islamic state cannot be tolerated in the Islamic Middle East, then that dogma is to be repudiated as categorically as the Jewish fundamentalist claim to the whole of Palestine on biblical grounds.

Since partition is the only just solution, therefore every attempt to prevent it must be considered unethical. That applies to all the propaganda that emanated from Arab sources until recently, and to a large extent still does, to the effect that the State of Israel has no right to exist. It applies still more to the vicious anti-Jewish hatred purveyed by much of that propaganda, and even instilled into school children.[24] And it certainly applies to the countless acts of terrorism carried out against the State of Israel ever since its creation. For if ethical judgements are to be made at all about the Middle East conflict, then violence, especially against civilians, must be unequivocally condemned, whether perpetrated by one side or the other.

Admittedly, the 1967 war, largely provoked by Colonel Nasser of Egypt, created a new situation in that, following Israel's victory, the Palestinians of the West Bank and Gaza found themselves under a foreign occupation which UN

Resolution 242 sought to bring to an end. (Previous occupations, by Jordan and Egypt, had been less resented.) But for the failure to implement that resolution, including its demand for Israel to withdraw from the conquered territories, the Arabs must take a large share of the blame, not least in view of their Khartoum summit of September 1967 with its Three Noes: No peace with Israel, no negotiations with Israel, no recognition of Israel.[25]

It is true that with the years the Israeli occupation became increasingly intolerable from a Palestinian point of view, leading ultimately to the first *intifada*, and then to the second, which is still going on. But though the Palestinians cannot be blamed for their attempt to throw off the occupation, and would have been widely admired for it if they had adopted a strategy of passive resistance *à la* Mahatma Gandhi, Martin Luther King and Nelson Mandela, the atrocities, including the suicide bombings, perpetrated by their terrorist organisations cannot be condoned.

It should be added that the pressures and persecutions, to which the half-million Jews living in Islamic countries of the Middle East and North Africa were subjected from 1948 onwards, prompted most of them to seek refuge in Israel. (Clearly, this is a major factor to be taken into account in determining what would constitute a just solution of the conflict.)

That, in short, is the ethical case against the way the Middle East conflict has been handled by the Palestinians and their Arab sponsors.

THE JEWISH-ISRAELI RECORD

But it does not exonerate the Jewish people. For from its very beginning the Zionist movement failed to take sufficiently seriously the presence, let alone the grievances and aspirations, of a large Arab population in the land in which they proposed to establish their homeland, and the paramount importance of cultivating their good will.[26] Although that was perhaps understandable in the days when colonialism was still commonly considered acceptable, it became less excusable as the twentieth century wore on, yet has tended to persist.

Admittedly, the bitter hostility of the Arabs towards the Zionist state before, during and after its birth did not encourage magnanimity towards them. Nevertheless it is now known from a number of recent historical studies[27] that during the 1948 war the Zionists did a great deal more than defend the portion of the land allotted to them by the UN. They also aimed for as large a territory as possible with as small an Arab population as possible.[28] In that process they drove out the populations of more than 400 Arab villages,[29] and some of their armed units, I am deeply ashamed to say, committed atrocities[30] which, in turn, created a general panic and caused some hundreds of thousands of Arabs to flee the country. Consequently, for the *naqba* (the Palestinian tragedy) the creators of the State of Israel must bear a substantial share of responsibility.

Since then, Israel has consistently failed to cultivate a moderate climate of opinion which might have encouraged a like tendency on the Arab side. And though it has commendably made peace with Egypt and Jordan, it has not yet done enough to launch, or to respond to, initiatives aiming at a solution of its much more fundamental conflict with the Palestinians.

In addition, Israel has during most of its history practised a policy of fierce retaliation for any attack launched against it, in the false but nevertheless persistent belief that this was necessary for its security. In fact, far from deterring further violence, every reprisal has merely provoked a counter-reprisal and deepened anger and hatred on both sides.

This policy reached its nadir in 1982 with Ariel Sharon's unprovoked and disastrous invasion of Lebanon, fraudulently named 'Peace for Galilee', of which Abba Eban said that it marked 'a dark age in the moral history of the Jewish People'.[31]

In recent years Israel's policy of building more and more settlements in the occupied territories in brazen defiance of world opinion has had the effect, if not the intention, of making the attainment of a peace settlement more and more difficult. It goes without saying that these actions, as well as the confiscations of Palestinian land, demolitions of houses, and collective punishments, are indefensible from a Jewish ethical point of view.

CONCLUSION

I am bound to conclude that for the fact that 54 years after the UN Partition Resolution the Middle East conflict has still not been resolved, Jews and Arabs, Israelis and Palestinians, are *both* to blame – in what proportion, can indeed be debated. But so as not to conclude on a negative note, let me add that on both sides of the conflict there have also been ethically commendable efforts to reach an accommodation.

On the Arab side, we should remember the courage and imagination which Anwar Sadat showed when he flew to Jerusalem to speak so eloquently in the Knesset for a peace agreement, for which he was assassinated. We should honour the memory of King Hussein of Jordan for the statesmanlike, conciliatory role he played in his later years, as his brother Prince Hassan continues to do. In view of the allegation so often heard nowadays that the Palestinians don't want peace, we should recall that in September 1993 Fatah activists led marches of tens of thousands of Palestinians through the streets of the West Bank, Gaza and East Jerusalem in support of the Oslo Agreement. We should acknowledge that many eminent Palestinians have long co-operated with their Israeli counter-parts in organisations such as IPCRI (the Israel/Palestine Centre for Research and Information) and the Jewish-Arab Centre for Peace at Giv'at Haviva (which has won the UNESCO Prize for Peace Education), and have co-signed the Joint Israeli-Palestinian Declaration of 25 July this year. Mention should also be made of the fact that Sari Nusseibeh, President of Al-Quds University and the Palestinians' chief envoy in East Jerusalem, has condemned violence and urged a peace agreement that does not include the contentious 'right of return'.

On the Jewish side it needs to be said that Israel is a democratic country in which Jews and Arabs alike enjoy freedom of speech; that it has had many brave peace activists, including Israel Shahak and Uri Avnery, as well as pro-peace writers like Amos Oz and David Grossman; that Prime Minister Yitzhak Rabin, although a late convert to the cause, showed both vision and courage when he addressed the peace rally, which cost him his life, in Tel Aviv in 1995; that there are in Israel several active peace organisations including *Shalom 'Achshav* (Peace Now), *Netivot Shalom* (Paths of Peace), *Gush Shalom* (Peace Bloc), *B'tzelem* (the Israeli Information Centre for Human Rights in the Occupied Territories); also *Shomrey Mishpat* (Rabbis for Human Rights) which has won the prestigious Knesset Peace Prize. Their aim, in their own words, is to prove that 'Judaism is a religion of justice, truth and peace, of tolerance, compassion and righteousness'.

With so much good will among some of the people on both sides, we should not despair. But it has to be admitted that just at present it is difficult not to. Nevertheless it is still possible to return to the path of reason and justice, of moderation and restraint, of reconciliation and peace. At least let us hope and pray that it is not too late.

NOTES

1. Cf. Psalm 11:7, Jeremiah 9:22f.
2. Cf. Genesis 1:26f., 5:1; Midrash Genesis Rabbah 24:7.
3. Leviticus 19:18; *Sifra* ad loc.
4. See *Principles of Jewish Ethics*, Rabbi John D. Rayner, New Jewish Initiative for Social Justice, 1998.
5. Leviticus 19:34.
6. *Gittin* 61a.
7. Amos 1–2.
8. Amos 9:7.
9. Isaiah 19:25.
10. Isaiah 2:4, 11:1–9, 32:16f., Micah 4:1–4.
11. *Avot* 1:18.
12. Obadiah Bertinoro ad loc.
13. Cf. Psalm 24:1, Joel 4:2.
14. Genesis 12:2, 13:15, 15:7,18, 17:8.
15. Genesis 26:3.
16. Genesis 28:13, 35:12, 48:4.
17. Exodus 3:8, 6:8.
18. Joshua 1:3.
19. Deuteronomy 32:8.
20. Leviticus 18:26ff., 26:27–39, Jeremiah 18:7f.
21. On Jewish fundamentalism, see John D. Rayner, *Fundamentalism* (pamphlet), Union of Liberal and Progressive Synagogues, 1998. On the relevance of this to the Middle East conflict, see chapter 24 ('The Land, the Law and the Liberal Conscience') in John D. Rayner, *Jewish Religious Law: A Progressive Perspective*, Oxford, 1998.
22. See James Parkes, *A History of Palestine from 135 A.D. to Modern Times*, London, 1949.
23. For instance, Judah L. Magnes and Martin Buber.
24. However, Professor Nathan Brown of George Washington University has demonstrated that Palestinian school textbooks are not as hostile to Israel as anti-Palestinian propaganda has alleged (Anglo File, Ha-aretz, 30 November 2001).
25. There is reason to think, however, that these negations were not meant as categorically as they sound. See Avi Shlaim, *The Iron Wall: Israel and the Arab World*, London, 2000, p. 258f.
26. That point was strongly made by Walter Zander, Secretary of the Friends of

the Hebrew University, in 1946 and 1948. See the article by his son Michael Zander in the *Jewish Quarterly*, Autumn 2001, No. 183. The same point has been made, for example, by Simha Flapan in his *Zionism and the Palestinians*, London, 1979.

27. For example, Benny Morris, *The Birth of the Palestinian Refugee Problem, 1947–1949*, Cambridge, 1987; *Tikkun Ta'ut* ('Correcting a Mistake: Jews and Arabs in Palestine/Israel 1936–1956'), Am Oved Publishers, 2001; Avi Shlaim, *The Politics of Partition: King Abdullah, the Zionists and Palestine, 1921–1951*, Oxford, 1998; *The Iron Wall: Israel and the Arab World*, London, 2000; Eugene L. Rogan and Avi Shlaim (eds.), *The War for Palestine: Rewriting the History of 1948*, Cambridge, 2001; Anton La Guardia, *Holy Land, Unholy War: Israelis and Palestinians*, London, 2001.

28. To call that 'ethnic cleansing' is not quite fair since the word 'cleansing' implies a racial contempt which was not there.

29. Eugene L. Rogan and Avi Shlaim, *The War for Palestine*, p. 14.

30. For example, at Deir Yassin, Lod and Kibya. See also *The War for Palestine*, p. 54f.

31. *Jerusalem Post, International Edition*, 8–14 August 1982. The invasion was unprovoked and fraudulently named in that, with the exception of one minor incident, the PLO in Lebanon had observed a cease-fire for nearly a year.

Open Letter to David A. Harris, Executive Director of the American Jewish Committee

16 December 2002

Dear Mr Harris,

Your ten-page 'Letter from One Jew to Another' of 29 October 2002 is a brilliant piece of sustained rhetoric, which expresses as powerfully as anything I have read the currently dominant attitude of the leadership of our people both in Israel and in the Diaspora. But though the facts you cite – as distinct from the generalisations you derive from them – are true enough, you omit a whole lot of other facts, inconvenient to your thesis. That makes your letter an exercise in demagoguery rather than a sober appraisal.

Briefly summarised, your thesis is that there is a worldwide conspiracy to destroy the State of Israel and that in these circumstances it behoves all Jews to stand solidly together in support of its present government. In my opinion that thesis is profoundly mistaken, and the policies that flow from it are hugely inimical to the best interests of the State of Israel and the Jewish people.

You begin by documenting how until 2000 all was going swimmingly for Israel and the Jewish people, then everything went wrong. So sudden, as you see it, was this *volte-face* that 'any serious supporter of Israel had to be stunned by the rapidity of Israel's changed international standing after September 2000'. But there is no mystery. Historical developments have causes, though they may take time to produce their full effects. So let me try to unravel the mystery for you.

- The Oslo Declaration of Principles raised high hopes, and boosted the peace camps, on both sides. On the other hand, the very prospect of a peace settlement, involving territorial compromise, provoked the rejectionists, who refused to accept anything less than 'Greater Palestine' and 'Greater Israel' respectively. On the Palestinian side, Hamas immediately launched a new series of terror attacks against Israel. On the Israeli side, Baruch Goldstein massacred 29 Palestinians praying in a Hebron mosque, and Yigal Amir assassinated Yitzhak Rabin.

- Under Shimon Peres the Oslo process made some headway, under Binyamin Netanyahu it was virtually halted, then resumed by Ehud Barak. But throughout all those years the building of Jewish settlements in the occupied territories, begun in 1967, went full-steam ahead, in stubborn defiance of UN resolutions and world opinion. This crucial fact, which you don't bother to mention, was bound to arouse ever-increasing resentment among the Palestinians, and slowly to erode their initial faith in the Oslo process.

- Furthermore, the settlement programme entailed the deployment of large detachments of the IDF to defend the settlers, the criss-crossing of the West Bank with connecting roads strictly for Jewish use only, the confiscation of Palestinian-owned land, the destruction of olive groves, the seizure of water supplies, and the strangulation of the Palestinian economy. In addition, the measures Israel felt compelled to take to suppress the resultant unrest included collective punishments, house demolitions, curfews, and daily humiliations at the checkpoints. All this intensified the resentment still further and by September 2000 it was like a powder keg. Then Ariel Sharon, by his Temple Mount walkabout with a huge police escort, ignited it and so triggered the Second *Intifada*.

- Israel's counter-measures became increasingly harsh, incited the Palestinian terrorists to step up their murderous activities, including suicide bombings, and caused the general Palestinian population, even though most of them continued to disapprove of violence, nevertheless to sympathise with them and to become a source of recruits for them. Hence the vicious cycle of attack, reprisal and counter-reprisal which we have witnessed in the last two years.

- All this was sensationally reported by the world's media and so brought the escalating conflict graphically to the attention of the general public. Most people were horrified by the tactics, especially suicide bombings, of the Palestinian terrorists, but scarcely less so by the brutality of Israel's reprisals, including helicopter gunship raids and targeted assassinations. Considering, further, Israel's persistent defiance of UN resolutions, relentless colonisation of occupied land, vast military superiority, and the consequent disproportion between Israeli and Palestinian casualties, it is hardly surprising that many came to see the conflict as a grossly unequal one and to sympathise with the underdog.
- This climate of opinion, in turn, gave the dormant forces of anti-Semitism and anti-Zionism an opportunity to express themselves with a new brazenness, further feeding the growing animosity towards Israel. However, what this phenomenon calls for is not blanket denunciation but sober analysis. Not all anti-Zionism is anti-Semitism. Still less is all condemnation of Israel's present policies anti-Zionism. Consequently your assertion of a worldwide conspiracy to destroy Israel is a gross exaggeration.

You ask: 'What is Israel to do in the absence of a credible peace partner and faced by an unending war of terror?' Regarding the second clause, Israel must of course take all necessary steps to defend its population. Nobody has questioned that, as distinct from some of the methods employed. As for the first clause, Israel has had several opportunities to make peace with the Palestinians but blown them, beginning in 1967, when David Ben Gurion vainly urged its government to relinquish the conquered territories in exchange for peace. In 1982 Sharon invaded Lebanon for the very purpose of destroying the PLO as a potential peace partner, just as in Operation Defensive Shield in 2002, for the same reason, he all but destroyed the PA. Similarly, he repudiated the Oslo process as soon as he became Prime Minister, and his whole record shows that what he wants is Greater Israel rather than a peace settlement involving the sort of territorial compromise that has any chance of being acceptable to the Palestinian people. Since he has done everything possible to *prevent* the emergence of a credible peace partner, to complain that Israel has none is perverse.

Again, you ask: 'Are we to succumb to a moral equivalence between Israeli and Palestinian behaviour over the last two years?' No, we are not. But that does not entitle us to condone Israel's violations of human rights, meticulously documented by its own impeccable watchdog organisations.

You refer to the UN as 'a world body hopelessly stacked against Israel'. On the other hand Israel owes its very existence to the UN, whose General Assembly has consistently affirmed its right to exist in peace and security within internationally recognised borders.

You allege that there is 'A worldwide campaign being waged to isolate, condemn, and weaken Israel'. That is another wild exaggeration. Besides, to a large extent, Israel has isolated itself by its defiance of world opinion, condemned itself by acts of excessive brutality, and weakened itself by its settlements, which extend its defence lines and entail vast expenditure. Above all, the impression you seek to convey, that the whole world is out to destroy Israel, flies in the face of the following facts: that, as just mentioned, the UN has invariably affirmed Israel's right to exist in peace and security within internationally recognised borders; that the same holds true for most of its member states; that Egypt and Jordan have concluded peace treaties with Israel; that in 1993 Arafat, on behalf of the PLO, made a historic declaration recognising Israel's right to exist; that the Oslo process *nearly succeeded*; that less than a year ago, in Beirut, the Saudi peace plan, envisaging normalisation of Arab–Israel relations, was endorsed by nineteen member states of the Arab League. It constituted a major breakthrough.

Nobody pretends that the present situation is not fraught with great difficulties and dangers. Nevertheless the outlines of a realistically attainable solution have been crystal-clear for some time. They involve an agreement simultaneously to stop Palestinian terrorism and Israeli settlement building (as recommended by the Mitchell Report), evacuation of the settlements, acceptance of the 1967 Green Line (with minor adjustments) as Israel's border, the establishment of a demilitarised but viable Palestinian state with its capital in East Jerusalem, and massive world aid to build up the Palestinian economy and to resettle or compensate the Palestinian refugees in a way that does not threaten Israel's demography.

The achievement of such a resolution of the conflict is entirely possible. It only requires that the large majority on both sides, who want peace, should assert their will, if necessary against their political leaders. There is no other way forward, and your letter, far from advancing it, militates against it. It does so by bolstering the currently prevalent mood of the Jewish people, which is one of self-pity and self-righteousness, paranoia and hysteria, and adherence to the fatal illusion that peace depends on security rather than security on peace. It is the exact opposite of what responsible Jewish leadership requires at the present time.

Today the Jewish people face a fateful choice between two scenarios.

Scenario One: Continuation of the present policy. More of the same. An increasingly oppressive occupation of an increasingly resentful Palestinian population. An endless cycle of violence and counter-violence. Perhaps even resort to unconscionable expedients such as wholesale expulsions (ethnic cleansing) in a desperate attempt to remove the irritant and preserve the Jewish majority of Israel's population. Fortress Israel, loathed by humanity and defying humanity until doomsday.

Scenario Two: Israel negotiates a ceasefire based on the simultaneous cessation of terrorism and colonisation, then, with international help, a comprehensive peace. It withdraws to its 1967 borders and, within them, devotes its enormous energy and genius to the building of a democratic, just and prosperous society. It lives at peace with its neighbours, makes a positive contribution to the stability and progress of the Middle East, and regains the good will of humanity.

Woe to the shepherds of Israel (Ezekiel 34:2) who lead their flock in the wrong direction!

Now is a time to urge our people to embrace the way of peace because that is the most Jewish, the most Zionist and the most pro-Israel thing to do, and the only one that holds out any long-term hope for the future.

Yours sincerely,
Rabbi John D. Rayner